Protestant Hispanic Churches of Oregon

Protestant Hispanic Churches of Oregon

Deborah L. Berhó

With a Foreword by Leonard Sweet

WIPF & STOCK · Eugene, Oregon

PROTESTANT HISPANIC CHURCHES OF OREGON

Wipf & Stock
An Imprint of Wipf and Stock Publishers
199 W. 8th Ave., Suite 3
Eugene, OR 97401

www.wipfandstock.com

ISBN 13: 978-1-61097-013-6

Manufactured in the U.S.A.

To my husband, Benoit,
who has taught me so much
about Latino immigrants.
Thank you.

Contents

Foreword

DEBORAH BERHO BRINGS TOGETHER words that don't usually belong together: Hispanic and Protestant (most Latinos are Roman Catholic, aren't they?); Protestant and Oregon (the Pacific Northwest is notoriously "secular," postmodern and pre-Christian, isn't it?); and Hispanic and Oregon (aren't Hispanic populations concentrated in the Southwest and Texas?). In this fascinating and revealing study of Latino churches and Anglo responses, Berho probes the contours of cultural collisions with theoretical insight and take-home strategies for bridging these boundaries.

While reading Berhó's book, I could not help but think of Caucasia, a region where Europe and Asia come together. It prides itself on having more national boundaries per square mile than anywhere else on earth. It also boasts almost as much biological diversity as the Galapagos Islands, and the greatest diversities of language anywhere on the planet. An Arab legend ascribes this rich diversity to the narrowness of its mountain passages. God's mule, which was carrying a pouch of languages to be distributed worldwide, stumbled on one of those treacherous paths, the sack opened wide, and the languages were scattered all over and remained there for posterity.[1]

Each human being is a member of multiple tribes—a family, a region, a nation, an ethnic group, and the list goes on. For the "human" way to be the "humane" way we must come to see our tribalisms as ways of bridging to others, not barricading them. I am a follower of Jesus, not to shut other people out, but to cross over into unknown territory, to climb mountains and cross rivers, and explore unknown horizons. You particularize in order to universalize. If our tribal identity does not help us to globalize—to open to all, to be open to all—then our tribalism is the wrong kind of "ism."

---

1. Karny, *Highlanders*, xvi.

It was in the nature of Jesus to cross cultures and bridge boundaries—between cultures, sexes, races, divine and human, pure and impure, etc. The beginning of the Christian tradition is a star-crossed love story which brings together the star of Bethlehem and the cross of Calvary. "The Adoration of the Magi," one of the most frequently painted scenes in all of Christian art, testify that this birth has relevance not just to Israel, but to all humankind. This would be a Saviour not just of the house of Israel, but of all houses of all humankind. I am writing this on the 26th of December, when the church celebrates the martyrdom of Saint Stephen. Two days from now, on 28 December, the church remembers "the massacre of the innocents," the first-born sons whom Herod killed. In other words, the Christmas story is part of a larger story that addresses a world of injustice, suffering and even death. The joy of that first Christmas wasn't a cute joy, but a joy that overcame obstacles and barriers, even climbs mountains.

Berhő's book is a model of the kind of studies we need for a future which is tribalizing and globalizing us at the same time.

Leonard Sweet
E. Stanley Jones Professor, Drew University
Distinguished Visiting Professor, George Fox University
Chief Contributor, sermons.com

Preface

IN MY FIRST YEAR of college, my Spanish professor invited me to attend the local Spanish-speaking congregation with him. I was hooked, and this was the beginning of a lifetime of learning about Hispanics in the U.S. and their worship practices.

This was Idaho in the 1980s, and while Hispanics were present, they were not as visible as the longtime Hispanic populations of areas like the Southwest, Texas, and New York. At first, I made immature generalizations and quick, often erroneous, judgments. For example, when describing a Hispanic church sanctuary in a paper for an ethnographic study assignment in my Cultural Anthropology course, I wrote something about the bright orange fabric hanging behind the pulpit representing "these people's love of color." A capable singer, I was always frustrated that I got behind while singing the choruses and hymns, and observed, "they don't make a break between their words"—a phenomenon called "resyllabification" that I would later learn about in a graduate linguistics class.

Initially, all the people seemed to be about the same: one big happy Hispanic family who warmly welcomed this bumbling gringa who spoke Spanish poorly. I couldn't tell if the delicious food I ate at potlucks, a welcome change from the cafeteria, was Mexican, Salvadoran, or TexMex—I just enjoyed it. Slowly, I began to realize that my Spanish reading skills were superior to those of Hermano Jesse (short for Jesus—wondering who would name their kid Jesus, anyway?), who slowly sounded out each syllable as he read Scripture aloud. I learned that Pastor would rather not talk about leaving his homeland of Nicaragua, preferring to leave those memories of violence behind. I learned that there were Latinos attending the church who couldn't maintain a conversation in Spanish, but often resorted to English. I began to pick up on the distinctions of *tejano*, Central American refugee, second- and third-generation Mexican Americans, well-educated South Americans, illiterate fieldworkers, immigrant youth searching to define their personhood, and Anglo power within the Hispanic church.

I went on to marry a Chilean who served as pastor of two Hispanic churches in Oregon. I observed personally the difficulties caused by immigration, culture shock, learning English, relying on interpreters, and cultural misunderstandings and paternalism on the part of sponsoring Anglo churches. There was distrust toward a South American "newbie" from less recent immigrants and members of the dominant Mexican culture found in Oregon, partly due to national differences, partly due to class distinctions.

In the 1980s, Hispanic churches in the Northwest were few and far between. Denominational differences were downplayed—there were so few evangelical Hispanics that they banded together and focused on their commonalities instead of worrying about whether one was Calvinist or Arminian or something else. There was no systematic effort to train Hispanic pastors from among those already living in the U.S.— when a group wanted to start a Hispanic ministry, they often brought an outstanding pastor from somewhere in Latin America.

Over the past three decades, I have continued to participate in Hispanic churches in the Northwest in various nominal capacities, while completing a doctorate in Latin American Studies, becoming an academic at a Christian university and participating actively in English-speaking churches. The number of Hispanics living in Oregon has grown exponentially, as have the Spanish-speaking churches. However, in my daily interactions with colleagues, friends and family, and Anglo Protestants, I find a lack of knowledge about the Hispanic population and Hispanic ministries.

Because of my life and academic experiences, I am in a unique position as a bridge between Hispanic churches and the academy, and more importantly, between the Spanish- and English-speaking Church. This book is the result of my desire to provide information that will facilitate understanding and ministry in God's kingdom.

I am neither a theologian nor a social scientist, though I have had coursework and read extensively in both areas. This book has benefitted from the comments of experts in these fields, but any errors are entirely mine.

More importantly, I am not Latina. My apologies to my Latino colleagues and brothers and sisters in Christ who may resent being described by an outsider. The continuing stream of bright young Hispanics through my college courses gives me hope that soon Oregon Latino Protestants will be publishing their own works for the church and for academia.

While the research presented meets all the standards for academic rigor, it is written in a style that pastors or church leaders should find understandable. Those wishing to study immigrant congregations or the Latino church in particular will find references to many additional sources.

Acknowledgments

This project was supported in part by the George Fox University Grant GFU2006G0001 and GFU2007G0001, and the gracious extension of a sabbatical by George Fox University in 2011 to complete the manuscript. The author also gratefully acknowledges financial support from the Provost's Office for some publication costs.

Thanks is due to Newell Morgan for taking me to a Latino church back in 1984; Paul Freston and Gary Railsback for reviewing the research design; Chuck Zickefoose and Jeanne Curty for patiently proof-reading the manuscript and providing valuable insight from the lay-person's perspective; to Leonard Sweet for generously agreeing to write the foreword; to Paul Anderson and Clella Jaffe for giving me practical insight into the world of publishing; to Mark McLeod-Harrison and Tom Johnson for their comments on a very early draft of this work; to the missionaries, faculty, and students in Quito, Ecuador, on the North Andean Field of the Church of the Nazarene, and at *Seminario Teológico Nazareno Sudamericano* for their friendship and hospitality during my sabbatical.

Thanks to my department colleagues at George Fox University, especially Viki Defferding, Sylvette Norré, and Beth Boyce; and to my family for putting up with my "mental absence" as I was preoccupied with writing, and for providing child care so I could carry out the research for this book.

I thank the following pastors and their congregations for allowing me to visit and inquire about their ministries: Ben Trolese, City Bible Church, Tigard; Francisco Mateo, Salvados para Servir, Beaverton/Portland; Luis Ramírez, Iglesia de Jesucristo, Forest Grove; Rose Medina, Iglesia del Pueblo Assembly of God, Cornelius; Héctor Rodríguez, Iglesia Evangélica Cristo Viene, Hillsboro; Jeremías Diego, Ministerios Restauración Elim Internacional, Hillsboro/Aloha; Raúl Giménez, Nuevo Día/Vida Church, Aloha; Víctor Alvarizares, Casa del Padre, Beaverton/Portland; Mauricio Rivas, Village Baptist, Beaverton; Samuel

Morán, Ministerio Restauración Mennonite, Portland; José González, Luz del Pueblo Southern Baptist, Portland; Mario Macías, Reedwood Friends, Portland; Nelson Reyes, Manantiales de Vida, Gresham; Carlos Ortiz, Roca de Salvación, Portland; Alfonso Rodríguez, Rosa de Sarón and La Cosecha Foursquare congregations, Portland; Genaro Loredo, Nueva Esperanza Conservative Baptist, Hermiston; Tony Estey, Esperanza y Vida en Jesucristo Christian and Missionary Alliance, Hood River; Jiroo Kuroda, Nueva Esperanza Conservative Baptist, Newport; Jaime Pantoja, Iglesia Bautista Conservadora Bilingüe, Madras; Lowell Stutzman, New Hope Bible Mennonite Brethren, Grants Pass; Ulysses Vela, Monmouth Christian Church, Monmouth; Víctor Vargas, Iglesia Pentecostés Mennonite, Woodburn; and Santiago Argueta, Rogue Valley Fellowship, Medford. Thanks also to Roy Libby of Conservative Baptist Northwest and to these current or former pastors of long-established churches: Cathi Perez-Scrivner, Mardo Jiménez, Juan Bonilla, and Ramón Argüello.

1

Introduction

A Review of the Literature and Methodology

T HE FIRST CHAPTER OF this book provides background for the reader on themes regarding Hispanic[1] Protestants in the U.S. published in other studies, and describes the research methodology. Chapter 2 presents information on the history and demographic profile of Latinos in Oregon, as well as the history of Protestant churches in the state. It concludes with a basic description of the twenty-seven congregations included in this study (two of the pastors of the twenty-five churches in this study were leading two congregations each). Chapter 3 examines these Oregon Protestant Latino churches in three areas: their relationship (if any) with a denomination; their relationship with other churches, both Anglo and Hispanic; and their participation in the community. Heterogeneity within the congregations is discussed in chapter 4 in terms of race and ethnicity, language use, socioeconomic level, and generation of immigration. A rich and detailed description of the worship services in twenty-five churches is found in chapter 5.

THE NEED FOR THIS BOOK

In the twenty-first century, the largest minority group in the United States is Hispanic. Not all Hispanics are immigrants, but recent and ongoing immigration contributes significantly to the number of Hispanics in the U.S. Several studies observe that the evangelical Protestant popu-

---

1. Though there are different sociopolitical nuances to the terms "Hispanic" and "Latino/Latina," they will be used interchangeably throughout this book.

lation of the global South is growing rapidly,[2] and that immigrants from these nations are revitalizing faith in the secularized North, including the U.S.[3]

While many Hispanics are traditionally Roman Catholic, research indicates that between twenty and thirty-three percent are Protestants.[4] In some U.S.- or Europe-based denominations, Hispanic church growth is keeping U.S. church membership afloat, balancing the decline of Anglo members.[5]

As the Spanish-speaking population in the United States grows, many churches desire to begin Spanish-speaking ministries. While Texas and the Southwest have had large Hispanic populations for centuries, in other areas like the Northwest, the significant numbers of Hispanics are a relatively new phenomenon.

One broad-ranging examination of Hispanic churches in the U.S. is the study of Leadership in Latino Parishes (NSLLPC), carried out by the Program for Analysis of Religion Among Latinas/os (PARAL). This study recognizes the exponential growth of Hispanic immigration in certain parts of the U.S., and goes on to comment: "Faith communities have an enlarged role in such locales where the growth of the Latino population is both rapid and significant, because the secular and public agencies generally have few programs in place to accommodate Latinos' needs."[6] In other words, the role of the church is especially important in areas where Latino immigration is recent.

Oregon in particular was characterized by the PARAL study as being a "diaspora state." PARAL uses the term "diaspora" in a very specific way, indicating a state that does not have a historic Hispanic population, and which has seen the Hispanic population double in the period 1990 to 2000.[7] Though present in Oregon since statehood in 1859, Hispanics

---

2. Lewis, *Christianity Reborn*, 1–8 and as related specifically to Latin America, Freston, "Contours," 221–72; Escobar, *Changing Tide*, 7.

3. Sanneh, *Whose Religion*, 76; Jenkins, *Next Christendom*, 99, 107–8, 191–92, 204, 208–9

4. Jenkins, *Next Christendom*, 101; Maldonado Jr., *Protestantes*, 9.

5. Escobar, *Changing Tide*, 8; Lawson, "From American," 329; Darino, "Hispanic Baptist Worship," 85.

6. Stevens-Arroyo and Díaz-Stevens, "Density," 16.

7. Ibid., 15.

have largely been invisible,[8] but this is changing. According to the U.S. Census Bureau, the population of Hispanics in Oregon increased by 144 percent in the period 1990 to 2000, from 112,707 in 1990 to 275,314 in 2000. The 2010 census indicates that the 450,062 persons of Hispanic or Latino origin represent 11.7 percent of the state's population.[9] This is a 300 percent increase since 1990, and a 63 percent increase since 2000.

According to the PARAL study, "a key characteristic of a diaspora state is the lack of experience in state, society and church in accommodating a significant influx of Latinos."[10] Put another way, "diaspora" communities like the relatively recent Hispanic immigrants to Oregon present significant challenges and opportunities for religious organizations. Indeed, as the author mentioned her research to Anglo church-goers and leaders, she often found them woefully uninformed. The situation may be more complex because Oregon is one of the least churched states in the nation.[11]

This book responds to the call for greater study of the Protestant Hispanic immigrant churches in a diaspora state. It is hoped that the information provided will not only expand the field of knowledge from an academic point of view, but also aid church and community leaders in serving the Latino/a population of Oregon.

THEMES IN LITERATURE ON IMMIGRANT AND HISPANIC CHURCHES

Despite the growth of this population and a growing body of literature on Protestant Hispanics in the United States, nothing has been published regarding Protestant Hispanic churches in Oregon. This study seeks to begin to fill this void. The balance of this chapter provides a review of existing literature on Protestantism among Latino/as in the United States and the Latino/a population of Oregon and then describes the methods and terms used in this study.

---

8. See Stephen, *Transborder*, for further discussion of the concept of invisibility of Oregon Hispanics and Rodríguez-Díaz and Cortés-Fuentes, *Hidden Stories*.

9. U.S. Census Bureau, State and County QuickFacts: Oregon. http://quickfacts .census.gov/qfd/states/41000.html, accessed November 6, 2011.

10. Stevens-Arroyo and Díaz-Stevens, "Density," 16.

11. Gallup, http://www.gallup.com/poll/125999/mississippians-go-church-most-vermonters-least.aspx, accessed November 6, 2011.

There is an emerging body of research on immigrant churches in the U.S.,[12] including works focusing specifically on Protestant Hispanic churches.[13] Many of these studies are denominational histories or focus on geographic areas with longtime Latino populations such as New York, Florida, or the Southwest.[14] The literature includes mission efforts to formerly Spanish or French (Roman Catholic) areas as an extension of Manifest Destiny.[15] Indeed, one of the primary ways that Spanish-speaking congregations began was through the initiative or sponsorship of an Anglo congregation or individual.

The conflicts that have arisen between Anglo and Hispanic congregations are a main theme of much of the scholarship. Montoya claims that "[t]he Anglo church has made a mess of incorporating Hispanics into their churches" and goes on to mention pitfalls of these relationships, including prejudice, intimidation, acculturation, dependence, paternalism, and segregation.[16]

Paternalism, or at least a lack of understanding between the two cultures, is described in Barton's study of early Methodist Hispanic ministries in the Southwest: "The tension that has existed between Latino Protestants and Anglo-dominant denominations has a historical foundation in the Anglo American missionaries' embrace and promulgation of the idea of Manifest Destiny in the nineteenth century. Just as present-day Hispanics find themselves the objects of mission efforts based upon stereotypical views of them, so did the first generation of Mexican and Mexican American Methodists discover that Anglo American church leaders had misunderstandings about their culture and abilities."[17]

---

12. See for example, Hurh and Kim, "Religious participation"; Pozzetta, *American immigration*; Lawson, "From American church"; Warner and Wittner, *Gatherings*; Ng, "Seeking the Christian tutelage"; Ebaugh and Saltzman Chafetz, *Religion and the new immigrants*; Ebaugh and Saltzman Chafetz, "Dilemmas of language"; Ebaugh and Saltzman Chafetz, *Religion across borders*.

13. These include Cortés, *Protestantism and Latinos*; Rodríguez-Díaz and Cortés-Fuentes, *Hidden stories*; Stevens-Arroyo and Cadena, *Old masks*; González, *Alabadle*; Aponte, "Hispanic/Latino Protestantism"; Stevens-Arroyo, *Recognizing the Latino*; Maldonado Jr., *Protestantes/Protestants*; Espinosa et al., "Hispanic churches"; Sánchez-Walsh, *Latino Pentecostal*; and Martínez Guerra and Scott, *Iglesias peregrinas*.

14 Atencio, "The Empty Cross," 38–59; Barton, "Inter-ethnic," 60–84. Troyer, *The Sovereignty*.

15. Troyer, *Sovereignty*; Barton, "Inter-ethnic Relations," 60–84.

16. *Hispanic Ministry*, 75–78.

17. Barton, "Inter-ethnic Relations," 60.

An attitude of superiority is expressed by some Anglos to the Hispanic congregations. Some demeaningly call the Spanish-speaking members "little brothers and sisters."[18] In other cases, the diminished value of Latino churches can be seen in the space allocated to them in an Anglo church building. The common practice of relegating Spanish services to the church basement is documented at least as early as 1960.[19] Finding an appropriate meeting space has been a challenge for many Hispanic congregations. Speaking specifically of Pentecostal churches, Soliván observes, ". . . most Hispanic Pentecostal churches are located in the poorest of the urban barrios. Whereas mainline churches worship in buildings intentionally designed for Christian worship, most Hispanic Pentecostal churches worship in storefronts, or in other buildings rehabilitated for use as a place of worship. A growing number of Pentecostal congregations meet in the underutilized facilities of mainline churches in need of income."[20]

One of the consistent criticisms of researchers on Latin American and U.S. Latino Protestant churches is the imposition of European and U.S. worship styles. Costas, writing in 1974, stated, "En nuestro día resulta intolerable el imperialismo cultural que impone formas que han tenido un origen extranjero y responden a necesidades de otra cultura y época." (In our day the cultural imperialism that imposes forms that have had a foreign origin and respond to the needs of another culture and era is intolerable.)[21] He went on to assert that "todo culto debe ser 'indígena,' debe ser el reflejo de una Iglesia que surge, vive y actúa en medio de un ambiente cultural determinado." (every worship service should be 'indigenous,' it should be the reflection of a Church that arises, lives, and acts in the midst of a particular cultural envionment.)[22] Darino describes a similar problem in U.S. Hispanic Baptist churches in the first half of the twentieth century:

> From the cultural point of view in the majority of Hispanic contexts, worship was European-North American until the middle of this century. Hispanics worshiped according to established patterns. . . . as they opened their hearts to the gospel, they also

18. Maldonado Jr., *Protestantes,* 10.

19. Department of Church, *Report,* 89.

20. "Hispanic Pentecostal Worship," 45–46.

21. "La realidad de la iglesia evangélica latinoamericana," 48.

22. Ibid., 39–40.

received the forms of worship. Christian organizations that emerged from last century's revival began sending missionaries to different countries. Those missionaries . . . took not only the gospel with them, but also patterns of worship from different sources, both European and North American. In reality these patterns were transplanted . . . evidenced in hymnology, in the liturgy used at the time, and in the style of music and worship.[23]

In fact, music is the area most criticized as being non-native, both in style and lyrics, as most hymns were translations into Spanish of songs originally written in another language.[24] In an opposing view, the preeminent leader of Latino worship music, Marcos Witt, states specifically about Latin American churches, "Debemos honrar a ciertos grupos y denominaciones, como nuestros hermanos los bautistas, los presbiterianos y los metodistas, que por años han hecho esta labor de preparar, impulsar y apoyar a los músicos de sus congregaciones." (We should honor certain groups and denominations, like our brothers the Baptists, the Presbyterians and the Methodists, that for years have done this labor of preparing, propelling and supporting the musicians of their congregations.), though he goes on to say that due to this preparation, Latin Americans can and should now compose their own worship music.[25]

Anglos and Hispanics have had differing visions for what Spanish-speaking churches are to achieve. Gjerde explores these conflicting ideals in terms of immigrant churches in general,[26] as do Mohl and Betten.[27] Timothy Smith's influential study of immigrant churches in the U.S. suggested that they were a means of assimilation or upward mobility.[28] Just the opposite role of the immigrant church as an agent for preservation of language and culture has been proposed by other sociologists,[29] and is still a matter of debate within Hispanic congregations: "The role of the church as an institution of cultural resistance continues to be contested within Latino congregations."[30]

23. "Hispanic Baptist Worship," 80.

24. Ibid., 81, 83; Costas, "La realidad de la iglesia evangélica latinoamericana," 46.

25. ¿Qué hacemos con estos músicos?, 40.

26. "Conflict," 181–97.

27. "The Immigrant Church," 269–85.

28. Smith, "Religion," 1155–56, 1178;

29. Stout, "Vital Center," 378, 380; Greeley, Denominational Society, 117.

30. Chávez Sauceda, "Race," 191.

The diverse visions for Hispanic ministries are evident in the literature. Lara-Braud claims that they are seen as temporary while Hispanic immigrants assimilate.[31] The goal of combining Hispanic and Anglo congregations into one is described as difficult to accomplish.[32] The over-arching premise of Montoya's book is that combining two cultures in one church is not desirable: "Another source of great encouragement for anyone laboring in the Hispanic mission field is the great thought that your church can be independent. By that, I do not mean the ecclesiastical or denominational structure known as 'independent churches.' I mean the independence from the Anglo mother church, or as we often see it, 'the smother church.' The Hispanic church has come of age and is rejoicing in a newfound independence."[33]

Studies also report racial discrimination by Anglo church members against their Spanish-speaking counterparts. Troyer's 1934 booklet describes one incident, after one Anglo woman had given a cordial welcome to a newly-believing Mexican. Two other women standing nearby remarked in his hearing, "'Well, if they're going to receive Mexicans in this Church, I'm not coming any more.' He went away with a broken heart."[34] Sixty years later, Orozco Hawkins observed racism toward Latinos from Anglo churches of one denomination in Washington State: "The dominant Anglo churches are resistant, insensitive and even adversarial with regard to the process of empowering of our Hispanic constituencies. It is not an encouraging picture. The Presbyterian Church has begun to facilitate some ministry with Hispanics, but the racism, paternalism and fear of the white church makes authentic Hispanic ministry nearly impossible at this time."[35]

Several works describe the struggle for self-determination for Latino pastors and congregations.[36] Many observe that Hispanic pastors and congregations are not functionally included in their denominations:

---

31. Lara-Braud, "Profile," 267.

32. Department of Church, *Report*, 89; González, "Hispanic Worship," 17, 24–27.

33. *Hispanic Ministry*, 147.

34. Troyer, *Sovereignty*, 17.

35. Orozco Hawkins, "Hispanic/Latina Women," 118–19.

36. Rodríguez-Díaz and Cortés-Fuentes, *Hidden Stories*; Aponte, "Hispanic/Latino Protestantism," 397–98; Barton, "Inter-ethnic Relations," 78; and Machado, "Protestant Establishment," 85–106.

"While most Protestant Hispanic congregations belong and participate in denominational structures, it is only and mostly a formality."[37]

At the same time, several studies observe that immigrants to the U.S. are balancing a corresponding decline in Anglo members of U.S. churches.[38]

Some Hispanic churches are not in any way related to an Anglo denomination or congregation. Evangelical groups native to the global South are actively sending missionaries to the U.S. to minister to expatriates.[39] The Apostolic Assembly is a home-grown Hispanic denomination that has its roots in the Azusa revivals.[40] Other Latino churches have separated themselves from Anglo denominations or churches. The Methodist Mexican churches in the Southwest formed a separate structure in the 1930s that continues to this day. Barton observes, "The formation of an indigenous church is emblematic of the desire of Mexicans and Mexican Americans to determine the policy and direction of their church without the constraints of an Anglo-dominant denominational bureaucracy. This was a case of Mexicans using a separatist strategy to achieve political autonomy and cultural preservation. The establishment of an indigenous Protestant movement demonstrates the willingness of some Mexicans and Mexican Americans to enhance their self-determination when they felt constrained by existing denominational structures and practices."[41]

The issue of division predominates in the literature, for several different reasons. First, the rapidly growing Pentecostal movements in Latin America tend to schism; Espinosa terms it "chronic fragmentation."[42] Freston suggests that this is due to the leadership style of the pastors: "They are . . . good entrepeneurs but bad collaborators."[43]

37. Armendariz, "Protestant Hispanic Congregation," 250.

38. Lawson, "From American," 329; Darino, "Hispanic Baptist Worship," 85; Aponte, "Hispanic/Latino Protestantism," 391; and Hernández, "Cathedral to Storefront," 216, 220.

39. Jenkins, *Next Christendom,* 107–8, 192, 205–6, 208; Martin, "Evangelical Expansion," 275, 284.

40. Martín del Campo, "Apostolic Assembly," 53.

41. Barton, "Inter-ethnic Relations," 78.

42. Espinosa, "Pentecostalization," 276.

43. Freston, "Contours," 233.

Recent immigrants who participated in Pentecostal churches at home in Latin America may see church splits as the norm.

Secondly, "Latinos" or "Hispanics," while lumped together as a minority group in the U.S., are really quite diverse. They have different countries of origin, speak myriad variations of Spanish as well as English and indigenous dialects, represent different educational, class, and racial groups, and may be second- or third-generation immigrants who don't speak Spanish at all. Multiple studies emphasize that immigrant congregations are not as homogeneous as they might appear to the outside observer.[44]

The third reason for divisions within Latino churches may revolve precisely around generational differences. While some churches have only recent immigrants, many include second- and third-generation immigrants and those who immigrated as children. As these individuals grow up speaking English well, many leave the monolingual Spanish-speaking church for a bilingual or English-only church.[45] Choosing a language for worship services and Christian education is an on-going issue.[46] The differences between generations can cause significant tension in the church body,[47] especially as related to leadership and decision-making.

The book *Alabadle: Hispanic Christian Worship*,[48] provides the best in-depth description of worship services in Protestant Hispanic churches. Though it covers many denominations or types of churches, several themes emerge. First, it is very difficult to generalize about a "typical" Latino worship service in the U.S.[49] Though many do not follow a liturgy, and there is great diversity in the services, nonetheless, González states that there are common threads discernible in Hispanic worship services in the U.S.: "As one travels throughout the nation and worships . . . in a wide variety of Latino contexts, one senses a commonality that

44. Pozzetta, introduction to *Immigrant Religious Experience*, vol. 19, *American Immigration and Ethnicity: A 20 Volume Series of Distinguished Essays*, vii; Smith, 1169–1170; Aponte, "Hispanic/Latino Protestantism," 381; and Orozco Hawkins, "Hispanic/Latina Women," 118.

45. Department of Church, *Report*, 88.

46. Mohl and Betten, 279, 281; González, "Hispanic Worship," 10–11.

47. Stout, "Vital Center," 380; Hernández, "Cathedral to Storefront," 223–24.

48. Edited by Justo González.

49. González, "Hispanic Worship: An Introduction," 9, 13; Darino, "What is Different about Hispanic Baptist Worship?," 75.

somehow holds these various strands together. Latino churches, whether Catholic or Protestant, whether mostly Mexican, Cuban, or Salvadoran, have their own particular flavor in worship."[50] Some of the commonalities observed include participation by many of the church-goers, not just a pastor and a few leaders, based on the principle of the priesthood of all believers;[51] the use of *coritos*, "short, popular chorus[es]"[52] whose "exact origin . . . is unknown, but they are seen to have risen from the *pueblo*" (people);[53] themes of separation from the world;[54] the "expectation that the Holy Spirit will meet us as we worship;"[55] a relaxed attitude toward the length of the worship service,[56] and freedom to worship in the service as led by the Holy Spirit.[57] Several researchers have described Latino Protestant worship services as a celebration or *fiesta*,[58] while others use such terms as "passionate and participatory,"[59] and having "fervor"[60] and "enthusiasm."[61] The pastor and sermon are seen to have central roles in Hispanic worship services.[62]

50. "Hispanic Worship: An Introduction," 6.

51. Soliván, "Hispanic Pentecostal Worship," 59; Darino, "Hispanic Baptist Worship," 75, 78–79.

52. Aponte, "*Coritos* as Active Symbol," 60.

53. Ibid., 61.

54. Costas, "La realidad de la iglesia evangélica latinoamericana," 48, 59; Soliván, "Hispanic Pentecostal Worship," 47; Darino, "Hispanic Baptist Worship," 84, 86.

55. "Hispanic Pentecostal Worship," 51–52, 55; Costas, "La realidad de la iglesia evangélica latinoamericana," 50.

56. Santillán Baert, "Hispanic United Methodist Church," 70; Soliván, "Hispanic Pentecostal Worship," 55.

57. Soliván, "Hispanic Pentecostal Worship," 50–52; Darino, "Hispanic Baptist Worship," 74.

58. González, "Hispanic Worship: An Introduction," 20–21, 23; Costas, "La realidad de la iglesia evangélica latinoamericana," 50.

59. Soliván, "Hispanic Pentecostal Worship," 52.

60. Santillán Baert, "Hispanic United Methodist Church," 60; Darino, "Hispanic Baptist Worship," 88.

61. Santillán Baert, "Hispanic United Methodist Church," 60.

62. Costas, "La realidad de la iglesia evangélica latinoamericana," 63; Soliván, "Hispanic Pentecostal Worship," 54; Santillán Baert, "Hispanic United Methodist Church," 60.

THE RESEARCH PROJECT

This book is the result of a broad study of Protestant Hispanic churches in Oregon over the years 2006 to 2010, funded in part by Summer Research Grants from the Faculty Development Committee of George Fox University.

The researcher participates in an ongoing attempt to identify all the Protestant Hispanic congregations of Oregon. A listing was made from personal knowledge, phone books, the state business name registry, and the Internet. Aware of the issue of invisibility, the researcher sought other ways to make the list more complete, adding churches she passed while driving through neighborhoods and asking each pastor interviewed to identify other Hispanic churches in his or her area.

The researcher had certain hypotheses before beginning, based both on more than twenty years of participation in and observation of Hispanic Protestant churches in the Northwest and on themes emerging from literature on immigrant churches. Some of these are mentioned in the preface, and they are explored further in chapters 3, 4, and 5. However, the author also was aware that her observations of the churches and the pastors' responses to the interview questions might bring to light entirely new information or disprove her hypotheses. She hoped to realize Vasquez' directive: "Therefore, rather than starting from overarching assertions of type: 'Pentecostalism does x for Latinos,' studies of the role of religion for U.S. Latinos must be driven above all by empirical research that takes into account the multiplicity of local inflections."[63] She did not consciously set out with a single framework from which to pose her questions, although in retrospect recognizes that her non-Pentecostal, North American, denominational upbringing colors her inquiry and analysis.

The researcher worked with leading sociologist of Latin American religion, Paul Freston, throughout 2006 to more adequately formulate the method and research questions. A triangulated sociological method was developed that included purposive sampling of churches in both the Portland metropolitan area and rural areas of the state. It included participant observation of church services, literature collection, and pastoral interviews. The questions used in the pastoral interviews were reviewed by Gary Railsback and his graduate Qualitative Research Methods class

---

63. "Pentecostalism, Collective Identity," 631.

at George Fox University during the summer of 2007, and may be found in the Appendix.

After identifying all the Protestant Hispanic churches on Washington County, which has a mix of suburban and rural areas, and a high population of Hispanic residents, both long-term and recent immigrants, a purposive sample of eight churches was chosen based on their location, size, age, and type (independent, denominational affiliation). Some very young churches, including what those who attend older congregations disparagingly call *grupitos*—little groups not yet officially organized as fully functioning churches—as well as long-established bodies were chosen for study. In summer 2007, the researcher visited a regular worship service at all of them, collected any literature that was available, and followed up with interviews of their pastors, several of whom the researcher has known for over twenty years. The pastoral interviews were conducted in English or Spanish, as the pastor preferred. This process was repeated in 2008 and 2009 for Multnomah County, the most populous area of the state, which includes the city of Portland as well as rural unincorporated areas to the east. Two of the pastors interviewed were leading two congregations, and they included information on both in their responses. One of the Multnomah County pastors was not available for a follow-up interview.

While these two populous counties have many Hispanic residents and Spanish-speaking churches, they do not represent the entire state of Oregon. All identified Spanish-speaking churches were plotted on a map, and nine regional clusters of Protestant Latino/a churches emerged. In 2010, church visits were done at one church in each of these nine rural areas around the state. One of these pastors did not respond to requests for interviews, so additional information was obtained from a long-time pastor in that denomination.

The interviews obtained were transcribed and sorted. The research design is quite similar to that carried out in Philadelphia by David Aponte, a "qualitative approach . . . of in-depth focus interviews and participant observation, supported by archival materials when available" focused on a specific geographic area.[64] Additionally, the researcher visited several of the oldest congregations in the state and interviewed pastors of those churches and persons involved in their beginnings.

---

64. Aponte, "Hispanic/Latino Protestantism," 385.

Limitations and Delimitations

This study is limited in size. It focuses primarily on twenty-seven purposefully selected congregations within the state of Oregon. This study also excluded some arguably Protestant groups: Adventists, Mormons, Jehovah's Witnesses, and the Mexican-origin *Luz del Mundo*. While the material presented draws from both the author's observations during a worship service and pastoral interviews, the views of the congregation are not represented. As Luebke warns, "Indeed, one of the most serious hazards connected with research in immigration history is to attribute evidence drawn from the leaders of a group to the rank and file members of that group. Excessive reliance on such elite-type evidence may easily distort perceptions of group attitudes and behavior."[65] While the research design called for a review of all available literature collected at the site visits, in news articles and online, very little documentation was made available at the churches, and few churches have websites, limiting this source of information.

Although the researcher speaks Spanish at the Superior level as determined by the American Council for the Teaching of Foreign Languages, she is not Hispanic, and her presence in worship services never went unnoticed. The researcher is a practicing non-Pentecostal Protestant firmly rooted in a denominational tradition.

Definition of Terms

Anglo—A white person of northern European descent.

Evangélico—The Spanish term most often used to refer to a Protestant. It does not carry the same nuances that the English term "evangelical" has in the U.S. political or religious environment.

First-generation immigrant—A person who was born in another country and immigrated during his or her lifetime.

Hispanic—A person living in the U.S. who traces ancestry to any of the former colonies of Spain except Guam and the Philippines; does not include immigrants from the nation of Spain itself. Although many ascribe

---

65. "German Immigrants," 210.

different nuances to this term, in this work it is used synonymously with Latino.

Latino/a—A person who traces ancestry to any of the former colonies of Spain except Guam and the Philippines; does not include immigrants from the nation of Spain itself. In this study, used synonymously with Hispanic.

Protestant—Christian beliefs and practices separate from Catholicism, stemming from the Reformation.

Second-generation immigrant—A person born to parents who immigrated, after their immigration.

Third-generation immigrant—Grandchild of immigrants.

2

Latinos and Spanish-Speaking Churches in Oregon

THE LATINO POPULATION IN OREGON

History

THERE ARE VERY FEW studies on Hispanics in the Northwest. Historian Erasmo Gamboa has published several items describing the early history of Latino/a immigrants to Oregon.[1] The University of Oregon's Labor Education and Research Center also published a thorough, wide-ranging report in 2008.[2] Erlinda Gonzales-Berry and Marcela Mendoza's 2010 book, *Mexicanos in Oregon: their stories, their lives*, makes an important contribution to the publications on the Mexican population of Oregon. Those wishing to delve deeper into the history and current status of the Hispanic population in Oregon will be well-served by reading these documents, as the following very brief history serves only to set context for the history of Hispanic Protestant churches in the state.

The coast of Oregon was explored by Spanish maritime expeditions, and the territory was considered to be Spain's until the Transcontinental Treaty of 1819, when Spain ceded Florida and the "Oregon Country" to the U.S. in exchange for sovereignty over Texas. Oregon's southern border, California, was part of Mexico until 1848. A small number of Mexicans lived and worked in Oregon in the early 1900s, but the

---

1. See, for example, *Mexican Labor and World War II*; "Chicanos in the Pacific Northwest: Expanding the Discourse"; "Mexican Mule Packers and Oregon's Second Regiment"; and Gamboa and Buan, *Nosotros: The Hispanic People of Oregon*.

2. Martinez Jr., Charles R., et al., "Latino Immigrant Children and Families: Demographics, Challenges, and Promise."

bracero program[3] in the 1940s attracted over 15,000 Mexican workers to Oregon's many farms.[4] After WWII, many Mexicans stayed on as farm workers and participated with their families in the migrant stream that included the orchards and farms of Oregon. Most lived in labor camps. The Immigration Reform and Control Act of 1987 and its Special Agricultural Workers (SAW) provision brought a spike in immigrants from Mexico. An estimated 23,000 people applied for SAW status in Oregon.[5] The 1990s and first years of the twenty-first century saw greater stability in the Hispanic population of Oregon as those who had obtained residency moved into work in light industry and service occupations.

While Oregon is considered by many to be a progressive state, there is much evidence to the contrary in relation to legal and practical treatment of racial and ethnic minorities. When Oregon became a state in 1859, its constitution had clause excluding Blacks. Mixed-race marriages were illegal until 1951, and the Ku Klux Klan was able to operate with relative freedom.[6] Mexicans fared little better than Blacks, facing discrimination and "signs stating 'No Mexicans Allowed'" in many Eastern Oregon businesses in the early 1960s.[7] Nevertheless, many found Oregon more tolerable than the hostile environment they found in Texas.[8] There were efforts by the Oregon State Council of Churches and the Catholic Archdiocese beginning in the 1950s to improve conditions for migrant workers and their families. At the governmental level, the activities and reports gathered by these groups and others resulted in specific Oregon legislation regarding migrant farmworker housing, labor issues and education that took effect in the early 1960s.[9] For example, according to the Oregon History Project, "During the 1960s, state officials and the public became increasingly aware of poor housing conditions in labor camps—most of which were located on private lands. State officials

3. A term alluding to the arms (*brazos*) of the temporary agricultural laborers.

4. Gamboa and Buan, *Nosotros*, 41.

5. Ibid., 64.

6. Xing, introduction to *Seeing Color*, 6–7. See also Pascoe, "'Mistake to Simmer,'" 27–43 and Elizabeth McLagan, "Very Prejudiced State," 78–92 in the same volume.

7. López, *Oregon Journal*, July 19, 1962 as cited in Gonzales-Berry, "'Tired of cookies,'" 96–97.

8. Gonzales-Berry, "'Tired of cookies,'" 95–97.

9. Ibid., 98–99.

funded several studies of the housing conditions and closed the most dangerous and unsanitary camps, but the problem persisted. In 1986, the Oregon Department of Labor reported that ninety percent of the 118 camps that officials visited did not comply with state regulations for health and safety. They noted poor lighting, structural problems, over crowding, poor ventilation, lack of running water and bathrooms, and the presence of vermin at many sites."[10]

In addition to efforts by non-Hispanic civic groups and lawmakers, Oregon Hispanics have worked actively to bring about positive changes in their conditions and opportunities. In 1964, the Valley Migrant League was formed. In the 1970s, two health clinics serving mainly Mexican migrant workers were established. Centro Cultural in Cornelius began, as well as the only all-Chicano college in the U.S., Colegio César Chávez at Mt. Angel. The farmworker union PCUN (Pineros y Campesinos Unidos del Noroeste), centered in Woodburn, began in the 1980s. While a few of these organizations were short-lived, Hispanic immigrants have consistently worked and organized to assist one another and to participate in community life. More recent evidence is the creation of the Hispanic Metropolitan Chamber of Commerce in 1994, the formation of the Chicano/Latino Studies Program at Portland State University, and the opening of a Mexican Consulate in Portland in 1996.[11] The University of Oregon report comments that Oregon immigrants "are establishing their own institutions—churches, clubs, businesses—that provide vital services and create social cohesion in addition to participating in existing organizations that meet their needs."[12]

Current Oregon Hispanic Demographics

Detailed information from the 2010 Census was not yet available in late 2011 for Oregon, and census data is notoriously imprecise for the Latino population. However, in broad strokes, data from the 2000 Census may be useful for purposes of this study. According to the 2000 Census, there were some 275,000 persons of Hispanic origin living in Oregon (Factfinder, 2000), 8 percent of the total population. According to initial 2010 Census data, the estimated population of Hispanics in Oregon

---

10. Tucker, "Farm Labor Camp," ¶3–4.

11. Nusz and Ricciardi, "Our Ways," 123.

12. Bussel, *Immigrant Experience in Oregon*, 10.

had risen to 450,062 people, 12 percent of the total population.[13] The great majority are of Mexican origin, 84 percent according to the Pew Hispanic Center.[14] According to the 2010 American Community Survey of "Foreign-Born Persons" (thus not including the second and subsequent generations), there were 150,558 persons residing in Oregon who were born in Mexico, followed by 7,024 Guatemalans; 3,882 Salvadorans; 1,752 Hondurans; 1,625 Peruvians; and 1,001 Ecuadorians.[15] According to the 2000 census, there were 5,092 Puerto Ricans.[16] All the other Latin American countries had fewer than one thousand residents in Oregon.[17]

There is significant diversity among Mexicans and Guatemalans, who represent the two largest groups of Latin immigrants to Oregon: there are "more than fourteen indigenous groups of people from Guatemala and Mexico. With markedly distinctive languages and customs. . . ."[18]

There is also diversity in time of residence in the state and generation of immigration: "[S]ome data indicate that between 70 percent and 80 percent of Latino adults in Oregon are recent immigrants (i.e., ten years or less U.S. residency . . .). However, generational history varies widely in different areas of the state. . . . Many children of immigrants in Oregon are U.S. born."[19]

Though many Hispanics originally came to Oregon to work in agriculture in rural areas, by the year 2000 "Forty-four percent of the Oregon Latino population lives in three counties that comprise the greater metropolitan area around the city of Portland: Washington, Multnomah,

13. http://2010.census.gov/2010census/popmap, accessed August 25, 2011.

14. "Demographic Profile Oregon 2008," table 1.

15. U.S. Census Bureau, 2010 American Community Survey One-year Estimates, "Place of Birth for the Foreign-Born Population in the United States." File B05006, Oregon.

16. U.S. Census Bureau, American Fact-Finder, "Demographic Profile Highlights: Selected Population Group Puerto Rican," Census 2000, Oregon. Puerto Rico is part of the United States, so technically Puerto Ricans are not "Foreign-Born." Unlike the statistics above for the "Foreign-Born," this figure includes all persons of Puerto Rican heritage, not just those born on the island.

17. U.S. Census Bureau, 2010 American Community Survey One-year Estimates, "Place of Birth for the Foreign-Born Population in the United States." File B05006, Oregon.

18. Bussel, Immigrant Experience in Oregon, 10.

19. Martinez Jr., et al., "Latino Immigrant Children," 56.

and Clackamas."[20] Nusz and Ricciardi observe both the dominance of the Mexican population as well as their residence throughout the state: "The face of Oregon in the new millennium is quite different than it was fifty years ago. Today, the Mexican presence is well-established from Coos Bay to Nyssa, from Medford to Portland, from Milton-Freewater to Astoria."[21]

Many Latino immigrants to Oregon have a ninth grade education or less, and approximately 80 percent of the families are two-parent households.[22] An Oregon Center for Public Policy report in 2007 indicated that Latino immigrants to Oregon pay more in taxes than they consume in public services,[23] while earning substantially less than non-Latino families in the state. A 2005 study found the per-capita yearly income to be an average of $4,200 for Latino families and $13,500 for non-Latino families in Oregon.[24] A 2008 study estimated the annual income of Mexican immigrants to Oregon at $15,918, with a majority of Mexican immigrants working in production, agriculture and service industries although there is an increasing number of small business owners.[25]

OREGON PROTESTANT LATINO CHURCHES

History

As previously noted, there is little documentation of Protestant church activities among Hispanics in Oregon. The information presented here was obtained mostly from interviews of pastors.

Early Protestant activity centered on areas where many migrant workers came to pick berries and other crops, such as the Willamette Valley. Gamboa recalls that at the Golden Gate Hop Ranch migrant camp in Independence in the 1940s: "On Sundays, Baptists and other evangelical denominations visited the camp and vied for the residents' attention with prayer and offers of free coffee and doughnuts. Although there were few converts among the predominantly Catholic population

20. Thompson Jr., "Racialized Minority Demographics," 22.

21. "Our Ways," 117.

22. Martinez Jr. and Eddy, "Latino Youth," 841–51.

23. Oregon Center, *Undocumented Workers*, 1.

24. Martinez Jr. and Eddy, "Latino Youth," 843.

25. Aguilera, et al., "Work and Employment," 69–73.

it was not uncommon to hear children singing hymns like 'This Little Light of Mine' in English."[26]

Gonzales-Berry indicates that "[t]he Oregon State Council of Churches had been active in ministering to migrants as early as the 1940s,"[27] but provides no details as to specific activities during this decade.

In the early 1950s there was an interdenominational team comprised of members of American Missionary Fellowship, Mennonite, and Conservative Baptist who worked together to reach the migrants working in the fields. Individuals participating in this outreach included Papa Theissen, Ray Fisk, Tom Phuf, Don and Jeannie Flesch, and Verna Fast.[28] The Oregon State Council of Churches had services to "'Spanish Speaking' clients" in 1957 and activities for "'Texas Mexican' migrants in Eastern Oregon. . . . English, sewing and home nursing classes for adults, Spanish language radio programs, recreation, and summer church camps for children" and the Council worked with other agencies to pressure the state government for migrant labor reform throughout the late 1950s.[29]

Many of the pastors interviewed provided a history of their church. Information in the following sections comes from those formal pastoral interviews, unless otherwise noted. In October 1962 the Conservative Baptist association brought Ray Castro from Rio Grande Bible Institute in Texas to begin work as a Hispanic missionary. The association owned a plot of land on Brown Road NE, just south of Silverton Road in Salem. Craftsmen for Christ began a church building there in 1968 for a Spanish-speaking congregation. In April 1969, Primera Iglesia Bautista was organized with Ray Castro as pastor, and began meeting in the Brown Road building in July 1969, though it was not fully completed at that time.[30]

26. Gamboa and Buan, *Nosotros*, 15.

27. "Tired of Cookies," 98.

28. Roy Libby, e-mail message to author, January 15, 2011.

29. Gonzales-Berry, "Tired of Cookies," 98.

30. This congregation, like many beginning Hispanic congregation, has undergone multiple changes. It dwindled in size to around 20 members and was unable to maintain the financial responsibilities of the building. In 1983 the church was disbanded and remaining members accepted into the Halbert Baptist Church (which became North Salem Baptist) with a vision to create a single bilingual body. After several years, the Spanish-speaking congregation separated amicably from North Salem Baptist to be-

In 1964, a group of evangelical Mexicans began meeting under a tree outside the city of Woodburn, because the only Spanish worship services in the town were Catholic. They stretched out hammocks, shared tacos, and worshiped together without a pastor. Though they came from many denominational backgrounds, and the group participants were always shifting as part of the migrant stream, they eventually became what is now the Iglesia Menonita Pentecostés. Templo Gethsemane also opened in Woodburn in the 1970s.[31] Another early church was the Iglesia de Jesucristo, begun in Forest Grove in 1973.

As more Spanish-speaking immigrants arrived in the 1980s, the number of Protestant Hispanic churches also grew. According to Pastor José González, the first non-Catholic Spanish-speaking church in Portland was an Apostolic Church led by a blind pastor at Prescott and 82nd Avenue. It began in 1980. In 1981, a Spanish-speaking Church of God led by a female pastor began on 192nd Avenue in Gresham. Pastor Cathi Perez-Scrivner and her husband attended the English-speaking Church of God, and as a bilingual Texan, she was touched by the need to minister to the men she saw in the grocery stores returning large sacks of beer bottles for their deposit. On several occasions, she sought a male to lead Bible studies or ministries to the men, but it never worked out, and her pastor told her several times that perhaps God was calling her to minister. Despite her misgivings about cultural inappropriateness, she began ministries in the migrant camps in the agricultural areas east of Portland. She was received respectfully, and over time Ministerio Latino developed, and still meets in the Church of God on 192nd.

Pastor Mardo Jiménez moved from California to Salem in 1980 to pastor the Brown Road Primera Iglesia Bautista congregation. Shortly thereafter, he was invited by the Madras Conservative Baptist congregation in Central Oregon to provide them Spanish literature for the growing Hispanic population of that small town. He complied and frequently travelled there, finally moving there to plant the Spanish-speaking church that was organized in 1980. Pastor Jiménez and his congregation gained notoriety for regular public confrontations with the Bhagwan Shree Rajneesh and members of his religious sect.[32]

---

come Iglesia Bautista Cristo Vive. Roy Libby, e-mail message to author, January 15, 2011.

31. Conversation with Robert Nava, September 2009.

32. Epps, *Unknown God*, 76–77.

The Assemblies of God have also been active in opening churches in Oregon for over thirty years. Little is known about the beginnings of the two older AOG churches in the state, in rural Ontario and Nyssa, but according to Pastor Flora Vergara, they were more than thirty years old in 2011. She indicated that Pastor Ray Meza was a pioneer for this denomination in Oregon, opening a Spanish-speaking Assembly of God in Salem and recruiting pastors to start others. Pastor Rose Medina described how, in 1982, the Hillsboro Latin Assembly of God began as a Spanish-speaking Sunday School class in the English-speaking Assembly of God Church at 6th and Darnielle. Miguel Figueroa was the Spanish Sunday School teacher who had a vision for an entire congregation and was instrumental in calling Pastor George Sanchez as the first pastor.

Pleasant Home Baptist Church opened a Spanish speaking work (now Vida Nueva) in 1984 under the leadership of Pastor José González. In 1985, pastors José González and Mardo Jiménez planted a Conservative Baptist Church in Hillsboro. Costa Rican pastor Juan Bonilla has been in ministry in the Hillsboro area since at least the mid-1980s, and in 2009 was still pastoring a mainly Guatemalan congregation at the Forest Grove Christian Church and leading a jail ministry, though he was in his eighties.

The late 80s and early 90s saw a boom in the number of Hispanic immigrants and corresponding growth in Spanish-speaking churches. Pastor Ramón Argüello started Primera Iglesia Hispana Ebenezer (Ebenezer First Hispanic Church) in Portland in 1990. He recalls that there were only a handful of Spanish-speaking Protestant churches in the state at that time. Pastor José González noted that when he returned to Oregon in 1993 after attending seminary in Texas, there were suddenly all types of Hispanic churches in Portland.

Church planting has continued into this century. Some examples are: Portland Spanish SE Rim-La Cosecha Foursquare Church in 2005, Village Baptist in Beaverton and Reedwood Friends starting Spanish services in 2006, and the Oregon Pacific District Church of the Nazarene employing a full-time Hispanic Ministries coordinator to oversee training of pastors and Spanish-speaking ministries in 2008.

Spanish-speaking churches in Oregon have had many false starts, changes in location, leadership, and name, and many are still somewhat tenuous in nature. State of Oregon corporation records indicate that many Spanish-speaking churches were officially organized in the 1990s and the early 2000s, only to be dissolved an average of two years later.[33]

The researcher has identified 232 Protestant Hispanic churches in Oregon, although this number is certainly inaccurate. During the three years of her research, she has experienced first-hand the tenuous and invisible nature of many of these churches. She has called phone numbers of Hispanic churches and pastors listed on websites that are no longer in service, discovered that churches have changed names and locations multiple times, and driven to addresses listed on websites that are no longer churches. On the other hand, she has contributed to this list by making note of Hispanic churches that appear in no phone book or web listing as she notices them in church buildings and commercial properties as she drives by, or hears of them from friends, pastors, and colleagues.

Churches in this Study

With this background, the remainder of the chapter contains a description of the churches visited in this study from 2008 to 2010. The beginnings of each church, its current meeting place and relationship with a denomination (if any), and size are presented, followed by demographic information such as the national origin of the congregation and pastor, and education and employment of the congregation and pastor. Finally, the services provided by and most needed by the congregation are described, as well as the pastor's assessment of the strongest area of the church. Unless otherwise indicated, this information was compiled based on observations made during the researcher's visit to the church service and information provided by the pastor in a subsequent face-to-face interview.[34]

CHURCHES OUTSIDE THE PORTLAND METROPOLITAN AREA

The oldest church in this study is Iglesia Menonita Pentecostés (Pentecost Mennonite Church) in Woodburn, the city with the highest percent-

---

33. Based on a business name search of the Oregon Secretary of State, Corporation Division's online records, using search terms "Iglesia," and "Templo."

34. Pastor Tony Estey of Hood River Iglesia Esperanza y Vida en Jesucristo (Church of Hope and Life in Jesus Christ) Christian and Missionary Alliance Church and Pastor Lowell Stutzman of Grants Pass New Hope Bible Mennonite Brethren Church answered the interview questions by e-mail.

age of Hispanics in the state.[35] Its beginnings in a hammock under a tree were previously mentioned. The church underwent various name changes as it sought to create an identity acceptable to both congregation and pastor. The current pastor, Víctor Vargas, is from Costa Rica and has been ministering there since 1981. This body actively participates in the Mennonite Church U.S.A. Around 140 people regularly attend services, held in the church's own building. Most of the congregation is Mexican, although Costa Ricans, Guatemalans, and an Argentine family also attend. All of the adults are first-generation immigrants. Pastor Vargas received a pastoral call in his native Costa Rica. He obtained a *bachillerato* from the University of Costa Rica, and took pastoral studies and was ordained through the Mennonite Church in Costa Rica. In addition to his pastoral work, Pastor Vargas also recently began to work part time delivering flowers. Most of the congregation is employed in agriculture, and he estimated that 75 percent had completed only elementary school, another ten percent had completed their GED, and 2–3 percent had attended some college. This congregation has participated in several outreaches to the community over the years, including a food and clothing bank and an emergency shelter. Pastor Vargas commented that immigration reform was a pressing issue for the Hispanic community, and described his congregation's faith as their greatest strength.

Nueva Esperanza (New Hope) in the central coast town of Newport is also a CBNW congregation. At a time when the English-speaking congregation was between pastors, several members felt a desire to begin a Spanish-speaking ministry. The senior pastor hired shared this passion, and brought a missionary with experience in Latin America to start a Bible study in Spanish. A few years later, in 2002, the current Hispanic pastor, Jiroo Kuroda, was hired. Originally from Peru, he serves the English-speaking congregation as worship pastor as well. This church has a vision for one body which happens to speak two languages, and shares resources, leadership, and the building. (The Spanish service is on Sunday evenings in the sanctuary). Pastor Kuroda has a degree in Christian Education from Rio Grande Bible Institute in Texas. Most of the congregation are from Mexico, with a minority from Guatemala, and one Colombian. All of the adult congregation are first

---

35. According to the U.S. Census Bureau, Hispanics make up 56 percent of Woodburn's population. American Factfinder, 2005-2009 American Community Survey 5-Year Estimates: Woodburn City, Oregon.

generation immigrants. About sixty people regularly attended in 2010. Only eight of these people completed high school, and one has attended college. Most of them work as housekeepers in the many hotels in the area, while others work in the fishing industry or in agriculture. This church has a clothes closet and an emergency financial assistance program for the community and also provides employment connections as well as interpretation for appointments. It is also very active in supporting missionaries, and any visiting missionaries speak in both English and Spanish services. The pastor mentioned immigration advice as an unmet need, and described the congregation as one in which friendly fellowship prevails.

A second CBNW church called Nueva Esperanza (New Hope) participated in this study, although this one was in Hermiston, a small town in rural north central Oregon. Genaro Loredo has been the Spanish congregation's pastor since it began in 2003. At that time the English-speaking church board had been praying about a Spanish-speaking ministry. In 2010, the congregation of about ninety people met on Sunday mornings in a fellowship hall, at the same time as the English service in the sanctuary. The Hispanic pastor and congregation were fully integrated into the life of New Hope Community Church, pooling finances, serving in various ministries, and participating in a single youth group. All of the Spanish speakers were from Mexico but there had been a few Central Americans in the past. Eighty percent were first-generation immigrants. Pastor Lopez also immigrated from Mexico at a young age. About 10 percent of the congregation completed only elementary school, while about 70 percent completed high school, and 10 percent had gone on to college. Pastor Lopez had completed a course of study by extension in Spanish offered by CBNW, and a BA in theology from Newburgh Theological Seminary and School of the Bible in Indiana. He worked full-time in the ministry. Most of the congregation worked in agriculture, although some were medical or educational assistants. The Hispanic congregation participated in the broader church's support of various community ministries such as Agape House and a crisis pregnancy center, as well as supporting missionaries. Pastor Lopez indicated a need for opportunities for the Hispanic community to better their English and for translation and cultural orientation services. He described this congregation as loving, helpful, and able to carry burdens.

In the small Southern Oregon town of Grants Pass, a Mennonite Brethren congregation also called New Hope participated in the study. It is a fully integrated church with about half Hispanics, half Anglos, and a few from Africa. Total worship service attendance ranges from seventy-five to ninety people. These services are done in both Spanish and English. Songs are sung in both languages simultaneously, and praying and sharing are done in both languages, although the sermon is in English and is not translated, as the pastor indicated that all Hispanics currently attending have strong enough English listening skills to understand. Pastor Lowell Stutzman indicated that his parents began this church in the mid-1960s, and a retired Mennonite Brethren missionary from Mexico returned to the area in the early 1970s. He began visiting many of the agricultural camps and soon thereafter established a separate church which met in the building at a different time than the Anglo church. In the mid-90s the churches were combined. All of the Hispanic members in 2010 were of Mexican ancestry, and about 40 percent of them are first-generation immigrants. About 5 percent have completed only elementary school, another 75 percent have completed high school and about 20 percent have gone on to college. Nearly all of them worked in "blue collar" jobs. (The timber industry has traditionally been the mainstay in this region). Pastor Stutzman is a bi-vocational Anglo, who describes himself as being able to "reasonably communicate" in Spanish. He has a BA but has not attended a seminary and is mostly trained through personal study. The pastor described the Hispanic community as needing strong advocacy, and his congregation as being "truly one family," "a place of healing," high in caring and compassion.

Templo Betania (Bethany Temple) is an Assembly of God congregation in Ontario, Oregon. When the researcher visited in July 2010, the pastor was on a three-week vacation, and several attempts to contact him were unsuccessful, so the information here is incomplete and based solely on observations made during that site visit. The church owns its building, a small structure without air-conditioning taken up mostly by the sanctuary. There were about twenty in attendance for the Sunday service which was held at 6:00 p.m. Most, if not all, of the congregation were first- or second-generation Mexican immigrants— at one point a music leader asked if everyone present spoke *mexicano* (instead of *español*), and much of the music was distinctively Mexican in style. One of the worship instruments was a set of maracas painted like a Mexican flag. Based on the church's location in a rundown area, the sermon emphasizing oppression of the poor by the wealthy, and linguistic archaisms such as *ansina*, *haiga*, and *nadien*,[36] this congregation is at the lower end of the socioeconomic and educational spectrum. Many in the church are bilingual—the researcher and her Latino husband were greeted with "God bless you" in English and there were English Bibles in the pew racks.

Ulysses Vela is the pastor of the Spanish-speaking congregation of Monmouth Christian Church. Monmouth Christian does not consider itself to be part of a denomination but a sovereign church. It began when Pastor Víctor Álvarez came from Guanajuato, Mexico, to the community in 1997 or 1998, fulfilling the English-speaking congregation's desire to start a Spanish-speaking ministry. A core of people began attending this congregation soon after its creation as the result of a church split in the nearby town of Independence. The Spanish service meets on Sunday afternoons in the sanctuary and has full access to other parts of the building through a calendaring process. Pastor Vela has an office there and is a full-time paid staff member of Monmouth Christian. There are bilingual Hispanic representatives on the overall elder board, and all finances are held in common with the English-speaking congregation. About fifty people regularly attend the worship services. Three are Anglo women who are married to or dating the pastor's relatives. All others are of Mexican background, and about 40 percent are first-generation immigrants who immigrated at least a decade ago. The pastor's mother was born in Mexico, but his father was *tejano* (Texan), making him second generation on one side and fourth or fifth generation on the other side. His wife, however, was born in Mexico. The pastor estimated that about 45 percent of the congregation attended only elementary school, some 50 percent finished high school, and 5 percent went on to attend college, including one woman who obtained her medical degree in Mexico. Pastor Vela attended Salem Bible College, an Assembly of God school, for two years and had nearly completed his AA there at the time of the interview. All of the coursework was done face-to-face and in English. (Pastor Vela is most comfortable speaking English but also preaches and ministers in Spanish.) Two of the congregation were employed as teachers, while others worked in plant nurseries, canneries, factories or as janitors or

---

36. Gonzalez Pino and Pino, "Heritage Speaker," 35. In standard modern Spanish, these words are "así," "haya," and "nadie" respectively.

caregivers. The congregation had a community outreach called Helping Hands that gave food to the community, opened the church building for short-term emergency housing, and called on first-time guests with cookies. They also were supporting several missionaries along with the English-speaking congregation. The pastor indicated a need for clear information regarding laws in the U.S. for the whole Hispanic community, including his congregation. He observed a strong spiritual foundation in his church body.

Esperanza y Vida en Jesucristo (Hope and Life in Jesus Christ) Church was meeting in Hood River, Oregon, in the Christian & Missionary Alliance (CMA) Church building on Saturday evenings. It began in 1999 on the initiative of the English-speaking Alliance congregation to minister to the Hispanic population in the area, calling a pastor to start a Spanish-speaking church. Pastor Tony Estey is a Spanish-speaking Anglo, married to a Mexican woman. There were about 150 in regular attendance (including children) in July 2010 at their worship services, held Saturday evenings. The congregation was mostly Mexican, with several South and Central Americans and a number of Anglos who speak Spanish. The pastor estimated that 80 percent of the congregation had only a sixth-grade education or less, while 20 percent had finished high school and 3 percent gone on to college. His own training was in the CMA course of study for pastors. The pastor had been bi-vocational for many years but dedicated himself full time to the pastorate in 2006. Most of the congregation worked in the local fruit industry or hotels and restaurants. This congregation followed a small group system that met many of the material and spiritual needs of attendees. It also provided training in various areas through its discipleship school. The pastor described the church's strength as having a strong personal relationship with Jesus Christ and a strong biblical foundation. He believed that immigration reform was a pressing concern, as well as a need for the community to provide more opportunities for the Hispanic community to progress and advance.

Iglesia Bautista Conservadora Bilingüe (Bilingual Conservative Baptist Church) in the Central Oregon town of Madras (Jefferson County) was established in 1980 as part of a church planting effort of CB Northwest in the 1980s. It continued to have strong ties to this organization, participating in its events. It was first pastored by Mardoqueo Jiménez. The congregation shared space for many years in the English-speaking Conservative Baptist Church, starting in a small basement room, then moving up to the sanctuary, and eventually building their own 7,000 square foot building adjacent to the English-speaking church. In 2010, the Spanish speaking church was mostly autonomous from the English-speaking congregation, although they continued to receive spiritual and material support (about $200 per month), and many of the Hispanic children and youth participate regularly in the programs of the Anglo church. About 115 people were in regular attendance during July 2010. The pastor, Jaime Pantoja, was from Mexico, as was the majority of the congregation, although the volunteer youth pastor and his wife were non-Spanish-speaking Anglos, and there were also a few Panamanians, Nicaraguans and Salvadorans. Around 80 percent of the congregation were first generation immigrants, many settling in the Madras area twenty to twenty-five years ago. The pastor was a very recent immigrant who worked full time in the ministry. Most of the congregation was employed in area wood mills or in agriculture, although several worked for the local school district or social service agencies. The pastor estimated that about 35 percent of the congregation completed only elementary school, another 35 percent had finished high school, and that around 7 percent had attended college or were currently doing so. Pastor Pantoja obtained a *bachillerato* in theology from the Baptist Seminary in Nogales, Sonora, Mexico and was ordained by the Baptist Church. This church ministered to the community by preparing outreach events for targeted audiences such as married couples or children, and were supporting a missionary in Ecuador. They also participated in an annual Madras-area church fair; their role the past few years was washing cars. The pastor indicated a need for more space for Christian education in the building, as they have outgrown the classrooms, and a need for more stores in Madras. He cited fellowship as a strength of the congregation.

Rogue Valley Fellowship in Medford, Oregon, had a Spanish-speaking congregation pastored by Santiago Argueta. This independent, non-denominational church began in 2001. The Salvadoran pastor and his Mexican wife, along with another Mexican family, had been attending the English services. They tried providing interpretation into Spanish, but this really didn't work, so they started holding meetings in Spanish separately. This group outgrew the meeting room, so they moved to a larger room, which they also outgrew, and now they use the sanctuary, meeting for worship Sunday mornings at 10:00 a.m. and

6:30 p.m. The Spanish-speaking group did not pay rent and was considered part of the larger church. Pastor Argueta worked only in ministry and participated regularly in staff meetings and decision-making, but there was little interaction between the two congregations other than the Hispanic children attending morning Sunday School in English with the Anglos. There were about 150 in regular attendance in August 2010. The pastor was the only non-Mexican in the Spanish-speaking congregation. Nearly all the adults immigrated from Mexico and all the children and youth were born here. Approximately 5 percent of the adults also spoke an indigenous dialect. Most of the congregation worked in service industries, such as hotels, restaurants, landscaping, and in the famous Harry & David fruit packing center. Pastor Argueta has received no formal training as a pastor, nor has he been required to, although he has been ordained by the local church. He simply acceded to the request by the Anglo church to assume leadership for the Spanish speakers. The pastor calculated that perhaps 50 percent of the congregation had completed only elementary school, and did not know about any additional education for the rest. The congregation supports missions activities in Mexico and Central America and does spiritual outreach such as small Bible study groups in the community, but no material ministries like food banks. The pastor cited legalization as the most pressing issue for Hispanics in the community and fellowship as a strength of his congregation.

WASHINGTON COUNTY

La Iglesia de Jesucristo (Church of Jesus Christ) in Forest Grove was part of a group of independent churches that separated from the Apostolic Assembly in the 1970s, but kept the same doctrine. It is one of the oldest congregations in the state, founded in 1973. This church owned its building. Pastor Luis Ramirez was born in California to Mexican parents and was fully bilingual and bicultural. He attended the Apostolic Bible College in Hayworth, CA. He estimated that 75 percent of the congregation is first-generation immigrants from Mexico and Guatemala. Based on observation during the site visit, this immigration appears to have happened long ago. In 2007, there were about 120 regularly attending worship services. Most of the adult members had completed elementary school, with about 10 percent continuing on to high school and college. Most worked in factories and construction. At the time of the interview, the congregation was considering beginning a food bank as an outreach to the community. The pastor indicated that immigration information was an ongoing unmet need for the congregation, and that its strength was "our Lord Jesus Christ and the belief, the conviction that we have that the Bible is God's word, that bonds us together and gives us the strength we need."

One of the oldest Latin American Assemblies of God in Oregon is Iglesia del Pueblo (The People's Church). It was founded in Hillsboro in 1982, and at the time of this study was pastored by Rose Medina, widow of the former pastor. She immigrated to the U.S. from Mexico as a child and was completely bilingual, as was this church's ministry and most of its forty to fifty congregants. There were several first-generation families attending this church, but most were born in the U.S. Most of the people were from Mexico, but there were also Costa Ricans, Salvadorans and a few Anglos from the U.S. who spoke Spanish. The pastor estimated that about one-fifth of the congregation had completed elementary school only, another fifth had gone on to college, and the remainder finished high school. Pastor Medina had taken many seminars and courses through the Berean Bible Institute extension program of the Assemblies of God. There was a wide range of employment types, from engineers to janitors and assembly workers. This congregation shared a building with the Anglo Assembly of God in Hillsboro for many years, but wanted to build their own building and purchased land for this purpose. In 2007 they were saving to begin construction and meeting in a Baptist church building in Cornelius, a small town neighboring Hillsboro, on Sunday afternoons. The pastor indicated that a strength of the congregation was its initiative, citing that many had taken advantage of classes in the community to improve their knowledge and skills in various areas. She stated that information on immigration and marriage and family counseling were needs of the Hispanic population in her area.

As mentioned previously, the Conservative Baptists Northwest (CBNW) were early and active church planters among Hispanics in Oregon. Iglesia Evangélica Hispana Cristo Viene (Hispanic Evangelical Church Christ is Coming) in Hillsboro began in the mid 1980s as a CBNW church, and its pastor, Héctor Rodríguez, arrived in 1987. In the mid 1990s, it became independent of CBNW, although the congregation was occasionally participating in CBNW activities at the time of the pastoral interview in 2007. The congregation was sharing space with

Hillsboro First Baptist Church. In the early years, the Spanish-speaking services were held in the basement, but for more than a decade they had been meeting in the church gymnasium on Sunday mornings, while the English-speaking services were held simultaneously in the sanctuary. The pastor and many of the congregants were Guatemalan, in line with the Hispanic population in the area, although there were also Mexicans, Salvadorans, Venezuelans and even some non-Spanish-speaking U.S. Anglos. In 2007, there were about 200 in regular attendance. The pastor estimated that about 50 percent had completed only elementary school, another 15 percent finished high school and 10 percent college. They worked in a wide range of jobs, from nurses and small business owners to hotel maids and construction workers. Pastor Rodríguez holds several degrees, including two from Guatemalan institutions. He studied English at Seattle Pacific University and completed an MA in theology and advanced studies in missiology at Western Baptist Seminary. This church had a regular summer outreach to the nearby migrant camps. The pastor indicated that this church had a strong leadership development program. He cited a need for cultural communication between Hispanics and the Anglo community, for the Hispanics to be accepted as human beings.

City Bible Church is an independent nondenominational church native to Portland. A small nucleus of people had a desire to open a ministry in Spanish. After some time and prayer, they began a Spanish Bible study in 1998. At the time of the site visit in 2007, Spanish speaking services were held in the sanctuary of West (Tigard) campus on Sunday afternoons, and children's activities occurred in other parts of the building. The Spanish congregation was completely integrated into the financial plans of the City Bible Church (all funds from both congregations went into and drew from the same general fund), and they were not paying rent to use the building. At the time the pastor was interviewed, Sunday service attendance ranged from 160 to 200 people, including children. The pastor was the child of North American missionaries, raised in Central America. This congregation was one of the most diverse in the study as far as countries of origin, although the majority were Mexican. The pastor estimated that 50–60 percent of the congregation had completed high school and that perhaps 5 percent had completed college and a few people graduate programs. The congregation had a wide variety of occupations, from business owners and store managers to construction and food-service workers. The pastor was educated and worked as an engineer before he became part of the full-time church staff. He had not had formal pastoral training at a Bible college or seminary but completed a City Bible course for lay pastors and cited his upbringing as a child of missionaries as significant preparation for his role. The church was using a small group system through which "common care" counseling and encouragement were provided, as well as access to the church's food, clothing, and furniture banks. They also had a Bible-based program for addiction recovery and offered ESL classes. The pastor indicated a need for computer training and for immigration law advice. The pastor felt that the diversity of the congregation in terms of national origen and being multigenerational was its greatest strength.

Several Oregon churches trace their origins to Latin American denominations. Iglesia de Restauración Elim Internacional (Church of Restoration Elim International) in Hillsboro began in 1997 and maintained strong ties to the Elim home office in Guatemala. Pastor Jeremías Diego indicated in 2009 that he travels there frequently. This church was completely economically independent. They rented commercial properties for several years but found it hard to adapt them for ministry purposes and to pay high rent, so since the time of the research observation visit in 2008, they moved to share space with a large independent Anglo church in Aloha. The pastor was Guatemalan, as was the majority of the congregation, although there were also Mexicans and other Central Americans. Two-thirds of the congregation were first-generation immigrants. Some of the congregants spoke an indigenous dialect in addition to Spanish, while the youth preferred to use English. In 2008, there were around 400 in attendance for worship services. The pastor indicated that about one-third of the congregation had completed only elementary school, another one-third high school, and another one-third college prior to immigrating. Most of the congregation worked in factories or plant nurseries. Pastor Diego had an MDiv from a California school and was working on his doctorate. The pastor characterized the congregation as spiritually strong and filled with the Holy Spirit, and indicated a focus on the youth, with many activities and trainings for them as "the future of the church."

Although it became independent from the denomination in 2006, Iglesia Cristiana Salvados para Servir (Saved to Serve Christian Church) in Southwest Portland traces its beginnings to Iglesia de Dios

Pentecostal, Movimiento Internacional (IDPMI) (Pentecostal Church of God, International Movement), from Puerto Rico. This church was completely independent and self-sustaining economically at the time of the pastoral interview. The main pastor, Neftali Franco, was Salvadoran and the associate pastor, Francisco Mateo, was Guatemalan. About 90 percent of the congregation were first-generation immigrants, mainly Mexican, but persons from all over Central America as well as Puerto Rico, Ecuador and Peru also attended. When the church observation visit was done in 2008, the congregation was renting space from a Korean congregation in Beaverton, but it moved and was meeting on Sunday evenings in the sanctuary of a very large Nazarene church building in the west hills of Portland. Around 400 regularly attended. The associate pastor calculated that around 70 percent of the congregants had completed only elementary school, another 20 percent high school and that only about 3 percent had attended college. Pastor Franco studied at the Mizpa Bible Institute in Los Angeles, which is sponsored by IDPMI and Pastor Mateo had completed two and one half years of a Bible school and leadership development program through the church. Both of these pastors worked full time in the ministry and were not bi-vocational. The congregation had varied jobs, from nurses to electricians to other construction workers and managers. This church followed a strict cell group system and ministered to the material needs of people through this system. They also had evangelism activities and were sponsoring two new churches in Yucatán, Mexico. The associate pastor remarked that he did not see any unmet needs for those attending his church, indicating his gratitude for the many ways "this country has given us a hand" and that the church taught its members to be self-sufficient, not looking for a government handout. He described the friendship in the cell groups as the greatest strength of the church.

Like many Protestant Hispanic churches in Oregon, Vida (Life) Church has passed through a series of changes and moves. In the early 1990s, the pastor sought an Anglo church with which to begin a Spanish-speaking ministry. New Song, another independent, non-denominational church in Portland, was open to this and the congregation worshipped there for about twelve years, meeting in various New Song spaces, but not in the sanctuary. The Spanish-speaking church then became independent. They purchased a house which served as office space and ministry center, but it was not large enough for worship services.

They rented space from two churches in the Beaverton area over the ensuing years. Most recently, the congregation moved to Life Church, an Assemblies of God congregation with over 600 members in Aloha, a suburb west of Portland. They were paying rent and were not financially or structurally integrated with Life Church. Most of the congregation lived close to this church building. Pastor Raúl Giménez was from Argentina, and the congregation was mostly Mexican, but there were also Guatemalans, Salvadorans, Panamanians, Venezuelans and two North Americans married to Hispanics. In 2010, about ninety people, including children, regularly attended. Most of the adults finished high school, with about five continuing to college, and one had a master's degree. Most worked in service professions, and none worked in agriculture, although during the summer months the congregation ministered in one of the area migrant camps. They also had a bread distribution ministry, but their most active ministry was counseling. The pastor cited praise, worship, and teaching as strengths of this church and a need for public transportation near the church building.

Another Spanish-speaking congregation with ties to CBNW is Village Baptist in Beaverton. The Spanish-speaking congregation was founded in 2006, although the church has had different ethnic or linguistic ministries for much longer. The Spanish-speaking group is adamantly part of the larger church. According to the Hispanic pastor, Mauricio Rivas, the broader church's vision is "We are one family"; those who speak English, the Spanish-speakers, and the Korean and Chinese congregations. In 2008, services in Spanish were being held in the sanctuary on Sunday afternoons. The pastor emigrated from El Salvador to Canada at a young age and was bilingual and bicultural. This congregation had mostly very recent immigrants from Mexico, most of whom were indigenous Mixteco dialect speakers, for whom Spanish is a second language, although there were a few from Central and South America as well. In 2008, there were about 170 in regular attendance. Most of the congregation was employed in agriculture or other service jobs such as house cleaning. The pastor indicated that very few of the congregation, perhaps 15 percent, had completed elementary school and that there were several who were illiterate, that only 5 percent had finished high school and even less had gone on to college. These latter were U.S.-born. Pastor Rivas holds a seminary degree from CETECA in Guatemala (affiliated with Dallas Theological Seminary), and in 2008 was working to complete a master's through Logos University in Florida. The Spanish-speaking congregation has a summer outreach to area migrant camps that includes food, medicine and clothing along with evangelization. Village also provides English-as-a-second-language (ESL) classes, and the pastor has a wide service network, although he cited legal advice as an unmet need. This includes immigration issues but goes beyond to having a basic understanding of laws in the U.S. The pastor indicated that a strength of the church is its love, acceptance and support provided by the pastor and his wife for the congregation—they find constant friendship in them.

MULTNOMAH COUNTY

Casa del Padre (Father's House) had large congregations in both Washington and Multnomah Counties and they shared the same pastor, Víctor Alvarizares. Thus, the description of these congregations here serves as a bridge between the two counties. The church first began in Portland in 1997 by persons who had belonged to El Shaddai in California. The El Shaddai "denomination" can be traced to the Elim movement in Central America.[37] The Beaverton church began in 1999, having been a cell group of the Portland church. At the time of the site visit, the Beaverton congregation was renting space from an Anglo Free Methodist Church, and the Portland congregation rented from a Russian congregation that had adapted a commercial building for use as a church, although both congregations began in homes. According to the pastor, the Portland church at one time had over 500 members and was the fastest growing, largest Hispanic church in the area. Due to allegations of sexual misconduct by the former pastor, it had fallen in attendance to about 150 in 2008. The Beaverton church was averaging around 225 people. Most of the participants in both congregations were first-generation immigrants. The majority were from Mexico, followed by Guatemalans, with a smattering of persons from nearly all other Latin American countries. About 25 percent of the congregants had completed high school, and about 5 percent went on to college, some through a cooperative agreement with the church and the College for

---

37. So stated Pastor Víctor Alvarizares in his interview, but sociologist of religion Paul Freston indicates that El Shaddai was begun in Guatemala by a member of the Guatemalan elite ("Contours," 238). Whatever the case may be, the Casa del Padre churches in Oregon trace their origins to Central America.

Global Deployment in Washington State. Most of the people in both congregations worked in construction or service industries. The pastor immigrated from Guatemala at a very young age and was bilingual and bicultural. He and his wife both held doctorates from the College for Global Deployment. These congregations emphasized education through cell groups and leadership training called "The Ladder of Success," and in 2008 had both just begun a ministry called "The Father's Arms" focused on meeting the material needs in the community. The pastor and his wife cited increasing legal restrictions such as requirements to obtain a driver's license as a problem for many in the congregations, and described leadership as a strength of both churches.

Iglesia de Jesucristo Ministerio de Vida Eterna Luz del Pueblo (Church of Jesus Christ Ministry of Eternal Life Light of the Town/People) was the result of two ministries (one formerly Assembly of God and the other Apostolic) that had joined just before the research visit in 2008. It was meeting in the fellowship hall of an English-speaking Apostolic church in the afternoon. There were nineteen in attendance, of whom eight were children or youth. In the parking lot prior to entering, the researcher heard fluent English speakers, indicating that they had lived in the U.S. a significant amount of time. This group was short-lived, as the pastor, Víctor Rojas, indicated that it dissolved shortly after the site visit. As a result, there is no additional data to share.

Manantiales de Vida Eterna (Streams of Eternal Life) is a church organization that began about twenty years ago in California, according to Gresham church pastor Nelson Reyes. There are just three or four congregations of this denomination, all on the West Coast. The original pastor in Oregon was a Venezuelan who had a ministry in the migrant camps in Damascus beginning in 1992. He fell ill, and asked Pastor Reyes to continue the ministry. In 2008 the congregation was meeting in a building belonging to an Assembly of God congregation in Gresham, paying monthly rent. A large upstairs room had been adapted as a chapel specifically for the Spanish-speaking group. A Phillippine congregation was meeting downstairs in the afternoon at the same time the Spanish service was held. Among the thirty-five to forty people who regularly attended were Mexicans, Salvadorans, Guatemalans, and a Chilean. The pastor estimated that 60 percent are first-generation immigrants and that about half of the adults completed only elementary school, while the other half are high school graduates. They were employed in plant nurseries, restaurants, factories, and as nannies or maids. The pastor himself has had no formal Bible or theological training and completed the second year of *bachillerato* in his native El Salvador.[38] He suffered a fall in his work on a construction site several years ago and was disabled. He was not receiving a salary from the church and only ministers as his physical health allowed. This congregation participated in personal evangelization in the community and supported orphan children abroad. The pastor indicated that dental and medical care was a pressing need for his congregants that is not being adequately supplied. He characterized his church as being one of fervent prayer and strong faith to continue ahead.

Ministerio Restauración (Restoration Ministry) is Portland's Mennonite Latino church. It began in 1992, when the pastor of a Hispanic Mennonite church in another town had the vision to plant more churches, and Pastor Samuel Morán, was invited to move to Portland from California. This congregation first met in Portland in the Hawthorne District in the English-speaking Mennonite church building, then moved to Oak Grove in Clackamas County to the south because many of the congregation lived in that area. Over time, families moved, and at the time of the pastoral interview in 2009 the congregation had moved back to the first building in Portland because it was closer to the current members' homes. They were meeting in the afternoon, and paying a symbolic rent of fifty dollars to the English-speaking congregation for use of the building, although the pastor did not have an office there. The pastor was Guatemalan, and the congregation of about sixty people was made up equally of Guatemalans and Mexicans, with two or three Spanish-speaking Anglos born in the U.S. About 60 percent of the congregation was first-generation immigrants, and the pastor estimated that about 85 percent of the adults had completed high school, with the remainder having completed some portion of elementary education but none going on to college. Pastor Morán studied at the Monte Basán Bible Institute (a denomination native to Guatemala) prior to immigrating, then completed a full course of study at the interdenominational Spanish pastoral institute led by Felix Rosales and housed at George Fox Evangelical Seminary, and in 2010 completed another two-year course of study through the Mennonite Seminario Bíblico Anabautista

---

38. Equivalent to approximately 11th grade in the U.S. educational system.

(Anabaptist Biblical Seminary) in Texas.[39] The pastor was not bi-vocational, and he reported that most of the congregation worked in factories or service occupations. This church did not have ministry programs such as a food cupboard, but it occasionally brings in attorneys through the Mennonite Conference to give legal advice. Nonetheless, the pastor cited legal advice as an ongoing need for this congregation. He indicated that a strength of this church is worship.

Iglesia Luz del Pueblo (Light of the Town Church)[40] is a Southern Baptist church in Gresham that began in 1998, out of a Latino Baptist church split. At the time of the site visit in 2008, the congregation of 140 to 180 people was meeting in an Anglo Southern Baptist building on Sunday afternoons, paying a token amount of rent. A majority of the congregation were first-generation immigrants from Mexico, as was the pastor, José González. There were representatives from other nations such as Guatemala, Cuba, Chile, Honduras, and El Salvador, and the pastor´s wife was one of several Anglos born in the U.S. The pastor estimated very few of the adults in the congregation had attended school beyond the primary level in their home countries, but that about 50 percent of them had gone on to obtain a GED in the U.S., and four individuals had obtained college degrees. The pastor attended seminary at Río Grande, Texas, where he obtained a degree in theology taught in Spanish. Many of the congregation worked in factories, but others were electricians, teachers, administrators and mechanics. The pastor himself was bi-vocational, working part time in a warehouse to obtain insurance and retirement benefits. This church had a ministry to addicts and prostitutes seeking to make life changes, as well as a food bank and clothing ministry. It participated annually in a community fair sponsored by area churches and was very active in foreign missions. The pastor described this church as being very loving and its greatest need being fully bilingual people to interpret in social and legal situations for monolingual Spanish congregants.

Two Foursquare Churches in Multnomah County were included in this study. Rosa de Sarón (Rose of Sharon) met in northeast Portland, and La Cosecha (The Harvest) was on the eastern edge of Portland. At the time of the site visit, they were sharing the same pastor, Alfonso

39. Allyn, "Pastor Samuel Moran came to Portland to lead exploding Hispanic Mennonite community," *Oregonian,* June 24, 2010.

40. The Spanish word *pueblo* could also be translated as "people."

Rodríguez, who was from Mexico. Rosa de Sarón started in 1993 when the denomination brought a Cuban pastor to Oregon to start a Spanish-speaking ministry and was renting space in a Presbyterian Church building. La Cosecha began in 2005 and was sharing a building with an Anglo Foursquare congregation. Most of the congregants in both locations were from Mexico, with a few Guatemalans. In the northeast Portland church, about 70 percent were from the Yucatan Peninsula and spoke a Mayan dialect as well as Spanish. A majority of the members had completed high school, but none had attended college. Most worked in service industries such as restaurants and hotels. Some were small business owners while others worked in construction or factories. The pastor worked exclusively in the church and had attended the Instituto Bíblico Ebenezer, an institution of the Iglesia de Dios Pentecostal Puerto Rico, in Chicago. He also had training through and was ordained by the Assemblies of God. The church did not have outreach programs other than evangelism in the local community, but supported several churches in Mexico. In 2008 they had recently done a needs assessment of the congregation and had identified a need for training and counseling around areas of self-esteem, responding to racism, and conflict resolution. The pastor indicated that fellowship was a strength of these churches.

Roca de Salvación (Rock of Salvation) was part of the North American Pacific District of the Assemblies of God in 2008 but became independent shortly thereafter. Pastor Carlos Ortiz is Mexican and bi-vocational. This church had been meeting since 2002 in a building belonging to an Anglo Life Fellowship Church in the urban St. John's area of Portland, giving a monthly love offering for its use. Nearly all the church-goers were first-generation immigrants, mainly Mexican, although there were some Salvadorans and Guatemalans, and nearly all of them had some previous contact with a Protestant church before immigrating. About seventy people regularly attended, of whom approximately 50 percent of the adults completed elementary school, some 20 percent high school, and less than 5 percent hold a college degree. Most of the adults worked in manufacturing, as did the pastor, who was a quality inspector. The church had a limited emergency ministry to those already associated with it, and a regular outreach to the community in a nearby park in conjunction with City Team Ministries. They also supported three missionaries abroad. The pastor cited a need for English and computer classes at a time and place accessible to his congregants, and a more general need for educational services for the Hispanic community. He described his church as one where the love of God is very present.

Reedwood Friends (Quaker) Church began a Spanish-speaking ministry in 2006. It was the youngest congregation in this study, with about ten people present during the 2008 site visit, although the pastor indicated at that time that between twenty and thirty were often in attendance. The group was made up mostly of recent Cuban immigrants, and they were meeting in a small chapel of the Reedwood Friends building. Pastor Mario Macías was Mexican, and he emphasized in the interview that the Anglos and Latinos were one body, two cultures, at least two different languages, but one church. The pastor earned an MDiv from Fuller Theological Seminary, and the majority of the congregation had at least a high school education. Many worked in factories. The church participated with Reedwood Friends' food bank and missions emphases, and the Hispanic and Anglo pastors worked together to connect the Spanish-speaking congregants to local social services. However, the pastor cited an ongoing need for psychological and emotional healing for many of these recent immigrants after traumatic journeys. On the other hand, he described the spiritual freedom and respect that attendees were discovering in their new church home to be a strength.

DISCUSSION AND ANALYSIS

This final section reviews the composition of the congregations in this study in terms of their countries of origin in relation to the larger Oregon Hispanic population. A brief discussion of legal status follows, and the section concludes with a summary of the needs and strengths of the congregations, as described by the pastors. Relationships with denominations and other churches, including building sharing, are discussed in more depth in chapter 3. Heterogeneity within the congregations in terms of race and ethnicity, language use, socioeconomic level, and generation of immigration is examined in detail in chapter 4. A detailed description of the worship services attended by the author at each church is found in chapter 5.

Congregation's Nationality in Relation
to Oregon's Hispanic Population

The churches in this study were representative of the general Oregon Hispanic population in terms of country of origin, for the most part. The great majority of the Oregon Hispanic population is Mexican. There is little heterogeneity of national origin, and the Puerto Rican presence that is significant in the eastern part of the U.S. is overshadowed by Mexicans and by the Central Americans as a group.

Focusing on first-generation immigrants, nearly all the congregations were majority Mexican. Several churches had only Mexicans in their Spanish-speaking congregations. These congregations were all outside Portland metropolitan area. They were Newport Nueva Esperanza, Grants Pass Mennonite Brethren, Hermiston Nueva Esperanza, and Medford Rogue Valley Fellowship. According to 2000 Census data, the largest Hispanic population in the counties where all these churches are located was Mexican,[41] as indeed it was for the entire state, but among foreign-born Hispanics in the Portland-metropolitan area, only 81 to 87 percent were Mexican-born.[42] In other words, rural counties had a higher percentage of Mexican-born Hispanics, and the churches reflected this reality.

The second-largest group of foreign-born Hispanics in Oregon is Guatemalan. Elim had mostly Guatemalans while Ministerio Restauración in Portland had an equal amount of Guatemalans and Mexicans. Three congregations had mostly Mexicans and a smaller group of Guatemalans, but no other nationalities: Forest Grove's Iglesia de Jesucristo and the two Foursquare congregations in Portland. Data from Census 2000 indicates these congregations to be in line with the trends of the Latino population in Oregon. Approximately one-third of the Guatemalans in Oregon live in Washington County where Elim and Iglesia de Jesucristo are located. Another third lives in Multnomah

41. The foreign-born Hispanic population in Lincoln County (Newport) was 95 percent Mexican; in Josephine County (Grants Pass) 81 percent Mexican; Umatilla County (Hermiston) 95 percent Mexican; Jackson County (Medford) 91 percent. U.S. Census Bureau, American Fact-Finder, "Place of Birth for the Foreign-Born Population by Year of Entry by Citizenship Status." Census 2000 SF4, Oregon.

42. Multnomah County had 81 percent Mexican-born Hispanics, Washington County had 87 percent, and Clackamas County had 85 percent. U.S. Census Bureau, American Fact-Finder, "Place of Birth for the Foreign-Born Population by Year of Entry by Citizenship Status." Census 2000 SF4, Oregon.

County, home to Ministerio Restauración and the two Foursquare congregations in this study.[43]

Most of the churches in Washington County reported attendees from many nations. According to the 2000 Census, there were Washington County residents from every Spanish-speaking nation. Multnomah County had people from all but the Dominican Republic, and Clackamas Counties had persons born in every Latin American country except Bolivia.[44] There were Puerto Ricans in each of these counties, as well.[45]

Reedwood Friends, which had mostly Cubans, was not representative of the Hispanic population. Although the Cubans in this congregation arrived after the 2000 Census, over 60 percent of Oregon's small Cuban population were living in Multnomah County (where Reedwood Friends is located) in 2000.[46] However, this same census data indicated there were only 883 Cubans in the county, compared to 20,144 persons born in Mexico.[47] The pastor's sense of call to ministry among Cubans is clearly a factor in the national composition of this congregation.

Among the rural churches, the Hood River Christian and Missionary Alliance was the most diverse in terms of national origin. Its congregation had persons from six Spanish-speaking countries, in addition to Brazil. Year 2000 census data indicated only persons from Mexico, Guatemala, Honduras, Panama, and Venezuela residing in Hood River County. Four of the countries of origin mentioned by the pastor are not in the census data. If the data is reliable, either the population of the county has shifted since the 2000 census or the church is drawing congregants from other counties.[48]

---

43. U.S. Census Bureau, American Fact-Finder, "Place of Birth for the Foreign-Born Population." Census 2000 SF3, Oregon.

44. U.S. Census Bureau, American Fact-Finder, "Place of Birth by Year of Entry by Citizenship Status for the Foreign-Born Population." Census 2000, Oregon.

45. U.S. Census Bureau, American Fact-Finder, "Census 2000 Demographic Profile Highlights: Selected Population Group: Puerto Rican." Oregon All Counties.

46. U.S. Census Bureau, American Fact-Finder, "Region and Country or Area of Birth of the Foreign-Born Population: 2000." SF 3, Oregon All Counties.

47. U.S. Census Bureau, American Fact-Finder, "Place of Birth for the Foreign-Born Population: 2000." SF3, Oregon.

48. It is the author's opinion that the census data is flawed, as she personally knows several Chileans who were living in Hood River County in 2000, but the census reported zero Chileans.

Most of the congregations, then, are similar to the surrounding Latino population in terms of national origin. Other background factors such as ethnicity and generation of immigration, as well as the interplay between the pastor's nationality and that of most of the congregation, are explored in chapter 4.

Legal Status

The pastoral interview included a question about the percentage of congregants that the pastor estimated to have legal status, with the option to decline answering (as they could choose to do with any of the questions). Not surprisingly, the researcher did not obtain this data for several of the churches. One of the pastors jokingly told the author that he would remember her if an immigration raid took place shortly after the interview.

The percentage of legal residents in the congregations varied widely, from 5 percent in one rural congregation to 90 percent in several Washington County churches. Nonetheless, there were rural churches with high percentages of attendees with legal residency, and churches in the Portland Metropolitan area with small numbers of persons with legal documents. Most of the churches with a majority of congregants in the U.S. legally have also been established the longest—though one of the oldest churches in the study also had one of the lowest percentages of legal residents in its congregation. The Immigration Reform and Control Act of 1986 allowed many to obtain legal status, and some may have been attending those churches since that time. Several of the largest congregations also had low percentages of legal status, but there were other large churches with high percentages. Likewise, many of the small congregations had high numbers of legal residents, but there were congregations of similar size with few legal residents. No strong correlations emerged among the congregations in this study between legal status and geographic area, size of the congregation, affiliation with a denomination, or length of existence of the church.

Immigration status is a significant and delicate matter for Hispanic churches. For example, in the Willamette Valley in January 2009, "a van from the department of immigration parked right outside the [Hispanic] church as the service ended. . . . [The pastor] and another member went out to try to talk with the officials in the van. The van left without talking with them, but simply circled the block and then returned. To the people in the church, it felt like intimidation. No arrests or any type of contact was made."[49] In a worship service of a Hispanic church not included in this study that the researcher attended in 2010, information was given and prayers offered for a congregation member who had been detained by immigration officials and sent to an immigration court in Washington State that very week. Immigration status and policies are an urgent issue for Oregon Hispanic churches, as evidenced by these events.

Needs and Strengths of the Congregations

Indeed, legal or immigration advice or reform was the need most frequently indicated by the pastors interviewed. The second most commonly-cited need could be characterized as cultural acceptance, although pastors varyingly described it as "cultural orientation," "opportunity for advancement," "cultural communication and acceptance," and "self-esteem, racism, and conflict-resolution." Finally, pastors said that education was needed, most often mentioning English acquisition and computer classes.

Fellowship, support, and caring friendship were strengths cited by ten of the pastors. Sociologists have postulated that emotional support and friendship are drawing factors for church participation among immigrants.[50] Other pastors focused more on purely religious or spiritual characteristics, describing their congregations' strengths in terms such as "praise," "prayer," "faith," "spiritual foundation," "personal relationship with Jesus Christ," "biblical knowledge," "spiritually strong," and "spiritual freedom." Finally, three pastors mentioned leadership development or personal initiative to obtain further education or skills as the strong points of their congregations.

CONCLUSION

Overall, the Oregon Protestant Hispanic churches in this study have congregations that are representative of the state's Latino population. Most are Mexicans, followed by Guatemalans and other Central Americans. The legal status of those attending churches is mixed, as it is

49. C. Saxton, quoting G. Koskela in e-mail message to author, February 17, 2009. Anglo church representatives contacted immigration officials who denied having a van in the area that day and stated that their policy was not to practice "random sweeps."

50. Hurh and Kim summarize these ideas as the "comfort theory" in "Religious Participation," 22.

among the general population. According to the pastors, church-goers need legal advice and reform, acceptance by the majority population, and educational opportunities, as do most of the Hispanics living in Oregon. Those who choose to attend these churches find a supportive community and opportunities for spiritual growth and development of their leadership skills.

3

Inter-Church and Community Relationships

INTRODUCTION

THIS CHAPTER EXAMINES PROTESTANT Latino churches in three areas: their relationship (if any) with a denomination; their relationship with other churches, both Anglo and Hispanic; and their participation in the community. Prior to beginning this research, the author had formed set impressions of Protestant Latino churches and these relationships.

These ideas were shaped over nearly twenty-five years of participation (sometimes more active than others) in Spanish-speaking churches and confirmed by a review of the literature about Hispanic churches in the United States. They included observations such as denominational distinctives being down-played among U.S. Latinos and cultural misunderstandings between Anglos and Latinos in both church and community settings. The latter were often accompanied by a sometimes unconscious sense of superiority on the part of the Anglos. These misunderstandings revealed themselves in decisions made by sponsoring churches for Latino churches without their participation, in "importing" successful pastors from outside of the U.S. for Spanish-speaking congregations without grasping the difficulties this entailed, in leaving monolingual Spanish-speaking pastors out of denominational meetings, and in allotting the Spanish-speaking services a small or out-of-the-way space in a building. In sum, the author's impressions of these interactions were generally negative.

While some of these impressions were confirmed, the author found several surprises as she carried out this study. She learned of denominations native to Central America and the Caribbean, multiple ethnic minority congregations sharing a building, and a very positive vision of sharing and unity across language and cultural groups for several congregations.

The first section of this chapter presents the data collected in pastoral interviews regarding denominations and denominational ties, coincident with a look at where and when Oregon *evangélicos* converted to Protestantism. A description of several Latin American denominations operating in Oregon follows. Pastors' responses to interview questions about their participation in their denomination and issues of control are presented. Information is presented on pastoral education, both that of the pastors in this study and available pathways of education and preparation for future pastors. This is followed by a discussion of physical meeting places and their impact on the congregations, including descriptions of several congregations that have a vision for a unified church body, albeit with two (or more) languages. Next, the pastors' description of each church's interaction with the broader community (both the Christian and civic community) is presented, including other Hispanic churches and pastoral associations. All quotations are from the pastoral interviews unless otherwise noted, and all translations are the author's.

This chapter concludes with the author's analysis of this data on inter-church and community relationships and a comparison of this information with previous studies, when available. It includes the point of conversion to Protestantism (most often from Roman Catholicism) relative to the time of immigration; the changing importance of doctrine; competition for members; church independence; the impact of denominational ties in terms of size, stability, and longevity; pastoral preparation; building and space issues; and relationships with the broader Christian community and civic society. The final paragraphs discuss what the author considers the most significant finding of this study—congregations with at least two language groups for whom a unified body of Christ is a purposeful objective and practice.

TIME OF CONVERSION TO PROTESTANTISM

The majority of pastors interviewed said that most of their congregation were nominally practicing Roman Catholics who converted to evangelical Christianity in their local church. Significantly, this was the case in all of the rural churches, where there are fewer choices of Spanish-speaking Protestant churches in the area. Only seven pastors, all in the Portland Metro area, said at least half of their congregation were evangelicals prior to coming to that church. (Four of these indicated that conversion happened pre-immigration; one mentioned people moving from other U.S. states where they were attending a Protestant church, and two said about half came from other churches in the area.) Several pastors made specific mention that only those from Guatemala were Protestants before immigration. Three congregations with high percentages of pre-immigration evangelical believers (Iglesia Restauración Elim, Ministerio Restauración Mennonite in Portland, and Iglesia Evangélica Cristo Viene of Hillsboro) also had sizeable Guatemalan representation in their congregations. The fourth (Manantiales de Vida Eterna) had a majority of Mexicans but significant percentages of Guatemalans and Salvadorans. Pastor Alfonso Rodríguez of the Foursquare Rosa de Sarón noted that his congregation was made up of about 70 percent immigrants from the Yucatán Peninsula in Mexico and that all of them were already Christians before immigration.

The pastor of Manantiales de Vida Eterna also said that about 50 percent of his congregation had come to worship there after trying other churches in the area and being rejected: "Muchos han conocido otros lugares y no los han aceptado."[1]

Five of the pastors interviewed said that many in their congregations were "reconciled" or "restored," meaning that they had been evangelical Christians prior to immigrating but slipped into a "worldly" lifestyle after immigration, and then found their way back into the fold in that specific church. The period away from any church often included drugs or alcohol, and one pastor attributed it to the disconnection and loneliness resulting from the immigration process itself.

DENOMINATIONS

In choosing churches for this study, an effort was made to include churches from a broad variety of denominations, geographic locations, sizes, and lengths of existence. While a few of the following churches adamantly denied being part of a denomination, indicating they were "sovereign" or "fully independent," for classification purposes here the

---

1. The pastor's assessment of his congregation as a place for those rejected by others is consonant with the author's observations made during the site visit.

author will indicate them by the general denominational or doctrinal heritage.[2] This study included:

- one Christian and Missionary Alliance,
- one Mennonite Brethren,
- one Quaker (Friends),
- one Iglesia de Dios Pentecostal Movimiento Internacional (Church of God Pentecostal International Movement-IDPMI),
- one Southern Baptist,
- one Christian Church,
- one Church of Jesus Christ with an Apostolic background,
- one Manantiales de Vida Eterna,
- two Mennonite,
- two Foursquare,
- three Assemblies of God (AOG),
- three Elim/El Shaddai,
- three nondenominational churches,
- and five Conservative Baptist congregations.

Given the movement away from denominationalism in the United States and in Latin America, perhaps this prism is not the most adequate for examining the Latino Protestant churches of Oregon. However, it is one with which the author is familiar and perhaps many readers as well, and provides a beginning point for analysis.

In the early years of Protestant Latino churches in Oregon, denominational distinctions were not emphasized. Pastor Victor Vargas described the beginnings of the Woodburn Mennonite church in 1964 as a constantly morphing mixture of all area believers who weren't

2. The classification of churches is extremely complicated, especially when including myriad splits and groups originating in Latin America. See Freston, "Contours," 234–37 for a discussion of several typologies and their challenges. The movement toward non-denominationalism in the U.S. has made categorization difficult in the northern hemisphere as well. Two of the Elim-rooted congregations, one Assembly of God, and the IDPMI congregation became independent since identification of congregations for this study in 2004; one group here identified as Conservative Baptist began with CBNW but became independent in the mid–1990s.

Roman Catholic, most of whom were migrant workers: "dos, tres familias, comenzaron a reunir y luego pues crecía y se deshacía y venían de muchas doctrinas—apostólicos, evangélicos, pentecostales, y otros. Entonces como que el grupo seguía pero ya no se mantuvo muy estable con su membresía." (two, three families, they started to meet and then later, well, it grew and it came apart and they came from many doctrines—Apostolics, evangelicals, Pentecostals, and others. So it was as if the group continued but it didn't stay very stable in its membership.)

The pastor of two Foursquare churches in this study attended Ebenczcr Bible Institute of the Puerto Rico-based Iglesia de Dios Pentecostal, and was later ordained by the Assemblies of God. While this does not represent extreme doctrinal difference, there are multiple other examples. A Mennonite pastor studied first in the seminary of the Guatemalan denomination Monte Basán [Mount Bashan]. The pastor of the Southern Baptist congregation has been ordained by the Conservative Baptists, the Friends Church, and the Mennonite Church. The Friends pastor in this study comes from a Baptist background. In 1987, the author's husband was enthusiastically invited by Mardo Jiménez to pastor the Madras Bilingual Conservative Baptist Church, although his seminary training, beliefs, and sermons were decidedly Wesleyan. Pastor Jiménez exclaimed, "¡Me has caído como anillo al dedo!" (lit. "You've fallen like a ring on my finger"; better understood as "You've come at just the right time and are a tailor-made fit"). These examples all indicate that doctrinal differences within Protestantism have been overlooked by many churches in this study.

However, other pastors said that doctrinal matters were important. The Foursquare pastor indicated that a group of Guatemalans had left his congregations, seeking a "more conservative" church. Southern Baptist pastor José González expressed sadness over a lack of sound doctrinal teaching that made people an easy target to be "stolen" by large neo-Pentecostal churches offering an emotional experience and indicated that two of the three founding families of his congregation have left for such churches. Several pastors stated that they rarely join in activities with Spanish-speaking congregations of other denominations due to doctrinal differences or fear that their members will switch churches. There is a sense of competition for members, not with the Roman Catholic Church or "the world," but between Protestant groups or even churches within the same denomination. Pastor González lamented,

El problema que aquí, como le digo, gente no se queda estable
en una iglesia. O Ud. les llama la atención, les dice que cómo
están, que debemos de participar, debemos de madurar, debemos de ser fieles a la iglesia local, tenemos que ser fieles y todo,
entonces cuando no resisten, se van a otra iglesia. Pero, digamos
si es iglesia bautista, a ellos no les importa, se van a otra iglesia
bautista, hasta aquel pastor les hace lo mismo también así, se van
a otra iglesia bautista. Es interesante, como mucho—será porque
no han tenido una estabilidad, o ya son mañosos.

[The problem [is] that here, as I say, people don't stay stable in
a church. Or if you call them on something, you ask them how
they're doing, that we should participate, we should mature, we
should be faithful to the local church, that we have to be faithful
and everything, then when they can't handle it anymore, they go
to another church. But, say if it is a Baptist church, they don't
care, they go to another Baptist church, until that pastor does the
same thing to them, so they go to yet another Baptist church. It
is interesting how so many—it might be because they haven't had
any stability or maybe they are just difficult.]

The issue of flock-stealing or church-hopping is developed further in
this chapter in the section on participation in the broader Christian
community.

Latin American Denominations in Oregon

Prior to beginning this research, the author was entirely unaware of denominations native to Latin America. Their growth in Latin America is
an important trend that U.S. church leaders and sociologists of religion
need to track, as many Latino immigrants to the U.S. come with this
background. The great majority of them are Pentecostal. According
to Espinosa, "Mexican Pentecostals are served by more than 166
Pentecostal denominations, of which approximately 159 are completely
independent and indigenous."[3]

The author identified four Latin American origin churches in this
study: Elim (also know as MIEL), El Shaddai, and Monte Basán from
Guatemala, and Iglesia de Dios Pentecostal Movimiento Internacional
(IDPMI) based in Puerto Rico. As many readers may be unfamiliar with
these groups, they are described briefly in the following paragraphs, al-

---

3. "Pentecostalization," 267.

though the ongoing schisms of Pentecostal churches in Central America make it difficult to trace them precisely.

According to Holland, Elim in Central America began in Guatemala in the 1962.[4] A pastor from the Guatemalan group went to El Salvador in 1977 to extend the movement. In 1983 there was a definitive doctrinal rupture between the churches of these two countries, and since that time, Elim Guatemala and Elim El Salvador have been two distinct organizations. Elim in Guatemala was estimated to have 714 congregations and a total membership of 50,000 in 1994.[5] Elim El Salvador is "modeled explicitly after the Yoido Full Gospel Church in South Korea."[6] According to Wadkins, Elim El Salvador's principal outreach is to the "very poor," and, referring specifically to the church center in Ilabasco, El Salvador, "It has an active membership of over 150,000 and is widely considered the second largest church in the world."[7] Both national churches strictly adhere to a cell group structure that is innately growth-oriented, and this, coupled with emigration patterns from Central America, has produced many Elim churches in many countries. According to Comiskey, "Elim now has more than 115 churches around the world with about 200,000 attending them. Before Elim officially establishes a church, they wait until there are at least five cell groups fully operating."[8] Wilson characterizes the Elim church as neo-Pentecostal, that is, "consisting initially of Pentecostalized elements of the historical denominations" that "emphasize empowerment in the form of prophetic authority expressed in emphases on miracles, healing, exorcism, and prophecy."[9] Freston adds a class distinction between neo-Pentecostal and traditional Pentecostal churches of Central America, noting that the former are "middle-class and elite charismatic churches. . . . privileged city dwellers."[10]

---

4. "Chronology of Protestant," PROLADES-RITA database, http://www.prolades .com/historiografia/2-Guatemala/guate_chron.pdf (updated March 18, 2011; accessed June 3, 2011), 3.

5. Wilson, "Guatemalan Pentecostals," 147.

6. Wadkins, "Pentecostal power," *Christian Century* 123, no.23 (November 14, 2006), 27.

7. Ibid.

8. Comiskey, *Passion & Persistence*, 148–49.

9. "Guatemalan Pentecostals," 146.

10. Freston, "Contours," 238.

According to Freston, El Shaddai was founded by a "former lawyer from a prominent family" and attended by former Guatemalan president Jorge Serrano.[11] McCleary and Pesina identify El Shaddai as a result of a 1983 schism from Elim Guatemala.[12] Wilson places El Shaddai in the neo-Pentecostal category and estimated it had one church with 10,000 members in 1994.[13]

Less information is available on the nature and origins of the Monte Basán Church. It was founded in Guatemala in 1968.[14] Wilson characterizes it as "popular Pentecostal" and estimated there to be one hundred organized churches with 10,000 members in 1994.[15]

The Pentecostal Church of God, International Movement (IDPMI) is based not in Central America, but in Puerto Rico. According to Espinosa, a Puerto Rican named Juan Lugo was converted as a result of the Azusa Street revival. He went back to his home in 1916 and began preaching. The Iglesia de Dios Pentecostal was incorporated in 1922 in cooperation with the Assemblies of God, and by 1929 there were twenty-five churches on the island and several in New York City. In 1957, the leaders in Puerto Rico decided to end their association with the Assemblies of God because they perceived discrimination. The church has continued to grow and "is now the largest Protestant denomination on the island."[16] According to their website, the church now has mission activities in thirty-eight countries around the world outside of North America, and the U.S. is divided into seven ecclesiastic regions.[17]

Two of the congregations in this study stem from what Espinosa terms "native U.S. Latino Pentecostal denominations:"[18] the Iglesia de Jesucristo in Forest Grove and Manantiales de Vida Eterna Church in Gresham. There were Mexicans and Mexican-Americans present at the Azusa Street revival in Los Angeles in 1906. While the revival was ini-

11. Ibid.

12. "Religious Competition," 49.

13. Wilson, "Guatemalan Pentecostals," 147.

14. Holland, "Chronology of Protestant," PROLADES-RITA database, http://www .prolades .com/historiografia/2-Guatemala/guate_chron.pdf (updated March 18, 2011; accessed June 3, 2011), 3.

15. "Guatemalan Pentecostals," 144.

16. Espinosa, "Pentecostalization," 279.

17. http://idiospenmi.net /index-4.html#.

18. Espinosa, "Pentecostalization," 281.

tially multicultural, as churches organized they did so along racial and ethnic lines. The Apostolic Assembly is one such group that today has thousands of adherents and various derivations, including the Apostolic Church of the Faith in Jesus Christ that operates on the southern side of the border.[19] The Iglesia de Jesucristo is part of a group of independent churches that separated from the Apostolic Assembly of the Faith in Christ Jesus in the 1970s but keep the same doctrine.

According to Pastor Nelson Reyes, Manantiales de Vida Eterna is a group of Latino-serving churches that began in the 1970s in California. There are only three or four congregations total, all on the West Coast, and his congregation is the only one in Oregon. This church began after the pastor had moved to Oregon for employment and wanted to continue participating in a church like the Manantiales de Vida Eterna congregation he had been attending in Los Angeles.

Denominational Participation

All the denominational pastors were asked about their congregations' participation in denominational events and their perception of the willingness of their denomination to include them in decision-making.

Pastor Rose Medina of Iglesia del Pueblo explained that the Assemblies of God have a separate governing body in the U.S. for Spanish-speaking churches. For Oregon it is the North Pacific Latino District. She indicated that her congregation participates regularly and enthusiastically in activities organized by this district, and that she presents regular reports to this body on the church she pastors. She said that Latino congregations are increasingly listened to in General Council meetings, since the Spanish-speaking churches are the fastest-growing segment of the Assemblies of God in the United States.

Pastor Carlos Ortiz of Roca de Salvación also enthusiastically endorsed the assistance and role of the North Pacific Latino District of the Assemblies of God, citing its importance as a legal, non-profit entity, but also as a spiritual authority. He indicated that submitting to such a body could prevent the abuses sometimes seen in independent churches.[20] At

19. For greater detail on the history of this group, see Martín del Campo, "Apostolic Assembly of the Faith in Christ Jesus" in *Los Evangélicos: Portraits of Latino Protestantism in the United States,* 51–75.

20. Ironically, the author later learned from Flora Vergara that this congregation had become independent from the Assemblies of God. Telephone interview, June 7, 2011.

the time of the pastoral interview, this congregation was still a "mission" church, not fully organized as a sovereign church of the Assemblies of God, but its members participated actively in regional events for women and youth. Pastor Ortiz said that beyond feeling welcome to participate in denominational events, "se nos insta" (we are urged to) and their expenses to do so were paid by the denomination.

Iglesia de Jesucristo in Forest Grove participates regularly with "sister" churches from all over the West Coast. They rent space in a school for their annual meetings, which are attended by as many as 500 people. They send money for missions and literature distribution to a central office in Salinas, California, but this office does not supervise the activities of the churches in any way.

The Oregon Elim churches meet together once a month, and Pastor Jeremías Diego travels frequently to Guatemala where he participates in trainings and other events at the central Elim church. The Oregon congregations do not depend financially or give reports to Elim, Guatemala.

The Reedwood Friends congregation is often invited to participate in joint services with the other Spanish-speaking Friends congregations. They were doing so infrequently, because at the time of the pastoral interview, the pastor indicated that his flock was made up of recent immigrants with many emotional and psychological needs, and that they were not ready for these events. He himself had frequent contact with Pastor Angel Diaz, the director of Spanish-speaking ministries for the Northwest Yearly Meeting of Friends. He was giving a monthly report to the Meeting. He did not sense any struggle for his congregation in particular or for the Spanish-speaking churches in general to be included or taken into consideration by Northwest Yearly Meeting.

Pastor Alfonso Rodríguez of the Portland Foursquare churches observed that his two congregations held joint services regularly and that they also participated in denominational activities.

Ministerios Restauración's pastor met monthly with the pastors of the other four Spanish-speaking Mennonite churches in the area. Members of his congregation participated in national and international Mennonite activities, and he himself has served as president of some of these committees. He described "enough space" for Latino voices within his denomination. Pastor Víctor Vargas of the Woodburn Mennonite congregation confirmed that his congregation also participated often in denominational activities, adding that the Latino churches's agenda was heard every year at the conference, their voices were heard, and they had voting rights. He noted that all documents at these meetings have been provided in Spanish and English for the past five years.

Luz del Pueblo members participated in Southern Baptist activities for women and youth as their schedules permitted. They also were sending money to the Southern Baptist central offices to support missionaries. Pastor José Gonzáles indicated that he did not render a regular report to the denomination, because his congregation had become self-supporting and self-governing, but that new churches receiving institutional support needed to do so. He said he felt very comfortable within the Southern Baptist denominational activities and that his participation in annual conferences was paid for by the organization.

The Hood River Iglesia Esperanza y Vida en Jesucristo (Church of Hope and Life in Jesus Christ) Christian and Missionary Alliance (CMA) congregation participated very little in denominational activities due to cultural and language barriers. The pastor said he was in constant communication with his district office. He indicated disappointment in his denomination for not having "sufficient intent to meet the need of reaching the large Hispanic population in our country with the Gospel."

The Grants Pass Mennonite Brethren congregation participated in both their regional and national conference activities, as well as activities primarily for Spanish-speaking conference churches. Although not one of the churches included in this study, Pastor Ramón Argüello of Iglesia Ebenezer in Portland wrote that less than a year after starting this congregation, he felt the need to affiliate with a denomination for accountability and spiritual and financial support. After much prayer, they joined the Mennonite Brethren and has continued in this relationship since 1991.[21]

All the Conservative Baptist Northwest (CBNW) congregations regularly sent participants to denominational activities such as Men's Roundup and youth rallies. The Hermiston, Newport, and Madras churches related that their distance from the Portland metropolitan area sometimes made this difficult. While the Madras and Hermiston pastors indicated a good relationship with CBNW, the other pastors hesitated when asked if they felt their voice was heard. One pastor who has distanced his congregation from the association over the years said

21. "Historia de Primera Iglesia Ebenezer y las iglesias pioneras del área metropolitana de Portland," (unpublished document, n.d.), 2.

that the growth was becoming a groundswell and that sooner or later the association would have to consider the Latinos' voice. Another who described a very distant relationship with CBNW said he has repeatedly criticized "zero Hispanic presence" in annual meetings. A third said that he had served at one time as leader of the CBNW Hispanic pastors' association but has become frustrated because the plans that were so carefully made came to nothing, due to "lack of interest" on the part of the denomination.

All the pastors were asked if they sometimes felt that decisions were made for them or their congregations without their input.[22] Fifteen of the pastors, an overwhelming majority, said "no." The pastors of Salvados para Servir [Saved to Serve] and Luz del Pueblo indicated that they sometimes felt overlooked or overridden regarding building use, noting that another congregation owned it and had first priority in this matter. The Foursquare and Hood River Christian and Missionary Alliance pastors indicated "rarely" without specifying any situations. Only the Village Baptist and Woodburn Mennonite pastors emphatically replied "yes." Both indicated that this happened at the state or national denominational level. Pastor Rivas elaborated, "Nos toman en cuenta en cosas que a ellos los convienen. Pero en cosas que convienen en nosotros somos ignorados." (They consider us in things that are in their interest. But in things that are in our interest we are ignored.) Pastor Vargas observed that it used to happen more frequently, but that sometimes in the Mennonite Council, leaders who had little spiritual maturity or respect among the Latino body had been imposed or had named themselves leaders.

PASTORAL TRAINING

The preparation of pastors can be closely related to the type of church in which they serve. Six of the pastors in this study had completed a denominational course of study by extension or in the local church, and of these, two have gone on to further education. Three of the pastors held college degrees that were unrelated to ministry. Sixteen of the pastors have studied in some type of Bible institute or college. Six of the foreign-

---

22. Iglesia de Jesucristo in Forest Grove is not included here, as it is independent and does not share a building. The pastor of Ontario Templo Betania was not available for an interview.

born pastors in the study completed pastoral training before immigration. The institutions providing pastoral education were:

- the College for Global Deployment in Vancouver, WA;
- two IDPMI schools: Instituto Bíblico Milpa in Los Angeles and Instituto Bíblico Ebenezer in Chicago;
- an Assemblies of God college in California;
- California Bible University;
- Western Baptist Seminary;
- Río Grande Bible Institute in Texas (for two pastors);
- the Apostolic Bible College in California;
- Salem Bible College (AOG);
- Seminario Baustista in Sonora, Mexico;
- Monte Basán Bible Institute in Guatemala;
- Seminario Anabautista in Texas;
- SETECA (Seminario Teológico Centroamericano, affiliated with Dallas Theological Seminary but located in Guatemala, for two pastors);
- California Baptist University;
- Newburgh Theological Seminary in Indiana (online); and
- Logos University of Florida (online)
- Fuller Theological Seminary.

Several held advanced degrees:

- Pastor Héctor Rodríguez of Iglesia Evangélica Cristo Viene in Hillsboro has an MA in theology and had completed all coursework for a doctorate in missiology at Western Baptist Seminary;
- Pastor Victor Alvarizares holds a doctorate from the College for Global Deployment;
- Pastor Jeremías Diego of Elim has an MDiv from California Bible University and was working on a doctorate at an unspecified school in 2007;

- Pastor Raúl Giménez of Vida Church has a master's in Christian education from Calvin Seminary;

- Pastor Mario Macías of Reedwood Friends holds an MDiv from Fuller Theological Seminary;

- Pastor Mauricio Rivas was working on a master's through Logos online in 2008.

In contrast to those pursuing more education, another group exhibited little or no formal studies to prepare them for their ministry. Instead, they tended to rely on on-the-job-training or divine inspiration. Two of the pastors in this study had absolutely no theological training, not even through a local church or by extension. One pastors the small Manantiales de Vida Eterna congregation in Gresham; the other leads the large and growing Hispanic ministry at Rogue Valley Fellowship in Medford. Both started out as participants in these congregations and have become pastors. In fact, much of the Medford pastor's sermon during the site visit was anti-intellectual or anti-education. Based on 1 Corinthians chapter 1, he emphasized that those who seem wise by wordly standards are made foolish by God, using statements such as "Los que no saben leer, saben más de Dios que algunos." (Those who don't know how to read know more of God than some.) City Bible has its own course of membership, leadership, and lay pastor training. Pastor Trolese observed, "we don't feel that . . . a Bible College degree or any-thing is a prerequisite necessarily to full time ministry." The pastor of the Southern Baptist congregation in this study called this lack of pastoral preparation "a great danger," noting that some persons who see no need for pastoral training, preferring to rely on the Holy Spirit alone, have had ethical failures and give a bad name to Latinos. He described the lack of training as being more prevalent in certain denominations or independent churches.

Six of the Latino pastors in the study received a call to preach be-fore they immigrated. Only one of them was called directly from Latin America to the church he currently pastors. This finding was contrary to the author's previous experiences in the Church of the Nazarene, a de-nomination not included in this study. According to Pastor Tony Estey of the Hood River Christian and Missionary Alliance, that organization also uses this approach: "developed ministers are recruited from foreign countries where missions have developed strong ministries that now supply leadership here."

The remaining Latino pastors had come to the U.S. or Canada for other reasons such as education and were living here when they began pastoring. Pastor Jiroo Kuruda of Newport had emigrated from his native Perú to study for music ministry at Río Grande Bible Institute in Texas, but ended up becoming not only a minister of music for the English-speaking congregation but pastor for the Hispanic group as well. Four of the pastors were born in the U.S. The remainder either accepted or returned to Christ after immigration.

Recognizing the need for more formal education, several institutions have developed programs for Latinos in Oregon pursuing ministerial careers, both in terms instruction and language needs. Seeing few opportunities for face-to-face preparation for pastors in Spanish in the Pacific Northwest, Pastor Felix Rosales began the Instituto Teológico Hispanoamericano (Hispanic American Theological Institute) along with Héctor Rodríguez in 1994 at Western Evangelical Seminary (WES). It provided a diploma in theology that was granted by WES until the latter merged with George Fox University. The courses have continued in classrooms on the George Fox Portland campus, although without university accreditation. In this seventeen year span, over 400 Spanish-speaking church leaders have completed the programs of study.[23]

Additionally, many denominations and the large independent churches now have methodical training in Bible and ministry available in Spanish. These include Educación Teológica por Extensión (ETE) through CBNW; the Ladder of Success training through Casa del Padre; and AOG Berean School of Bible (now Global University). Salvados Para Servir and Elim both have intensive Bible study courses and leadership training; the Foursquare churches of Oregon initiated their own denominational course of study in Spanish; the Christian and Missionary Alliance has a International Intercultural Ministries department and several seminaries; the Mennonites have the Instituto Bíblico Anabautista de Formación Ministerial; according to Pastor Mario Macías the Quakers are also offering a course of study online in Spanish; and the Church of the Nazarene offers a complete course of pastoral study leading to ordination in Spanish in Oregon. City Bible offers courses in English through Portland Bible College. Nearly all of

23. Félix Rosales, telephone comm., June 9, 2011.

the pastors indicated some path of study in which they would direct persons who felt a call to ministry. Two of them indicated work under close supervision in the local body as the only training, and a third was unable to articulate any plan for pastoral formation.

MEETING PLACES AND CONSEQUENT IMPACT

The following section addresses sharing between various minority groups, the actual issue of space used, the impact the sharing has had on the host congregation and the Spanish-speaking congregation (as reported by the Latino church pastor), and the degree of integration of groups. The section concludes with an examination of eight congregations that describe themselves as fully part of a larger church with no vision for separation. Given the paternalism, racism, and conflict described in the literature on immigrant churches in the U.S. and the author's previous experiences, the latter situation was a pleasant surprise.

Churches with Multiple Ethnic or Racial Minorities

Several Hispanic congregations share space with other ethnic or linguistic minorities or have done so in the past. Village Baptist describes itself as a multicultural church, with Korean, Spanish-speaking, Chinese, and English-speaking congregations. The Assembly of God building in Gresham where Manantiales de Vida Eterna church meets also houses a Philippine congregation. The Southern Baptist Spanish-speaking congregation meets in a building owned by an Anglo congregation, but a Russian congregation meets there as well. Salvados Para Servir was renting space from a Korean Assembly of God in Beaverton during the site visit, although it has since moved. Casa del Padre in Portland rents from a Russian congregation that has adapted a commercial building for worship purposes, and in the past shared a building with a predominantly African-American congregation. The Beaverton Casa del Padre congregation also shared a building with Indonesians and Koreans in the past and held occasional joint services with the Indonesians.

Churches that Own Their Buildings

Iglesia de Jesucristo in Forest Grove, Iglesia Menonita Pentecostés in Woodburn, Templo Betania AOG in Ontario, and Iglesia Baustista Conservadora Bilingüe in Madras have their own building which they do not share with any other congregation. All these congregations have been established for at least thirty years. The first three are in small, older buildings, while the Madras church building is newer, having been built especially for them in 1997. The Forest Grove and Ontario buildings are mostly sanctuary, and the Woodburn and Madras buildings have some classrooms, but they are inadequate for the current congregations's needs. The Woodburn church was in the process of fund-raising for a larger building.

The Madras congregation shared space with the Anglo congregation in a nearby building for many years, starting in a classroom in the basement adjacent to the gym, then moving upstairs to use the sanctuary after the congregation grew too large for the classroom. At a service celebrating the 30th anniversary of the Spanish-speaking congregation, the widow of the former Anglo pastor spoke nostalgically of those years of sharing, of passing in the foyer as one service let out and another began. She remembered affectionately the care the Hispanic group had given her family during her husband's illness, saying of the Spanish-speaking ministry, "We thought we were ministering to you all, but it was always really you ministering to us."

One Building, Separate Identities

The other congregations all shared buildings with another church body. In the pastoral interview, all were asked what impact they felt sharing a building had on their congregation, as well as on their hosts. The pastors' replies to these questions, as well as observations on the degree of integration between the two groups, follow.

As previously mentioned, the two Casa del Padre congregations met in other church buildings. Casa del Padre Portland met in a commercial building adapted by a Russian congregation for worship purposes, while the Beaverton congregation met in a Free Methodist building. Pastor Alvarizares indicated that he felt this sharing had a positive impact on his congregations as it helped them to "see the Body of Christ beyond racial barriers." Mrs. Alvarizares was present in the interview, and she added that, "Our goal has always been to have that relationship with the [host church] pastors, and the times when we're struggling with something, we know this is not only our congregation, but that the people who we're renting from are going through that." Both Casa del Padre congregations paid rent to use these buildings, and the pastor emphatically told the author that he felt that paying rent was important as it helped the congregation mature:

> . . . as Hispanic churches we need to have a healthy self-esteem, that's one of the things I've seen between the Anglo churches and Hispanic churches, they look on us as a mission field, "Let's give them a handout." I've talked to all the pastors that we've had a relationship with, "We're the same as you, the same God that supplies for you supplies for us, so challenge us in that area." In all of the buildings that we've been in, we've always paid rent; that helps us as the body to grow in all the areas. I do believe that God will continue to move in the Hispanics, the biggest growth is in our children being born here, not people crossing the border, we have to be aware of that, and us being seeing as equals, not as people of lower class.

The short-lived Ministerio de Vida Eterna was meeting in a fellowship hall adjacent to a kitchen in an Apostolic church building.

Manantiales de Vida Eterna was meeting a run-down, labyrinthine Assembly of God building in Gresham, after leaving the Damascus area. Pastor Reyes called on the English-speaking pastor, seeking a new meeting place for his small congregation. In the same time period, the English-speaking pastor had been praying about opening a Spanish-speaking ministry, so he welcomed the Spanish-speaking congregation to his building.

At the site visit in 2009, the Latinos had exclusive use of a large upstairs room that they had made into a sanctuary. They also had use of a small kitchen nearby and could request to use other areas of the building if needed. This congregation initially gave voluntary love offerings for use of the space. When the English-speaking congregation went into financial decline, it asked the Latinos to begin making a regular monthly rent payment.

They have been meeting in this building for ten years but are completely independent from the host congregation, neither have they held joint activities with the Philippine congregation that also uses the building. They previously had an annual joint service with the English-speaking congregation up until about 2006. The Hispanic youth do not participate in activities with the Anglo youth group, as Pastor Reyes cited doctrinal differences, indicating that the Anglo congregation was more liberal.

Pastor Reyes postulated that the presence of his congregation may have affected some in the English-speaking group negatively, as they didn't have an open heart towards those of other nations. He stated that there were others with open hearts to obey Jesus' commandment to go and preach the gospel to all nations, who would have been positively impacted by the Hispanic congregation.

The two Foursquare congregations in this study have different situations: one Foursquare congregation rents the sanctuary only from a Presbyterian church and the other uses an English-speaking Foursquare congregation's building. In the latter, they have had joint services with both the English- and Spanish-speaking congregations, as well as provided Vacation Bible Schools together. There have been some scheduling conflicts and disagreements over keeping the building clean.

Iglesia del Pueblo AOG rented space in the English-speaking AOG building in Forest Grove for many years but wanted to construct their own building and purchased land to do so. Feeling both a financial and space squeeze, they moved out of the AOG building to an English-speaking Baptist church in the neighboring town of Cornelius, where they give an offering and maintain the building and grounds in exchange for full use of the building Sunday afternoons. They see this as temporary until they have raised enough money to construct a building on the land they purchased.

The North Portland AOG Roca de Salvación was meeting in the building of Life Fellowship church, where they had full use of the building and used a scheduling process so as not to interfere with the activities of the English-speaking congregation. Pastor Ortiz described how he felt called to minister in North Portland, but there were no Assemblies of God buildings in that area, so he prayed and went knocking on church doors in the area. He saw it as a sign of God's providence when, after consulting with his board, the pastor of Life Fellowship opened the building to them at no cost whatsoever. At the time of the pastoral interview in 2008, Roca de Salvación was giving an unsolicited monthly love offering to the Anglo church and had just purchased its own music equipment so as to not cause so much wear on Life Fellowship's equipment. Pastor Ortiz expressed tremendous gratitude to the Life Fellowship church, but lamented the lack of their own building because he envisioned having many more services for the community such as a food bank, a clothing bank, ESL classes, and a center for translation assistance or orientation to community services. Pastor Ortiz reported a good relationship with Life Fellowship, being in constant communication via e-mail and occasionally praying together. When asked how he thought the presence of the Spanish-speaking congregation had affected Life Fellowship, he replied that they had told him that Roca de Salvación was a blessing, since Life Fellowship's denomination doesn't have any Hispanic ministries. Sharing their building with the Spanish-speaking congregation was allowing them in some small measure to reach out to Spanish speakers and the mission field in their backyard.

Ministerio Restauración, the Mennonite congregation in Portland, was paying a symbolic rent of fifty dollars per month to the English-speaking Mennonite church for use of the building. They used the foyer and sanctuary every Sunday afternoon for Sunday School and worship service, and had access to the rest of the building except the offices. Pastor Morán characterized the relationship with the English-speaking congregation as "very good," noting that the presence of the Spanish-speaking congregation enabled them to have a hand in the mission of expanding God's kingdom and that the Hispanic church attributed some of the fruit of its ministry to the Anglos as well.

As previously mentioned, Salvados para Servir was renting space from a Korean Assembly of God congregation in Beaverton and had use of the sanctuary in the afternoons and other rooms at times if they made previous arrangements, although the Korean congregation always had preference for usage. The associate pastor characterized the relationship between the two churches as one of mutual respect. Salvados para Servir had its offices in a remodeled house directly across from the church building at the time of the pastoral interview, and the associate pastor commented that, while he considered it a privilege to be renting a building from another congregation, having no classroom space and having to find places for special activities at other locations was difficult. At the time of the site visit, the Hispanic congregants filled the entire sanctuary for the worship service. Within a year after the pastoral interview, this congregation had moved and was renting a larger building for Sunday afternoon services from Portland First Church of the Nazarene, approximately twenty minutes from its previous location. There is very little interaction between the English-speaking Nazarene congregation and Salvados para Servir.[24]

24. Karen Garrison, Executive Administrator, Portland First Church of the Nazarene, e-mail message to author, June 8, 2011.

As noted above, Iglesia Vida has moved multiple times. During the site visit, it was sharing space with another congregation in a commercial building near Highway 26 that had been poorly readapted for use by a church. It now meets in Aloha, paying rent for use of the sanctuary of Life Church, and Pastor Raúl Giménez has an office in the building as well. Although the two congregations are not institutionally tied, Pastor Giménez is considered part of the pastoral staff of Life Church and is in constant communication with the English-speaking church. He stated that the Spanish speakers have felt "very pampered" by their positive reception from Life Church, and that in turn, the English speakers had expressed appreciation for the contributions of the Spanish speakers as far as the church extending to other cultures and in their ethics and care for the building.

Elim church was also renting a large commercial space during the site visit. It had created a sanctuary and had outlying areas for a bookstore, offices, and classrooms. The sanctuary was filled to capacity during the worship service the author attended. However, during this service the difficulty of paying the lease was mentioned. In a follow-up visit with Pastor Jeremías Diego in 2010, he indicated that they had moved and were renting space from a large non-denominational church called Our Place in Aloha, but he did not comment on interactions with the English-speaking congregation.

As indicated above, the Southern Baptist Luz del Pueblo congregation as well as a Russian congregation use a Southern Baptist church building owned by the English-speaking congregation. Luz del Pueblo pays a sum to help the Anglo church that they do not consider rent but an expression of thanks. According to Pastor José González, these immigrant congregations have kept the church doors open, since the Anglo congregation is mostly aged and dwindling in size. Pastor González indicated deep respect for the English-speaking church and especially its organization and hard work.

Finally, the Christian and Missionary Alliance Spanish congregation pays rent for use of the English-speaking congregation's building in Hood River. They have exclusive use of the facility on Saturday evenings. Pastor Estey described the relationship between the Hispanic church and the Anglo church as "Excellent . . . though there is little interaction due to the cultural differences." He indicated that sharing the building had "made them [the Anglo congregation] more aware and appreciative of their neighbors' culture and role in the local community and in the kingdom of heaven."

While several pastors interviewed acknowledged the challenges involved in calendaring and sharing space with the host church, the dominant theme in their responses was one of gratitude for the use of the space. Only one pastor indicated that there are real difficulties and conflicts between some congregations that share space. It is possible that more pastors held this view but did not feel comfortable sharing it with the author. The multiple moves by other congregations could also indicate inter-group conflicts.

Two (or more) Languages, One Church

In contrast to the above congregations that were essentially separate from their "landlords," the remaining congregations shared space with others, but instead of paying rent or having a separate identity, they considered themselves part of a larger church body. One pastor described it as being one body in which one part just happened to speak Spanish.

Pastor Héctor Rodríguez described Iglesia Evangélica Cristo Viene as a ministry of Hillsboro First Baptist Church, not as a separate congregation. He is part of the pastoral team and has an office in the building. The Spanish-speaking congregation meets in the gym (having literally moved up from its beginnings in the basement in the 1980s) and contributes financially every month to cover utility costs. While the pastor described the relationship with the English speakers as harmonious and positive because it gave them access to sources they would not otherwise have, there is infrequent interaction between the two linguistic groups. Pastor Rodríguez noted that a few of the Anglos don't feel comfortable with the Hispanics in their building, but that in general, there is a good relationship between the two groups.

Another church that describes itself as a ministry of the larger Anglo congregation but has infrequent contact between groups is the Ministerio Hispano at Rogue Valley Fellowship in Medford. Pastor Santiago Argueta explained how his family and another Spanish-speaking family started attending the English services there, using a translator and headsets, without much success. The church leaders appointed him Spanish-speaking pastor, and he began holding services in a small room in the building, which they quickly outgrew. They have moved through several rooms as the group has grown, and now meet in the sanctuary on Saturday evenings and in a large room Sunday mornings at the same time as the English speakers hold their services. The Hispanic children attend Sunday School with the Anglo children in English, but the Hispanic teens and Anglo teens do not meet together. The pastor has an office in the building and is part of the pastoral team and attends staff meetings. They have not had joint events, and the pastor indicated hesitancy on the part of the Spanish-speaking congregation to do so, citing a sense of inferiority or shame due to not being able to speak English.

Pastor Ulysses Vela said, "We're part of Monmouth Christian, except we're Hispanic." His congregation does not pay rent and uses the sanctuary for services on Sunday afternoons, and can use any other part of the facility, scheduling it in cooperation with the English speakers. The pastor has his office in the church building and is a paid member of the pastoral staff. Members of the Spanish-speaking group have served on the elder board, and all of the money is held in common. The pastor chooses his own curriculum and makes his own decisions: "I make most choices, I just run it by the elders, and they say it's OK." The Hispanic children attend Sunday School along with the Anglo children. The pastor commented, regarding the English-speaking congregation, "They love us a lot. . . . everything they've demonstrated so far. I've been here since 2000, you know, first of all most churches charge you rent or they give you the ugliest building, most Hispanic pastors don't get paid as church staff, usually they don't let you use all the things, from what I've seen, they just have been so accepting, it's true what it [the church mission statement] says, 'Love God and Love people.'" However, the pastor noted that it has been a challenge to get the two groups together often because of language and cultural barriers, though they have tried several different plans to do so.

The Spanish-speaking congregation is an integral part of the church body at New Hope Community, a Conservative Baptist church in Hermiston. There is a large banner along the roadway in front of the church announcing "Servicios en español" (Services in Spanish). Pastor Genaro Loredo was hired by the English-speaking church elders to begin a Spanish ministry within the broader church context. He has his office in the building and is part of the church leadership team. Bilingual members of the Spanish-speaking group participate in leadership roles for the entire church, such as serving on building or missions committees. The Spanish-speaking congregation purposely meets at the same time on Sunday mornings as the English speakers, so that the children and youth of both groups can meet together, and Hispanics (mostly second- or third-generation) who prefer to worship in English may do so. They do not pay rent for any facility use, and all funds are held in common. During the site visit, they were meeting for worship in the fellowship hall. This is sometimes a small challenge. A Sunday School class meets there immediately before the Spanish service, and one Sunday a month the senior adults have a potluck in the same room immediately after services. There is pressure for both the Sunday School class and the Spanish service to end on time, but Pastor Loredo said this issue has not become a point of frustration. The church is currently adding an additional wing, and this will provide space for all the groups to work more comfortably. He described the relationship within the broader church as very positive, providing not only economic support, but spiritual and moral support as well:

> Yo diría que siempre es buena, bastante buena, aunque siempre hay lugar para mejorar, pero existe una buena relacion entre anglos e hispanos aquí en la iglesia. Yo creo que por lo mismo que estamos involucrados en las diferente areas de toda la congregación y eso ayuda mucho.

> [I would say that it is always good, very good, even though there is always room for improvement, but a good relationship between Anglos and Hispanics exists here in the church. I think it is due to this same thing that we are involved in the different areas of the whole congregation and that helps a lot.]

The author observed this good relationship during the site visit. Prior to the service in the ladies' restroom, an Anglo woman gave a hug to a Hispanic woman and chatted about a topic the two had obviously discussed before. In the hallway, another older Anglo woman was giving out chewing gum and hugs to the Hispanic children and youth as they went in to the Spanish service. Individuals from both language groups appeared to have genuine relationships with one another.

City Bible describes its Spanish service as just one more service of the church. It has worked on unity in many ways. All funds are "100 percent integrated" and no rent is paid for facilities. The pastor is a member of the pastoral staff who was first employed to run a youth internship program and later took on the role of Spanish-speaking pastor.

The Spanish-speaking congregation has a leadership team. According to Pastor Trolese, its members

> know that one of their primary job descriptions is to connect with that ministry for the whole church, and likewise that ministry knows it is now their responsibility to provide and cover and help with this. So, I'm always just ensuring that that connection is happening. . . .on that level it has made everyone think, . . . discussing all the fall women's ministry and women's Bible study things, . . . all the other ladies know they have to always be thinking, 'How is this going to work?', If they are using a video curriculum, is it available subtitled in Spanish, are there Spanish books available. . . .

This church has deliberately not created a separate youth group, as it recognizes that many of the Hispanic youth were born in the U.S. and are more comfortable speaking English and identify more with U.S. culture than that of their parents. The church has encouraged them to participate in the City Bible youth group that serves all youth. The church holds a combined evening service several times a year, and the worship team for the Spanish-speaking group leads bilingual songs. During special services, "they know they will find a whole section of Spanish speakers somewhere in the auditorium." The pastor recognized that a unified mindset had not been reached completely, noting that he often had to remind ministry leaders to think about resources to accommodate Spanish speakers. At the time of the pastoral interview, he was the only representative of the Spanish speakers on the elder board, but he mentioned that several members of the elder board had deep interest and practical experience in missions and ethnic ministry. In fact, when the Spanish-speaking ministry started, only two of the ten or so persons who met regularly and prayed for Hispanic ministries actually spoke Spanish.

Village Baptist is also one church with several languages. The pastor said, "El grupo hispano y la iglesia no es un grupo más, somos una sola familia o sea yo soy pastor de la iglesia Anglo y somos . . . somos para todos y tenemos acceso para todo y todas nuestras ofrendas van para un solo fondo." (The Hispanic group and the church is not another group, we are a single family. In other words I am a pastor of the Anglo church and we are . . . we are for everyone and we have access for everything and all our offerings go to a single fund.) Each language group (Spanish,

Korean, English, East Indian, and Chinese) has a ministry budget. The Spanish-speaking congregation does not pay rent for use of the buildings, and they use any area of the campus according to their needs— Sunday evenings for worship in the sanctuary, some youth activities in the gym, Friday activities in a building known as "North Village." Saturdays there is a bilingual Spanish-English service. There is a single youth group for young people of all backgrounds. The church had asked Pastor Rivas to identify two from the Latino group to serve on the elder board, but at the time of the pastoral interview, he had deferred this representation, feeling that adequately preparing these individuals first was more important than having representatives. The pastor was called by the Anglo church to lead both a Spanish-speaking ministry and to do pastoral care for the whole church. He has responsibilities to the broader church and is on call several days each week for the needs of anyone associated with Village, regardless of their language. He stated that the church's multicultural vision was something that takes time to develop, but that was, in his opinion, the biblical model. He described U.S. society as multicultural, noting that public schools must offer services openly to every cultural group, but that they have only been partially successful in doing so. The church's vision is to emphasize that the gospel is open to all nations, and that this church body must also be so, respecting each group's cultural differences, but recognizing strength and beauty in a multicultural church.

Newport First Baptist Church (Iglesia Nueva Esperanza) also has a vision for one church, one family, but two languages. Pastor Jiroo Kuroda described it as follows: "Bueno, es bien sencillo. Es una sola iglesia en sí, diríamos la Primera Iglesia Bautista, que tiene dos servicios. Uno en inglés y uno en español. Por lo tanto, en la iglesia contamos con cuatro pastores, entonces los cuatro tenemos la misma autoridad dentro de la iglesia." (Well, it is very simple. It is one church in itself, we would say First Baptist Church, that has two services. One in English and one in Spanish. Therefore, in the church we have four pastors, so the four of us have the same authority within the church.) Pastor Kuroda serves as worship minister in the morning worship service in English and as Spanish-speaking pastor, and his title is not Hispanic pastor, but associate pastor. The senior pastor, youth pastor, and preschool teacher all attend the Spanish-speaking services on Sunday afternoons to support the ministry. The Latino youth, who are English-speaking, make up part of First Baptist's youth group along with the Anglos. The Spanish speakers use the entire building as needed and do not pay rent. All the money goes into a general fund and is dispersed as needed to the ministries of the entire church, whether Spanish- or English-speaking. Pastor Kuroda reported that the English-speaking church had accepted the Latinos very well, despite differences such as time, order, and music. He attributed this to the fact that a core group of English speakers had been praying for a way to minister to the growing Latino population in the area over ten years ago. When a new senior pastor was hired, he also brought a desire for a Spanish-speaking ministry. There have been bilingual Latinos on the board of deacons, and the pastor indicated he never felt left out of decision-making. A great effort is made to communicate with all. Missionaries who visit must speak in both the English and Spanish service. Financial reports and building issues are presented in both languages, and the church by-laws have been translated into Spanish. This has helped the Spanish speakers have a sense of ownership and responsibility for the church building and vehicles, and they have participated in remodeling or maintenance days at the church.

This church has a joint evening service every month that there is a fifth Sunday. The worship music is done in both English and Spanish, and instead of a sermon, individuals from both groups share their testimonies, which are interpreted into the other language. This personal storytelling allows members of both congregations to get to know one another. This is followed by a potluck or snack time in which both groups try to visit, in spite of the language barrier. Pastor Kuroda felt that the acceptance and flexibility of the English speakers was seen especially during these services, which are held at 7 p.m. (he deemed this "late for the Americans") and in their willingness to try to sing in Spanish. He indicated that many of the English speakers were older adults, and he particularly appreciated their attempts to step outside their habits to get to know the Spanish speakers. The pastor described these fifth-Sunday services as having successfully broken down the "our church—their church" mentality.

Reedwood Friends is yet another congregation that describes itself as one body with two language groups. The English-speaking congregation had desired a Spanish-speaking ministry for several years. The Anglo pastor spent his childhood in a missionary family in South America, and is bilingual in Spanish and English. Pastor Mario Macías spoke at length about his positive experience with the senior pastor and the congregation:

> tengo que hablar mucho porque este ministerio es algo completamente diferente, por mi experiencia como pastor en otras iglesias en Los Ángeles en California. Nosotros aquí con el pastor Ken, tenemos la misma visión y el mismo sentir. Lo que yo creo como ministro, hago énfasis en una palabra que no somos mediocres, que somos personas importantes, hablando espiritualmente. . . . cuando hablamos de visión, de tener un mismo sentir, o hablar de la palabra harmonía, yo incluyo a los anglos aquí, porque esa es la visión de nosotros aquí como iglesia. Aquí somos dos culturas, latinos o hispanos, pero somos una sola iglesia, con los anglos. Y los anglos nos han abierto la puerta, que es otra experiencia que yo nunca había tenido en más de 20 años. Que la iglesia no solamente está comunicando a nosotros que somos una iglesia sino que son hechos. Entonces la mentalidad de este grupo está a ese nivel, no somos un grupo. . . no somos "invitados" no somos de segunda clase, sino que somos igual.

> [I have to say a lot, because this ministry is something completely different, in my experience as a pastor in other churches in Los Angeles in California. We here with Pastor Ken have the same vision and the same views. I, as a minister, emphasize the phrase that we are not mediocre, that we are important people, spiritually speaking. . . . When we talk about the same vision, having the same views, or speak of the word harmony, I include the Anglos here, because that is our vision here as a church. Here we are two cultures, Latinos or Hispanics, but we are just one church with the Anglos. And the Anglos have opened the door to us, which is another experience that I had never had in over twenty years. That the church is not just telling us that we are one church, but they show it with actions. So the attitude of this group is at that level, we aren't a group . . . we aren't "guests," we aren't second class, but we are equal.]

This congregation was meeting in a small chapel area on Sunday mornings during the site visit, but the pastor anticipated moving to the sanctuary when the congregation grew, and indicated that they had access to any part of the building and did not pay rent. The pastor described the entire church (English and Spanish speakers together) as undergoing a "metamorphosis" as they sought together to become one church, something he had never experienced in his previous years of ministry. The English speakers frequently invited the Spanish speakers to participate with them in events, and the pastor indicated that the Spanish speakers did participate about 60 percent of the time. The author made two observations in accord with the pastor's effusive remarks on the desire for unity in the body of this church. During the pastoral interview, a poster was prominently displayed in the main church office with the statement "No human is illegal." Second, the English-speaking congregation was engaged in Spanish classes taught by the Latino pastor, actively seeking to be able to communicate more with the Spanish-speaking congregation.

The last congregation that described itself as "one church, two languages" is New Hope Bible Church, a Mennonite Brethren congregation in Grants Pass. Both Spanish and English speakers meet jointly Sunday mornings. About half of the congregation are Latinos. The worship music was projected in both languages for some songs and in English only for others. There were both Spanish and English hymnals in the pew—the number of the hymn was announced for both, and congregants sang in the language they preferred. The musicians included an Anglo pianist, three Hispanic guitarists and a drummer, and both Latino and Anglo vocalists. Several times during the service individuals addressed the congregation in their native language and someone interpreted for them (prayer, prayer requests). The sermon was preached only in English, with a bulletin handout that had most of the sermon text on it. Pastor Lowell Stutzman can "reasonably communicate" in Spanish but does not preach in it. Both the English speakers and Spanish speakers seemed very comfortable with each other and with this arrangement for the worship service. Pastor Stutzman indicated that there are "very strong associations between members of the different cultures. We truly are family." He did note that the decision to have joint services "has presented challenges with translation, worship songs and styles, and length of services." This church has a board with ten members, three of whom are from Mexico.

INTERACTION WITH BROADER CHRISTIAN COMMUNITY

Moving from the building situation emphasis, the concept of involvement in the church commuity at large was explored. In the interview, pastors were asked if they worshipped with other Spanish-speaking churches besides those of their own denomination, if they felt included in the broader Christian community, and if they participated in a pastoral association. Their responses are presented below. Although the author did not ask specifically about interdenominational events for Spanish speakers, several pastors offered information on them, and these are also included in this section.

In Washington County, Iglesia Evangélica Cristo Viene, Iglesia del Pueblo AOG and Village Baptist all occasionally joined with Spanish-speaking congregations of other denominations for activities. The pastors of the former two have known each other for years, and their two congregations have shared many activities. Iglesia Vida also infrequently shares events with a few other congregations whose pastors have known each other for many years. Pastor Mauricio Rivas of Village Baptist limits participation in events with other congregations to those that do not include doctrine, such as concerts. The two Casa del Padre congregations have also interacted with other churches with similar goals, mostly for concerts. Forest Grove Iglesia de Jesucristo, Elim, and Salvados para Servir do not join with Spanish-speaking congregations of different denominations. The associate pastor of the latter indicated that "Nosotros tratamos de lo mejor posible de irnos de la Palabra de Dios y mantener la santidad dentro de la iglesia. Y si algún otro ministerio puede, pensamos que puede, dañar la vida espiritual de nuestros miembros tratamos de evadirlo." (We try as much as possible to go with the Word of God and to maintain holiness within the church. And if some other ministry could, we think it could, damage our members' spiritual lives, we try to avoid it.)

In Multnomah County, Luz del Pueblo Southern Baptist, Manantiales de Vida Eterna, and Ministerios Restauración Mennonite participate in activities with Hispanic congregations of other denominations very infrequently. Pastor Ortiz of North Portland AOG Roca de Salvación said that he was open to doing so, but also mentioned a sense of competition among Spanish-speaking churches for believers. Reedwood Friends' Spanish-speaking pastor did not feel that the new Christians in his incipient congregation were ready to participate with other churches often.

Iglesia Bautista Conservadora Bilingüe in Madras did not participate in activities with non-Conservative Baptist churches. Regarding the central coast area, Pastor Kuroda noted, "No hay iglesias hispanas o hay grupitos pero son grupitos que no. . . . en vez de tener comunión parece que quieren o guerra o algo. . . . [una iglesia de] línea Pentecostal, ellos tienen servicios en inglés traducidos al español simultáneamente, y claro algunas familias se han encargado de sacar a las familias de aquí. Por eso, uno desea tener comunión pero cuando la gente actúa de esa manera, se roba la bendicion." (There aren't Hispanic churches or there are little groups but they are little groups that don't. . . . Instead of having fellowship it seems that they want war or something. . . . [A church of] Pentecostal type, they have services in English translated to Spanish simultaneously, and of course some families have taken it upon themselves to take families away from here. That is why, one wants to have fellowship but when people act like that, the blessing is stolen away.) Pastor Vela of Monmouth Christian said, "What I've noticed about Spanish churches is they're real jealous. I've had an event, a concert. I invited eighteen Hispanic churches and guess how many showed up. Zero. Two of 'em called. And it was free. It was on a Sunday, I understand, lot a churches you know, struggle with finances, but once a year? I don't understand that." The Hood River Christian and Missionary Alliance church indicated joint events three or four times per year with churches "with the same vision." The Grants Pass Mennonite Brethren congregation is part of a local fellowship of churches known as Church of the Valley and participates in its events. The Woodburn Mennonite church mostly participates in Mennonite activities but occasionally joins in events related to the Northwest Hispanic pastoral association. Pastor Santiago Argueta reported that the Spanish speakers of Rogue Valley Fellowship in Medford joined with a few other area Latino congregations twice a year for campaigns.

Eight of the Portland-metropolitan area pastors said that they did not perceive a struggle for them or their churches to be included in the broader Christian community. Two said that they were often invited but did not participate. Pastor Medina indicated that in her years in ministry she has seen a change toward more acceptance of Hispanic pastors and churches. She added that she had been invited to the pastors' appreciation event sponsored by Portland Christian radio station KPDQ. Pastor Alvarizares said that he felt welcomed but that people were sometimes hesitant, due to a perceived language barrier (ironic in his case, since he speaks fluent English).

Four pastors in the metropolitan counties indicated some type of struggle for acceptance or welcome in the broader Christian community. The Elim pastor said that he wished to participate more but had not found a way to plug in. Pastor Rivas of Village Baptist said that it has been a "struggle" but that events like the Luis Palau campaign were unifying the churches (implying both Anglo and Latino cooperation). One Multnomah County pastor said that he has felt excluded, not due to language or cultural differences but because his church has different doctrinal beliefs and practices. Another Multnomah County pastor indicated conflicting visions and contradictory messages: "The Anglo pastors say they want to start a Hispanic work but then they change their minds. They promise a salary that never materializes. There is cultural conflict between congregations. We need more than just them opening a building. Many churches reject having Hispanic ministries. We need mediation."

Two of the rural pastors said that there simply have not been events such as a mayor's prayer breakfast or other ecumenical meeting in which to participate, although it is possible that they were unaware of such events. One of these indicated that the Hispanic community and Anglo community were strongly divided and never came together. Three rural pastors said that they felt very welcomed in the broader Christian community, while two said they saw a struggle. The Hood River pastor, himself an Anglo, noted that the Anglo church community was, in his opinion, missing the point: "I believe that the Anglo churches don't grasp the opportunity for missions work in their own backyard. The problem that I have observed over more than twenty years of Hispanic ministry is that the Anglo Christian community assumes that the Hispanic Christians should assimilate into the Anglo church without regard for the richness of the Hispanic cultures and languages, and their need for their own cultural experience in the evangelical faith."

Woodburn has the densest Hispanic population of any city in the state, and it has been a place where many churches sought to begin Spanish-speaking ministries. The Woodburn pastor in this study related difficult experiences in the local Christian community and with the pastoral association many years ago, again bringing up the theme of competition between churches for participants:

> porque algunos grupos anglos quisieron establecer obras his-
> panas porque era la moda, entonces muchos dividieron nuestras
> iglesias, nosotros perdimos miembros, porque les daban más
> facilidades, les daban dinero, les daban comida, y se para un pas-
> tor de la asociación pastoral . . . y dice, 'ya tenemos 30 miembros

hispanos en . . . nuestro departamento hispano,' pero no trabaja-
ban ni evangelizaban nada, son miembros que agarraban de otras
iglesias. . . . me dolió mucho en el corazón y nunca más volví a
participar. Me han invitado, pero no quiero perder una hora de
hablar del amor Dios o del Espíritu Santo mientras los pastores y
los lideres están robando a ovejas de nuestra congregación.

[because some Anglo groups wanted to establish Hispanic works
because it was in fashion, so many divided our churches, we lost
members, because they made it easier for them, they gave them
money, they gave them food, and a member of the pastoral association stood up . . . and said, "We already have 30 Hispanic
members in our Hispanic department," but they didn't work or
evangelize at all, they are members that they grabbed out of other
churches. . . . that hurt me deeply and I never participated again.
They have invited me but I don't want to lose an hour to talk
about the love of God or the Holy Spirit while the pastors and
leaders are stealing sheep from our congregation.]

Several pastors brought up their participation in interdenominational events. One was a Luis Palau campaign held in Spanish for two
days along the Portland waterfront. Pastor Mauricio Rivas of Village
Baptist was a principal organizer of this campaign, and he commented,
"Unificó a la iglesia. Estuvimos casi diez mil personas en dos días. Yo
estuve muy cerca del evento, trabajando y unificando amistades entre
pastores con denominaciones. Fue una actividad inter-denominacional
y vimos a toda la iglesia apoyando." (It unified the church. There were
almost ten thousand people in two days. I was very close to the event,
working and unifying friendships between pastors and denominations.
It was an interdenominational event and we saw the whole church
supporting [it].) Hillsboro's Iglesia Evangélica Cristo Viene, Iglesia del
Pueblo AOG in Cornelius, and Ministerios Restauración Mennonite in
Portland all actively supported this Luis Palau campaign.

Willamette Celebration was an evangelistic event held in 2010
in Albany, sponsored by many area churches. Newport Conservative
Baptist Nueva Esperanza and Monmouth Christian church pastors reported that their congregations worked actively in this bilingual, non-
denominational event. The Monmouth church also participates in the
town's annual community church service held on July 4th.

Popular Spanish worship leader Marcos Witt came to Portland several years ago. According to Pastor Carlos Ortiz, when members of his

church asked to be included in this event, they were told that since Roca de Salvación AOG and Pastor Ortiz did not participate in the Hispanic pastoral association, they would be unable to do so.

When asked about the Asociación Evangélica Hispana del Noroeste (Northwest Evangelical Hispanic Association), the pastors of City Bible, Village Baptist, Reedwood Friends, and the Foursquare congregations all indicated they participate. The pastors of Iglesia Evangélica Cristo Viene of Hillsboro, Luz del Pueblo in Gresham, Ministerios Restauración Mennonite in Portland, Vida Church in Aloha, and Manantiales de Vida Eterna said that they used to participate in the past, but they no longer do so. Some said they didn't have enough time, while others felt excluded because of their doctrine, and others tired of what they described as constant requests for money. Pastor Rose Medina said that her husband often participated prior to his death, but that she does not due to time concerns.

Outside the metropolitan area, only Pastor Vargas of Woodburn participated in the Portland-based Hispanic association. He indicated having had very negative experiences with the Woodburn pastors' association that included English-, Spanish-, and Russian-speaking congregations. Another rural pastor termed the Northwest Evangelical Hispanic Association "muy cerrada" (very closed), noting that if he wanted to know about an event, he was always the one to seek out the information instead of receiving an invitation to participate. The Medford pastor said that several Latino pastors in the Rogue Valley area met together regularly, but this group had not yet become an official organization or pastoral association. Few rural church pastors participated in local (English-speaking) pastoral associations, and the Newport pastor indicated that such an organization had existed for a very short time in that area.

PARTICIPATION IN CIVIC COMMUNITY

All the pastors were asked if they or their church members participated in the community in non-church-related activities. Several said that certain individuals did out of personal interest but not as representatives of their churches. Three of the Washington County pastors said they did not at all, as did one of the Multnomah County pastors. Six of the pastors, including three from outside the Portland area, said that they or their church members did volunteer in the community, without indicating specifics.

The Elim congregation was doing jail visits and indicated a desire to be more involved in the community but uncertainty as to how to proceed. Village Baptist and Roca de Salvación members have helped clean local schools. The Mennonite church participates through its Council in providing immigration services. Luz del Pueblo Southern Baptist participates in food distribution, as did the Hermiston Nueva Esperanza church through its association with Agape House. Hermiston also supports the local crisis pregnancy center. Luz del Pueblo, Roca de Salvación, and Madras Iglesia Bautista Conservadora Bilingüe all have participated in a community fair. Roca de Salvación gave out backpacks with school supplies there, while the role of the Madras church members at the church fair was to wash cars. Iglesia Menonita Pentecostés in Woodburn, Roca de Salvación AOG, and Monmouth Christian had church members on the school board (although the latter was referring to representatives from the entire church, Anglo and Hispanic). Monmouth Christian's pastor volunteered often at his daughter's elementary school, and the senior pastor and youth pastor have coached youth sports in the community. The Newport pastor lamented the lack of community activities. He mentioned a "help center" for Latinos that was not well-regarded by the Hispanic community, and that he has often done translation or interpretation for community members. The Woodburn Mennonite church has a long-standing relationship with the local chapters of both Alcoholics and Narcotics Anonymous. The associate pastor of Salvados para Servir indicated that they taught the congregation to "be conservative and defend the faith" if it came under attack politically, and also to provide for themselves, to not look to the government for handouts. Finally, the pastor of Manantiales de Vida Eterna encouraged the congregation to vote Democrat, "otherwise they'll send our children to war."

DISCUSSION AND ANALYSIS

Time of Conversion to Protestantism

Only four of the pastors in this study indicated that most of their congregants were Protestants prior to immigration. Since the majority of Spanish-speaking immigrants to Oregon are from Mexico, and Mexico is one of the least Protestant nations of Latin America,[25] these findings are neither surprising nor out of line with research on the U.S. as a whole: "15 percent of all Mexican immigrants arriving in the U.S. are Protestant or Other Christian."[26] Several pastors made specific mention that only those from Guatemala were Protestants before immigration. Three congregations with high percentages of pre-immigration evangelical believers (Iglesia Restauración Elim, Ministerio Restauración (the Portland Mennonite congregation), and Iglesia Evangélica Cristo Viene in Hillsboro) also had sizeable Guatemalan representation in their congregations. The fourth (Manantiales de Vida Eterna) was majority Mexican but had a significant proportion of Guatemalans and Salvadorans. Two of these churches are Pentecostal, the fastest-growing type of Protestantism in Latin America.

The small number of pre-immigration *evangélicos* in Oregon is important to bear in mind. It makes previous church participation less likely to affect current behaviors and could make Protestantism more closely related to their status of immigrant in the minds of the congregants. Additionally, the transnational nature of some U.S. Latino churches described in some studies[27] was found in only three congregations: Restauración Elim with frequent contact with Guatemala, Rosa de Sarón Foursquare with three sister churches in the Yucatán Peninsula and continuous movement back and forth by Yucatán Christians, and Luz del Pueblo Southern Baptist. The latter supports a mission church in Oaxaca, pastored by the brother of one of the Portland church members. None of the other churches have ongoing contact with congregations south of the border. These two factors suggest that studies of religious trends in the Latin American nations may be limited in their usefulness when applied to Oregon congregations.

Latin American Denominations in Oregon

The growth of new forms of Christianity in the global South and their impact on Europe and the U.S. has been mentioned by various authors.[28]

25. Garrard-Burnett, "Christianity and Conflict," (panel presentation, National Defense University, Washington, DC, April 6, 2006).

26. Espinosa, "Pentecostalization," 268.

27. See, for example, Vasquez, "Pentecostalism, Collective Identity," and Ebaugh and Saltzman Chafetz, *Religion Across Borders.*

28. Sanneh, *Whose Religion,* 76; Jenkins, *Next Christendom,* 99, 107–8, 191–92, 204, 208–9.

Jenkins in particular predicted changes in the U.S. Protestant land-scape caused by missionary efforts from churches indigenous to Latin America as well as ongoing immigration.[29] The present study shows that four Latin American denominations influence church life Oregon.

Pastor Morán of Ministerio Restauración, the Spanish-speaking Mennonite Church in Portland, was trained at the Instituto Bíblico Monte Basán in Guatemala. He was ordained, pastored, and became a superintendent in this denomination prior to coming to the U.S. and working with the Mennonite Church.[30] The researcher did not identify any Monte Basán congregations in Oregon, and the phone number for a Monte Basán Christian bookstore in Salem had been disconnected. While there may be more Guatemalans with this background in Oregon, it appears that Monte Basán has not made any institutional inroads in the state.

Elim, El Shaddai, and Iglesia de Dios Pentecostal, Movimiento Internacional, however, have greatly impacted Oregon. The three largest congregations in the study began as part of these three denominations: Salvados para Servir (formerly IDPMI) with 400 in attendance, Elim in Hillsboro-Aloha with 390–400 in attendance and daughter churches in Beaverton and Salem, and Casa del Padre (formerly El Shaddai) with 225 attending in Beaverton and 150 in Portland. They did not start as official mission churches, but rather began as people who had partici-pated in the large congregations of these churches in the Los Angeles area moved to Oregon and desired to attend the same denomination. They called pastors from the California churches to Oregon. All three are Pentecostal, but only Elim has a majority of members who were practicing Protestants prior to immigration.

Denominational Participation

These Latin American origin churches operate in financial and admin-istrative independence. Two (Salvados and Elim) are strikingly inde-pendent, not participating in any ministerial association or joining with other local or Spanish-speaking churches for events, even though they both currently use buildings owned by English-speaking congregations.

29. Jenkins, 204, 208–9.

30. Allyn, Bobby, "Pastor Samuel Moran came to Portland to lead exploding Hispanic Mennonite community," *Oregonian*, June 24, 2010.

Elim is the only church in this group that still maintains ties with the denomination in Guatemala; the other groups had separated from their denominations in 2005 or 2006 but maintained the same doctrine. None of the pastors interviewed wished to elaborate on their reasons for splitting from the parent organization.

The author suggests that the cultural realities of operating in the U.S. as a minority- and immigrant-serving church created tensions with the home church. However, it is entirely possible that these bodies were merely continuing in a long tradition of Pentecostal church independence or division described in the literature in chapter 1, named "chronic fragmentation" by Espinosa."[31]

Movement toward independence was also seen in several of the churches with U.S. denominational backgrounds. Iglesia del Pueblo AOG in Cornelius and Madras Iglesia Bautista Conservadora Bilingüe moved out of a building shared with an English-speaking congregation of their denomination. Iglesia Evangélica Cristo Viene in Hillsboro, Village Baptist, and Nueva Esperanza in Newport all reported distancing themselves from the Northwest Conservative Baptist Association, the latter two preferring responsibility to and support from the local congregation. Roca de Salvación in Portland left the Assemblies of God and became independent between the time of the pastoral interview and this writing. Manantiales de Vida Eterna and Iglesia Vida worship in an Assemblies of God building but have no plans to join the denomination.

In addition to these independent churches with denominational ties, Monmouth Christian Church, City Bible, Iglesia de Jesucristo in Forest Grove and Rogue Valley Fellowship in Medford are independent, not depending on or responsible to a parent organization. The Southern Baptist model followed by Luz del Pueblo is self-governing and self-supporting. Thus, though the research design sought to study churches from a variety of denominations, spread out geographically and of varying periods of existence, approximately half of the congregations were independent of or separating from a denomination in some way. This theme of division confirms what previous studies have found, as noted in chapter 1.

Prior to undertaking this study, the author had the distinct impression that denominational ties were strongly negatively correlated to church size. The information collected throughout the research period

---

31. Espinosa, "Pentecostalization," 276.

confirms this hypothesis, although not overwhelmingly. Eleven of the churches had regular attendance of less than one hundred persons. Nine of these eleven were denominational churches. Six of the churches had 170 or more regularly attending. One of these (Elim) maintains strong ties to its Guatemalan denomination, one has always been nondenominational and independent (City Bible), and the other four (Salvados Para Servir, Village Baptist, Iglesia Evangélica Cristo Viene in Hillsboro, and Casa del Padre in Beaverton) began with denominational ties or support but have stepped away from them significantly. Village Baptist, Iglesia Evangélica Cristo Viene, and Newport Nueva Esperanza continue to participate occasionally in CBNW activities but do not see themselves as accountable to it.

As mentioned in chapter 2, Oregon Corporation records indicate that many Hispanic churches are short-lived.[32] It appears that denominational ties contribute to stability and longevity of Latino Protestant churches in Oregon, as all the churches in this study that existed prior to the "boom" of Hispanic church planting that began in the 1990s are denominational. They are:

- the Mennonite Iglesia Pentecostés of Woodburn (1964);

- New Hope Mennonite Brethren's Hispanic ministry in Grants Pass (1970s);

- Iglesia de Jesucristo in Forest Grove (1973);[33]

- Ontario's Betania Assembly of God (1980s);[34]

- Madras Iglesia Bautista Conservadora Bilingüe (1980); and

- Iglesia del Pueblo Assembly of God in Cornelius (1982).

Hillsboro's Iglesia Evangélica Cristo Viene began as a Conservative Baptist church in 1985 and is still meeting in the same building although it has since become independent of CBNW. As described in chapter 2,

32. Based on a business name search of the Oregon Secretary of State, Corporation Division's online records, using search terms "Iglesia" and "Templo."

33. Pastor Luis Ramirez indicated that this church is not part of a denomination but it has an extensive fellowship of sister churches. Interview, September 2007.

34. Pastora Flora Vergara indicated that the Spanish-speaking Nyssa and Ontario Assemblies of God were the oldest in the state and that she visited them thirty years ago. At that time the Ontario group was meeting in a house. Telephone communication, June 7, 2011.

the Conservative Baptists of the Northwest were purposeful in starting Hispanic churches. Pastor Flora Vergara of the Assemblies of God indicated that Ray Meza was a pioneer church planter for that denomination's Spanish-speaking churches in the state. The other early churches mentioned here were not denominationally orchestrated but began due to circumstances of individuals or individual churches.

One might argue that it is having a network of like-minded churches and leaders and not denominations *per se* that contributed to the longevity of these churches. This may be true in the case of the Iglesia Evangélica Cristo Viene and Iglesia de Jesucristo. However, all the other "old" churches except Iglesia del Pueblo are in rural areas and were (and still are) geographically isolated from their denominational counterparts. Perhaps the structure and accountability provided by an umbrella organization make for a longer existence. Financial support in the initial period certainly had an impact, but all the pastors of these churches indicated they are now financially independent of the denomination.[35]

The author also originally thought that denominational links contributed to stability of meeting place, which in turn might contribute to church size. The evidence in this study does not strongly support this theory. For example, the Ontario Betania AOG church, New Hope Grants Pass, and Iglesia de Jesucristo in Forest Grove have existed for at least thirty years and meet in their own building, but are among the smaller congregations in the study. Iglesia del Pueblo AOG moved out of the space provided for it in an English-speaking AOG building, seeking their own space, but has moved twice and is now sharing a Baptist building in a neighboring town. It is also one of the smaller congregations in the study, though founded in 1982.

Elim, Salvados Para Servir, and Casa del Padre in Beaverton and in Portland have moved several times in the past five years, and Casa del Padre has changed its name, yet these are three very large congregations and only Elim is denominational. However, Vida Church in Aloha is one congregation for which this lack of institutional support (that

35. The pastor of Ontario's Betania Assembly of God was unavailable for interview, thus the author does not have information regarding denominational support of this very small congregation. New Hope Mennonite Brethren Church's Spanish- and English-speakers are fully integrated into one self-supporting body, so there is local, but not denominational, financial support. The Madras Conservative Baptist Church still receives two hundred dollars monthly from the English-speaking congregation, but not from CBNW.

could have provided a meeting place or consistent funding to secure it) has impacted the church size. The author has tracked this pastor and a small core group since its inception in 1993. It has met in three different church buildings in Portland, three in Beaverton, in various homes, and is now sharing building space with Life Church AOG in Aloha without forming any denominational affiliation. The congregation has grown and dwindled and grown again, certainly due to a variety of factors, but the multiple moves have had an impact.

Previous publications on Latino Protestant churches in the U.S. have emphasized a sense of disenfranchisement or lack of voice in their denominations, as described in chapter 1. Two of the denominational pastors in this study openly and emphatically agreed that Latino churches are not included in decision-making at the denominational level. It is possible that others held this view but were hesitant to share it with the author. The tendency toward independence among many of the churches with past denominational ties may also be evidence that Latino pastors do not feel heard at the denominational level, and thus seek to distance their congregations from these organizations.

Pastoral Training

The lack of training for Pentecostal pastors has been observed in several studies. Regarding Latin America, Williams writes: "Pentecostals are constantly reminded that their communication with God is direct and does not have to be mediated through an ordained minister. . . . although some of the larger denominations now require that their pastors complete a minimum period of training and apprenticeship, in most of the smaller independent churches members can aspire to become pastors with little or no formal training."[36] Soliván describes an "absence of formal training in the [Pentecostal] movement";[37] and Vasquez mentions "Pentecostalism's long anti-intellectual tradition," quoting the pastor of a mostly-Salvadoran apostolic Pentecostal church in Washington, DC as saying, "We work with our hands, not with books."[38] Brazilian sociologist Francisco Cartaxo Rolim asserts a deeper meaning for the lack of educational requirements for Pentecostal pastors: "[P]entecostalism . . .

---

36. Williams, "The Sound of Tambourines," 195.

37. "Hispanic Pentecostal Worship," 50.

38. "Pentecostalism, Collective Identity," 627.

breaks with the traditional differentiation between qualified producers of religious discourse and practice (the clergy) and mere consumers of these religious products. In pentecostalism [sic] every believer is a direct and legitimate producer of his or her religious world. They thus defy not only the traditional way of doing religion, but the very structure of a classist society."[39]

While utter lack of training never crossed the author's non-Pentecostal WASP mind prior to initiating this study, she did have concerns that there was no systematic plan among U.S. denominations for identifying and training Spanish-speaking pastors for Latino churches, and that this led to the poorly-conceived practice of importing successful pastors from Latin America for congregations in the U.S. This had been her experience in the 1980s and 1990s with at least four pastors in the Church of the Nazarene in the Northwest. It was also observed by Lara-Braud: "The time-honored practice of relying on imported pastors is a reflection of the difficulty denominations have had finding and training pastors born and raised in the United States."[40] In this study, only one pastor had come to Oregon under these circumstances, though the CMA pastor acknowledged that his denomination also follows this practice. Nearly all the pastors have completed or are pursuing training through their denominations or through a wide variety of educational institutions, some to the doctoral level. Nearly all were able to describe a method of preparation for others who sensed a call to ministry. There are multiple opportunities for pastoral training in Spanish both in the Portland area and through local churches. Given that most of the pastors in the study became pastors after immigration, this availability is significant. It appears that denominations no longer have trouble identifying pastors from among the Hispanic population already in Oregon.

Meeting Places and Consequent Impact

Several publications on U.S. Latino Protestant churches identified the placement of these congregations in the basement or other out-of-the-way areas of an Anglo church building as a subtle form of discrimination. Indeed, the author has attended Spanish-speaking churches that were housed in the basement or fellowship hall of an English-speaking

---

39. Sepúlveda, "Pentecostal Movement," 72.

40. "A Profile of Hispanic Protestant Pastors," 256.

congregation. In 2009 she had a conversation with an Anglo pastor who wanted to start a Spanish-speaking ministry. During the building tour, he proposed a small classroom in the basement as the location for this group, indicating its proximity to a kitchen and restrooms. When the author asked why the sanctuary would not be available to the Latinos, the pastor said that this would require turning on the heat (apparently acceptable for the Anglos but not the Hispanics).

Though these attitudes still remain, locational discrimination did not surface as directly in the churches in current study. The poorest-quality meeting place was that of Manantiales de Vida Eterna, reached via a circuitous and smelly route of hallways and stairs with worn and stained carpeting, though the classroom-cum-chapel itself was attractive and full of light. However, the entire church building seemed poorly-maintained both inside and out, leaving the author the impression that all the congregations meeting there were on equal footing.

Soliván asserted that Pentecostal Latino congregations face special challenges for meeting places: ". . . most Hispanic Pentecostal churches are located in the poorest of the urban barrios. Whereas mainline churches worship in buildings intentionally designed for Christian worship, most Hispanic Pentecostal churches worship in storefronts, or in other buildings rehabilitated for use as a place of worship. A growing number of Pentecostal congregations meet in the underutilized facilities of mainline churches in need of income."[41] Ontario's Templo Betania AOG was in a very rundown neighborhood, although Ontario could not be termed "urban." Manantiales de Vida Eterna was meeting in a poorer area of East Portland. Casa del Padre in Portland met in a remodeled commercial building, as did Vida Church and Elim Restauración, although the latter two later moved to share space in a church building, and these were not mainline churches. Only two pastors mentioned that their financial contribution for the space shared with an Anglo church was significant to the financial health of that church: Luz del Pueblo Southern Baptist and Manantiales de Vida Eterna. Neither of those Anglo congregations were mainline; the only mainline church renting to any of the congregations in this study was Grace Presbyterian in East Portland, where Rosa de Sarón Foursquare uses the sanctuary.

Several pastors mentioned occasional difficulties due to sharing or renting space, and some of these congregations moved during the pe-

41. "Hispanic Pentecostal Worship," 45–46.

riod of research, seeking more adequate facilities. Most of the congregations met in the sanctuary, but those that didn't seemed comfortable in
the smaller spaces they were using and indicated that when they desired
to move to a larger room or the sanctuary, they would be able to do so.
Though not included in this study, Pastor Juan Bonilla of Forest Grove
Hispanic Church said that his small congregation would have felt even
smaller in the large sanctuary of the building where they meet, and were
quite happy in the diminutive chapel where they met. This seemed to be
the case with the Reedwood Friends congregation as well.

Several building-sharing arrangements came to light in this study
that have not been described in previous studies of Latino Protestant
churches in the U.S. In Oregon, several linguistic or racial minorities
share a building. In some cases, it would appear that certain English-
speaking churches have been especially open to sharing their building
with linguistic minorities in their community. In others, different minority congregations have opened their buildings for use by Spanish-
speaking congregations, perhaps finding some common ground in their
experiences.

Though the possibility of a united church with two or more language groups is recognized in previous studies by the Protestant Council
of the City of New York,[42] Montoya,[43] and Machado,[44] each points out
that such an approach is fraught with difficulties. González[45] poignantly
describes the lack of connection that a Latino fully competent in English
can experience in an Anglo worship setting. Furthermore, Montoya[46]
and the very popular *Purpose Driven Church* movement urge separation
into culturally-similar groups.[47] No successful multilingual or multicultural congregation was set forth in the literature on Protestant Latino
churches in this country.

Given the negative experiences of the author in Anglo-Latino
church relations prior to beginning this study and those described in
the literature, the nine Oregon church bodies with both a vision and
practice of unity were truly a revelation. In choosing a purposive

42. *Report*, 89.

43. *Hispanic Ministry*, 67–78.

44. "Protestant Establishment," 85–106.

45. "Hispanic Worship," 16–17.

46. *Hispanic Ministry*, 147–48.

47. Warren, *Iglesia con Propósito*, 182–89.

sample, the author was unaware of this model and did not use "unified body" as a characteristic in determining which churches to study. It is possible that because the researcher is a member of the majority community and identified herself as a fellow believer, the pastors were not completely forthcoming with their criticisms of a unified church experience. However, several of the pastors were especially emphatic about their positive experiences as part of a larger church body. Morever, the very existence of these nine churches as part of a unified vision over time speaks to the sincerity of their words.

For the analysis that follows, Iglesia Evangélica Cristo Viene in Hillsboro and the Hispanic ministry of Rogue Valley Fellowship are set aside, for though they describe themselves as one with the English-speaking church, share a building, finances and some decision-making, they have very little fellowship between groups.

The other seven churches had much more extensive mutuality, with New Hope Bible Church, the Mennonite Brethren church in Grants Pass, having the most radical model of integration. It is unusual in many ways, including that it has an Anglo pastor who doesn't preach in Spanish and that none of the Mexican congregants are recent immigrants. They all have at least some ability to understand spoken English. The sense of acceptance by the English speakers of both the Mexicans and parts of the service in Spanish was remarkable. The author postulates that this denomination's historic commitment to marginalized groups may be a factor in this church's vision for itself.

Aside from the Grants Pass congregation, having bilingual and bicultural pastors seems to be a key factor in the development of a church with a vision for unity. The pastor of Village Baptist left his native El Salvador for Canada as a child. The City Bible pastor (an Anglo) had been a missionary child in Central America. The Hispanic pastor at Reedwood Friends has lived in the United States for at least twenty-five years, and the senior pastor (Anglo) also had been a missionary child in South America and speaks fluent Spanish. The Hermiston pastor has lived in the U.S. since childhood and speaks English fluently, as does the pastor in Newport, although the latter immigrated at a slightly older age. The Mexican-American pastor of Hispanic Ministries at Monmouth Christian was born in the U.S. and is completely bicultural and bilingual.

Five of the eight rural churches had this vision of "one church family in two languages." One of these pastors mentioned that he often felt isolated from denominational activities due to distance. It is possible that this geographic isolation has made cooperation between linguistic groups more necessary or attractive. Proximity has overruled language and cultural barriers to unite those of a common faith.

Why has this vision and practice of church unity not been described in any previous study? The author originally thought that it was an emerging model, as some of the first churches of this type that she visited had only been in existence for three or four years. However, as she continued to research, she discovered others that have existed for more than twenty years, disproving the idea that they were ephemeral and would eventually give way to separation.

One plausible explanation for the unified Latino-Anglo churches is that Oregon is one of the least-churched states in the country.[48] According to O'Connell Killen, "The defining feature of religion in the Pacific Northwest is that most of the population is 'unchurched.' Fewer people in Oregon, Washington, and Alaska affiliate with a religious institution than in any other region of the United States."[49] Perhaps the sense of Christian unity in Oregon is more important than racial, ethnic, or linguistic backgrounds, as Christians of diverse national origins band together in a non-religious majority society.

Interaction with Broader Christian Community

Several pastors indicated that doctrinal differences within Protestantism have been overlooked by Oregon Latino churches. This finding is very similar to what Aponte described regarding the evangelical churches of Philadelphia prior to the 1950s:

> The recollections of surviving participants emphasized an absence of denominational partisanship within this early Protestant community in the face of the shared context of larger challenges, i.e., the difficulties of urban life in general, as well as the presence of a much larger Roman Catholic Hispanic population. In those early days when First Spanish Baptist Church was the only Hispanic Protestant congregation in Philadelphia, all *evangélicos* (i.e., Protestants) participated in the congregation while continuing to affirm their differing doctrinal positions. Baptists and non-

48. Gallup, http://www.gallup.com/poll/125999/mississippians-go-church-most-vermonters-least.aspx, accessed November 6, 2011.

49. *Religion and Public Life*, 9.

> Baptists, Pentecostals and non-Pentecostals were all members of
> this one church. . . .[I]n the social context of that time they had
> all found it useful and acceptable to be involved together in the
> First Spanish Baptist Church.[50]

However, based on input from several pastors, it appears that the
Hispanic churches of Oregon have entered into a new phase of existence
in which creedal differences are more important. In the early days when
the Hispanic population was very small until just after the initial immigration spurt in the 1980s, there were few evangelical churches and even
fewer Spanish-speaking pastors. This lack of options forced Protestant
Latinos to band together. At the present, the variety of evangelical
churches has greatly expanded, as have the programs for pastoral training and the number of pastors.

The competition between Protestant churches for members was
not a recurring theme in previous studies of U.S. Latino churches, but
Freston observes a similar fluidity among Protestants in Latin America,
stating "religious identity may include comings and goings."[51]

Participation in Civic Community

The churches in this study could be described as occasionally involved
in their communities, but only the Mennonite and Salvados para
Servir churches indicated any political involvement, though the pastor of Manantiales de Vida Eterna indicated from the pulpit how his
congregation should vote. They gave no other indication of being involved in community development or advocacy. Unlike their Catholic
counterparts that supported the development of organizations such as
Centro Cultural in Cornelius and the short-lived Colegio César Chávez
described in chapter 2, the Protestant Latino churches of Oregon appear
to limit their community and political involvement.

Armendariz observed a similar phenomenon in his study of eight
congregations, although they represented mainstream denominations
not included in this study of Oregon:[52]

---

50. "Hispanic/Latino Protestantism," 387–88.

51. Freston, 227.

52. They were Episcopal, Lutheran, Methodist, Presbyterian, and United Church of
Christ congregations.

"these congregations do not deal efficiently with the communities in which they are located. One particular survey . . . indicated, overwhelmingly, that its own members recognized their lack of involvement in the issues affecting the community. Part of the reason is that most members of these congregations do not actually live in the community. A large majority of the members of these sample congregations live outside and thus become commuters to church activities."[53] This cannot serve as an explanation for the lack of civic or political involvement for the Oregon churches, as only the Woodburn Iglesia Menonita Pentecostés pastor indicated that a majority of his parishoners lived outside the city of Woodburn.[54]

Latin Americans have a long tradition of participation in mutual aid societies, traceable back to the Spanish colonial period. Miller describes the development of these *mutualistas* in the 19th century in the U.S. southwest, heavily populated by Mexicans and Mexican-Americans.[55] Aponte notes that the in Philadelphia, "In a situation of growing social instability and decreasing public resources many Hispanic Protestant churches have stepped into the gap. . . . Hispanic Protestant churches have become agents of stability and hope in neighborhoods where the people . . . face a host of social ills."[56] Many Oregon churches, particularly those organized by cell groups, "take care of their own" and thus serve as a type of insular mutual aid organization.

Recinos described a loss of identity and purpose in relation to society for the mainstream Latino congregations in the Washington, DC area. He suggested that new waves of immigrants could serve as the impulse for changes he believes are needed in this area: "As Latino newcomers like the Salvadorans revitalize Hispanic mainline Protestant churches's belief and practices, these faith communities may be equipped to deal critically with the Latino community's history of conquest, colonization, racial oppression, poverty, family fragmentation, migration, and exile."[57]

53. "Protestant Hispanic," 240.

54. Other pastors said that a few families commuted from their homes in other communities, but the majority of church-goers lived in the area surrounding the church building.

55. Miller, *Latinos and Development of Community*, 21.

56. "Hispanic/Latino Protestantism," 396.

57. "Mainline Hispanic Protestantism," 197.

This would be a process in which the needs of the newcomers cause the settled Hispanic population to engage in activism.

Maduro observed that a large percentage of Hispanic political leaders in New York have Pentecostal backgrounds, but these presumably are bilingual Latinos who are at least second- if not third-generation immigrants or bilingual Puerto Ricans.[58] Vasquez' study of La Gran Comisión, a Pentecostal congregation in Paterson, New Jersey, indicates that it has a long history of civic involvement. It was founded in 1943, has around 600 members, and serves Latino immigrants from multiple nations, as well as their children and grand-children.[59] Aponte also observed that the Latino Protestant churches of Philadelphia (many of which were established in the 1940s and 50s) became more engaged in community issues as time went on: "these congregations all found themselves increasingly called upon to address the social conditions of their members."[60]

Undoubtedly an important factor in the lack of political participation is the relative youth of Oregon's Latino Protestant churches. Many are concentrating on consolidating their organizations. Most church-goers are first-generation immigrants for whom English is a struggle, making communication with the broader public difficult, let alone influencing groups or public policy. The coming years will reveal whether or not these congregations become active in the community like some of their older counterparts in the Eastern part of the country.

There are mixed reports of the influence of Protestantism on political and civic participation in Latin America. While Wilson characterizes members of the neo-Pentecostal churches of Guatemala as "activists with the means and the desire to engage in public life, [who] have a strong sense of civic responsibility and support schools, social service programs, and, inevitably political activities,"[61] he concludes his study of their political participation with the prediction that due to the relative newness of the movement, the inexperience of its members and its notorious fragmentation and independence, "political participation . . . is likely to be personal, pragmatic, and tentative."[62] He describes Pentecostalism

58. "Religion and exclusion," 45, 50.

59. "Pentecostalism, Collective Identity," 622, 632.

60. "Hispanic/Latino Protestantism," 390.

61. "Guatemalan Pentecostals," 146.

62. Ibid., 155.

in El Salvador as being similarly non-politically involved, noting that
the *Reglamento local*, the Assemblies of God's church operations manual
used in most of Latin America, includes a membership "pledge to respect civil authority and to refrain from political involvement."[63] He also
suggests that Pentecostals' other-wordly focus may preclude them from
working with secular community organizations.[64] Costas concurs: "Los
que participan en el culto se niegan, en gran parte, a participar en las
actividades comunales, a involucrarse en cuestiones políticas, a servir
al necesitado, etc., y si lo hacen, es con un propóstio ulterior: ganarlos
a la fe." (Those who participate in the worship service refuse, in great
measure, to participate in community activites, to get involved in political matters, to serve the needy, etc., and if they do, it is with an ulterior
motive: to win them to the faith.)[65]

Freston observes that Latin American *evangélicos'* political involvement "is not recent. But since the 1980s, it has increased tremen-
dously, especially with the involvement of Pentecostal denominations."[66]
However, his comments refer principally to Guatemala and Brazil.[67]
Brazilians were not included in this study, and while there are
Guatemalans in the Latino churches of Oregon, the majority of them
arrived in the 1980s, fleeing violence in their homeland, prior to the
time of the growth of Protestant political activity. Those evangelicals that
remained in Guatemala in the early 1980s under the rule of leader Ríos
Montt may feel betrayed or co-opted by his violent policies mixed with
evangelical rhetoric and hesitate to mix their faith with politics again.
Espinosa observes that "Protestant growth has translated into political
power" in Central America and claims that in Latin America "we are

---

63. "Sanguine Saints," 8.

64. Ibid., 2.

65. "La realidad de la iglesia evangélica latinoamericana," 49.

66. "Christianity and Conflict," (panel presentation, National Defense University,
Washington, DC, April 6, 2006).

67. Chile is another Latin American country where numbers of evangelicals have
grown dramatically and their presence is becoming noticed by politicians. One example
of this is the unanimous legislative vote and subsequent declaration by former president
Michele Bachelet of October 31 as National Evangelical and Protestant Churches's Day
in 2008. The number of Chileans in Oregon is negligible, so their political activism as
evangelicals is not germane to this study.

starting to see Catholics and Pentecostals begin to work together on key moral, social, and political issues on behalf of the Latino community."[68]

It is evident that scholars do not agree on the effects of religion on civic and political participation in Latin America, and that it varies from one country to another and between denominations. Furthermore, given the small percentage of Oregon Latinos who converted to Protestantism prior to immigration, trying to apply trends seen in Latin American churches to Oregon is questionable. For example, the *Reglamento local* was used by the AOG in Mexico, home to the majority of Oregon's Hispanic immigrants, but the percentage of evangelical Christians in Mexico remains so small that its influence on the political activity of Oregon Latino Protestants must be negligible.

Other factors certainly affect attitudes toward political and civic participation among evangelical Latino immigrants in Oregon. They are in the minority, not part of a growing majority as in Guatemala. The undocumented wish to call as little attention to themselves as possible, so participation in public meetings like a political rally is unlikely.

Although these factors were also true during the organization of the migrant health clinics, Centro Cultural, and Colegio César Chávez, the current social climate is significantly different. It appears that these agencies benefitted from the northward spill of the *Chicano* movement of the 1970s, whereas anti-immigrant sentiments flare across the nation at the turn of the twenty-first century. Since these organizations received significant Catholic support, it is also possible that the type of Christianity makes a significant difference. In Latin America, Catholic clergy "called for the direct and active involvement of church organizations with labor unions, human rights groups, and peasant and neighborhood organizations."[69] It is also possible that U.S. Latino Catholics may be more willing to participate in broader society than their Protestant counterparts.

There is mixed evidence regarding the influence of church creed and tradition on Hispanic community activism. Pentecostals supposedly steer away from involvement in this temporal world, but Puerto Ricans of Pentecostal heritage, if not practice, provide political leadership in New York.[70] Mainline churches such as Presbyterians and Lutherans

---

68. "Pentecostalization," 292.

69. Ibid., 50–51.

70. "Religion and exclusion," 45, 50.

have not hesitated to advocate for change in U.S. society, but Recinos claims that established Hispanic mainline congregations need to be prodded out of their complacency by seeing the needs of recent refugees from Central America.[71]

These contradictory findings make predicting social involvement for Oregon Protestant Latinos difficult. Mainline churches do not seem to have Hispanic ministries in Oregon.[72] It is likely that some churches will urge their members to stay aloof from political activity while others become increasingly vocal as times goes on, due to a variety of social, economic, and doctrinal factors, just as the Latin American churches have done.

CONCLUSIONS

The Latino churches of Oregon are young, compared to those in many areas of the country. Most of the Protestant Hispanics in Oregon, with the exception of those from Guatemala, began attending Protestant churches after immigration. Three denominations indigenous to Latin America are very active in Oregon, along with better-known denominations with roots in Europe or the U.S., such as Baptists, Mennonites, and the Assemblies of God. There are also many independent churches. Mainline churches have few, if any, Spanish-speaking congregations in Oregon. Denominational ties have contributed to the stability and longevity of Latino Protestant churches in the state. Most of the Hispanic pastors have participated in Bible or theological training, and opportunities for on-going studies in these areas, in Spanish, are available in the state and on-line.

As more options become available for Protestant worship in Spanish, creedal and doctrinal distinctions have become increasingly important. Oregon pastors report competition between Spanish-speaking congregations for participants. Those who do participate in Protestant Latino congregations are not very politically involved, regardless of their doctrinal background.

Few Oregon Latino churches have their own building. Most share with or rent from an English-speaking church. More than one third of

71. "Mainline Hispanic Protestantism," 197.

72. For example, "there are no Hispanic PCUSA [Presbyterian Church USA] churches . . . in the Cascades." Aleida Jernigan, Co-Executive Presbyter for the presbytery of Cascades in e-mail message to author, Sept. 28, 2011.

the congregations in this study described being part of a unified body, sharing and interacting in significant ways with the Anglo congregation. This report of unity is in stark contrast to the paternalism, racism, and divisions described in previous studies of Hispanic churches in other parts of the country. It is possible that the sense of Christian unity in Oregon is more important than ethnicity, as Christians of diverse national origins and languages join together in a non-religious majority society.

4

Congregational Composition and Language Use

INTRODUCTION

REGARDING RELATIONSHIPS WITHIN IMMIGRANT churches, several themes are prevalent in previous studies. First, many researchers point out that these churches are very internally diverse, much more so than outsiders perceive. This diversity in Latino churches can be traced to different countries of origin and regional differences within countries, urban vs. rural backgrounds, and educational and socioeconomic differences. In most places in Latin America, being indigenous or *mestizo*[1] or Afro-latino defines social groups. Legal status in the U.S. is another divisor. Finally, length of time in the U.S. and generation of immigration, coupled with fluency in English, Spanish, or an indigenous dialect cause further distinctions.

Second- and third-generation immigrants, who are mostly youth in Oregon, often speak little Spanish. Responding to their needs and including them in the Latino church is a challenge described by several researchers. Related to this issue are questions of assimilation into the host culture.

This chapter examines the composition of each congregation in terms of:

- country of origin, including a brief section on non-Hispanics attending Hispanic churches,

- ethnicity,

---

1. In simplest terms, of mixed European and indigenous ancestry. The complexity of this word's meaning is summarized by González in his introduction to *Alabadle*, 14–16.

- educational attainment and type of employment,
- generation of immigration, and
- language use.

These elements are described for each congregation outside of the Portland metropolitan area, followed by those in Washington and Multnomah Counties. The latter part of the chapter compares the national origin and generation of immigration information on the Oregon congregations with census data. Finally, the information presented in this chapter is examined in light of previous studies about relationships within U.S. immigrant churches and in Latino congregations specifically.

COUNTRY OF ORIGIN

Non-Hispanics Attending Hispanic Churches

Although not mentioned in the literature, the author has observed a few Anglos like herself attending Hispanic church services over the course of many years. All the pastors were asked if any non-Latinos attended their congregations. Phrases in quotes in the sections below are from their interviews, unless otherwise indicated. Rogue Valley Fellowship's Hispanic ministry, Manantiales de Vida Eterna, Iglesia Menonita Pentecostés in Woodburn, the former Assemblies of God congregation called Roca de Salvación, the two Foursquare congregations, and Casa del Padre in Portland did not have any non-Latinos attending.

Pastor Vargas of Iglesia Menonita Pentecostés in Woodburn said that they used to have many Russians join them, as they enjoyed the regular communion and foot-washing elements of the worship services. More recently, however, Russian congregations have developed and provide Russian speakers with opportunity to observe these ceremonies in their own language.

The pastors of Hermiston Conservative Baptist Nueva Esperanza and Forest Grove's Iglesia de Jesucristo said that they have had occasional visitors who are not Hispanic, but no regular attenders. As previously mentioned, the pastors of the Hood River Christian and Missionary Alliance Church, City Bible, and Grants Pass New Hope Mennonite Brethren Spanish-speaking congregations were Anglos.

All the other churches said that several non-Latinos regularly attended services. Twelve pastors indicated that family ties were the reason for this—many were bicultural couples.[2] In Madras, some of the non-Hispanic attendees are Native Americans from the Confederated Tribes of Warm Springs.

A second reason indicated by the pastors for non-Latino attendees was their desire to learn the Spanish language or maintain their Spanish after living abroad. This was the case for eight churches.

A related reason was a more general interest in Hispanic culture or a specific sense of call to serve Latinos. Interestingly, very few of these people spoke Spanish. Those who attended Reedwood Friends speak "very little," while those attending Casa del Padre in Beaverton, Madras Iglesia Bautista Conservadora Bilingüe, and Newport Nueva Esperanza didn't speak any Spanish. The Madras church had an Anglo couple that were members and volunteer youth ministers. The senior pastor, youth pastor, and the Sunday School teacher for preschoolers all regularly attended the Spanish service in Newport to show their support of the ministry. The Grants Pass service was bilingual with both Anglos and Hispanics attending at the same time. Only a few of the Anglos there had learned Spanish, but they worshiped together "because they have a love for the Latino people." At the Hood River church, several Anglos who attend had learned Spanish and enjoyed the "cultural dynamics" and the "biblical focus."

While worship style falls within the category of Latino culture, it was mentioned specifically by three Washington County pastors as a possible motive for non-Hispanic attendance. The worship styles of all the churches in this study are described in chapter 5. Vida Church in Aloha had six non-Latinos on its worship team, and Pastor Raúl Giménez attributed this to the "libertad de adoración" (freedom of worship). Associate Pastor Francisco Mateo of Salvados para Servir ventured that "consideran la iglesia latina como algo vibrante . . . porque el estilo de música les atrae quizás" (they consider the Latin church as something vibrant . . . because the style of music attracts them perhaps), and Pastor Alvarizares of Casa del Padre said that the number one reason Anglos attended services at the Beaverton church is "because of the expression of worship that we have." Soliván makes an interesting comment germane to this point, claiming that American Anglo European culture has

2. This includes the now-defunct Iglesia de Jesucristo, Ministerio de Vida Eterna. Although the pastor was not interviewed, the author observed during the site visit that his wife was an Anglo who spoke Spanish.

"passion-impairment" and that there are marked differences in the enthusiasm of Anglo and Hispanic Pentecostal churches.[3] According to the pastors mentioned in this paragraph, there are a handful of Anglos who seek to overcome this "impairment" by joining Latino congregations.

Nationality of Latinos in Churches

The following section first describes the nationalities of Oregon Latino pastors and the members of their churches, based on information provided by the pastor. All pastors were asked four questions about national origin:

- "If your church has people from different Latin American countries of origin, how does this affect the church body?;
- Do people from different countries mingle socially or stay separate?;
- Do you observe a sense that one group of origin looks down on another?; and
- Do you think the pastor's country of origin impacts whether people from other countries also come here or don't come?"

It also presents information on the generation of immigration of the congregants, the choice of language for various activities, participation of (often second-generation) youth, educational attainment and occupations of the congregation, and the characteristics of the leadership team or board members. Where pastors indicated a tendency toward assimilation to U.S. society or toward cultural preservation, these observations are included.

CHURCHES OUTSIDE THE PORTLAND METROPOLITAN AREA

The Hood River Christian and Missionary Alliance church was the most diverse of the rural Hispanic congregations. The approximately 150 regular attendees are primarily from Mexico (including the pastor's wife), but there are also individuals from Argentina, Chile, Guatemala, Honduras, El Salvador, and the Portuguese-speaking nation of Brazil. Including the U.S.-born Anglo pastor, there are eight nationalities represented. Regarding this diversity, Pastor Estey indicated that "[t]his

---

3. "Hispanic Pentecostal Worship," 55.

dynamic socially and spiritually enriches the congregation" and that during social events all the congregants mingle. He noted that among the immature some from one group may look down on those of another nationality, but that "as they grow spiritually the old patterns disintegrate." He acknowledged that his nationality impacts whether people from other countries attend the church "to some degree" but did not elaborate further.

Most of the congregation works in the local fruit industry or hotels and restaurants. The pastor estimated that 80 percent of the congregation had only a sixth-grade education or less, while 20 percent had finished high school, and 3 percent gone on to college. The board members of this congregation are all from Mexico and have completed a high school education.

About 50 percent of current attendees are first-generation immigrants, and the church has made the decision to become fully bilingual "for the sake of the second generation." Pastor Estey indicated that his church has a strong youth ministry and that they stay "plugged in" to the congregation. The Sunday School classes, worship services, and informal activities are all bilingual in Spanish and English. During the site visit, the author observed that many of the songs had English translations projected along with the Spanish lyrics, that scripture reading was done in both languages, and that there was consecutive interpretation of the exhortation on tithing done by a layperson, but that the sermon was preached only in Spanish.

While the Woodburn Mennonite Iglesia Pentecostés had mostly Mexican congregants, there were four Costa Rican families, one of which was the pastor's. There were also two Guatemalan families, one family from Argentina, and a Puerto Rican. Nearly all of them were first-generation immigrants. As the church was developing in the early years as described in chapter 2, it went through several name changes, and when Pastor Vargas arrived it was called Iglesia Pentecostés Mexicana (Mexican Pentecost Church). He believed the name reflected the occasional tendency of Mexicans to say they speak *mexicano,* meaning they speak Spanish. Since Pastor Vargas is not Mexican, he requested that they change the name to just Iglesia Pentecostés. Pastor Vargas indicated that the diversity of nationalities in the congregations had been a positive thing, piquing curiosity about other cultures, including unique word usages. He said that his congregation mixed freely without regard to nationality. He also believed that his Costa Rican nationality had been a positive aspect in the church, claiming that when people came and heard a Costa Rican accent instead of the Mexican accent they are accustomed to, they paid closer attention to the sermon.

Most of the congregation was employed in agriculture, and the pastor estimated that 75 percent had completed only elementary school, another 10 percent had completed their GED, and 2–3 percent had attended some college. The church board of Iglesia Pentecostés had mostly Mexicans, one person "born here," and one Puerto Rican. Pastor Vargas said that most of the board members had slightly more education than the average congregant, indicating that most of the board had completed middle school.

There were few youth and young adults in this congregation. Pastor Vargas said that many of them quit attending because they had to start working to help their parents financially. Some still participated in the migrant stream, working in grapes in California, strawberries in Oregon, and potatoes in Idaho. Others started attending Anglo churches, and yet others married and moved away. The second-generation young people who remained in his congregation were attending high school and college. Pastor Vargas stated that they recognized that they were being taught non-Christian values in the public schools and that they saw the church as their home and place of identity, even though they also may have had relationships with Anglos and Anglo churches.

> Aunque sean nacidos aquí, hablan el idioma bien, y está bien que aprecien las raíces. Personalmente he hecho énfasis hacia ellos no pierdan las raíces, que no se avergüencen de su origen, que en este país todos somos inmigrantes, que los únicos no inmigrantes son los indios de aquí que son ya poquitos, que no se sientan menos porque a veces les ponen como mojados . . . . Esa pugna por el racismo . . .

> [Even though they are born here, they speak the language well, and it is good that they appreciate their roots. Personally I have made an emphasis toward them not losing their roots, that they not be ashamed of their origin, that in this country we are all immigrants, that the only non-immigrants are the Indians from here that are now very few, that they not feel less because sometimes they are treated as wetbacks . . . . That struggle because of racism . . .]

All church activities are in Spanish,[4] though the youth use English when doing things like playing basketball together. The author noticed during the site visit that as soon as the service was over, the youth spoke with one another in English. The church has not made a conscious decision regarding language use; "It has happened spontaneously."

Though the pastor of Ontario's Templo Betania Assembly of God was unavailable for an interview, the author did make several observations during the site visit regarding the composition and language use of the congregation. She was greeted by, "God bless you" in fluent English, and there were English copies of the Bible in the pew racks. The hymnals were in Spanish, as were all the worship choruses. One of the maracas used in worship was painted with the colors of the Mexican flag, and before leading the congregation in prayer, a layman asked, "¿Todos aquí hablan *mexicano*?" (Does everyone here speak Mexican?)[5] This and the guest speaker's multiple references to events in Mexico,[6] indicate that the majority of this congregation is Mexican. Of the approximately twenty people present, two were in their twenties and the rest were middle-aged or older adults. Based on the church's location, the sermon that referred several times to the poor being taking advantage of by the rich, and linguistic archaisms, this congregation is at the lower end of the socioeconomic and educational spectrum.

At Newport's Nueva Esperanza, the pastor was Peruvian, his wife was Colombian, and there were three Anglo English speakers who regularly attended. All the other congregants were Mexican. (The single Guatemalan family had moved away from Newport seeking work just prior to the pastoral interview.) Before the Guatemalans left, the congregation joined together without regard to nationality for social activities like potlucks or baby showers. Pastor Kuroda stated that:

> Lo que hemos descubierto con el pastor americano es que no-sotros mismos estamos haciendo una cultura diferente. . . . son mexicanos . . . pero están viviendo una nueva cultura aquí en este país. Creo que el hecho de estar en contacto con ellos casi a

---

4. The author did note several calques from English in the pastor's prayer, such as *fil* "field" and *norsería* "[plant] nursery."

5. Again, meaning Spanish.

6. The pastor was on vacation for three weeks. The guest speaker lived in Ontario and was known to the congregation, but it was unclear to the author whether he was a member of this congregation.

diario, ya no hay esas barreras culturales . . . porque ya, o ellos se han hecho a mí o yo a ellos, algo ha sucedido que nos hemos complementado dentro del grupo de nosotros, no? Así que . . . creo que al principio del ministerio sí, había esas barreras, o choques culturales, ya sabe, palabras o frases o cosas que uno decía o malos entendidos. . . . Pero ya, ocho años después ya la gente te entiende, te comprende, y yo los entiendo o sé de lo que están hablando."

[What we have discovered with the American pastor is that we ourselves are making a different culture. . . . They are Mexicans . . . but they are living a new culture here in this country. I think that [due to] the fact of being in contact with them almost daily, there are no longer those cultural barriers . . . because by this time, either they have adapted to me or I to them, something has happened that we have complemented each other within our group, right? So . . . I think that at the beginning of the ministry, yes, there were those barriers or culture shocks, you know, words or phrases or things that one said or misunderstandings. . . . But now, eight years later the people now understand you, they comprehend you, and I understand them or I know what they're talking about. . . .]

Only eight of the sixty adults regularly attending had completed high school, and one had finished college. Most of the congregation worked as housekeepers in the many hotels in the area, while others were employed in the fishing industry or in agriculture. All the members of the board were Mexicans (as was all the congregation) and included the one college graduate. The others had all finished high school. Some of these bilingual people have also served on the board of deacons for the broader church.

Pastor Kuroda observed that the Hispanic population in this area is young, and most families have young children. There was only one teenager attending Nueva Esperanza in Newport at the time of the pastoral interview. He speaks English, and the youth pastor for the church includes this young man in his ministry to all youth, as part of the vision of a single church.

Nueva Esperanza in Newport had a mixed language program. The preschoolers were taught in English by the Anglo teacher previously mentioned, and according to Pastor Kuroda, the children knew this and had not had any problems with it. The children's church program had been done in English by Anglos, but they transferred responsibility to the Spanish speakers. They liked the Superchurch curriculum they had been using, but it was available only in English, so Pastor Kuroda translated it to Spanish each week. At potlucks and informal events, Spanish was used by the adults and English by the children. The Guatemalan family that had just moved also spoke Mam, an indigenous dialect. Pastor Kuroda indicated that he always spoke Spanish slowly with them, to facilitate their understanding, as Spanish was their secondary language. He described the use of various languages as something that had not been a conscious decision nor imposed by either congregation, but as occurring naturally, mostly based on the first language of the teachers. During the worship service observed at the site visit, only Spanish was used in all announcements, prayer, Bible reading, music, and preaching.

The pastor and most of the congregation at Madras Iglesia Bautista Conservadora Bilingüe were Mexican. In addition to the previously mentioned Native (North) Americans and Anglos who regularly attended, there were Panamanians, Nicaraguans, and Salvadorans. Pastor Pantoja had not observed that one group looked down on another, but asserted that a multicultural congregation was more dynamic than one of a single culture. He stated that at social activities, all the members mingled without regard for their national backgrounds. Though this congregation has had pastors of other nationalities in the past, including a Chilean and a Dominican[7], Pastor Pantoja felt that coming from the same country of origin as most of the congregants was a positive: "mi forma de trabajar va en harmonía con la cultura que ellos tienen" (my way of working is in harmony with the culture that they have).

Most of the congregation was employed in area wood mills or in agriculture, although several worked for the local school district or social service agencies. The pastor estimated that about 35 percent of the congregation completed only elementary school, another 35 percent had finished high school, and that around 7 percent had attended college or were currently doing so. All of the board members were Mexican, and they included persons who had little formal education to those with some college study.

---

7. On the date of the site visit, the former Dominican pastor and his wife were in attendance. Though Dominican, she used Mexican terms in her greeting to the church, and added, "como decimos los mexicanos" "as we Mexicans say," indicating her identification with the nationality of the majority of the congregation.

Around 80 percent of the congregation in Madras were first-generation immigrants, including two or three elderly women. Pastor Pantoja indicated that while the teens stayed active in the church's youth group, when it came time for them to attend college, they were forced to move to another city because there was no university in the town. The author learned during the site visit that some second-generation youth preferred to attend the youth group at the neighboring English-speaking Conservative Baptist congregation, and many of the Hispanic children participated regularly in the AWANA children's program there as well. She observed that several teenagers participated on the Spanish worship music team. Pastor Pantoja recognized that the presence of the second generation presented a challenge: "Representa un reto para la iglesia porque nosotros tenemos que pensar en la filosofía del ministerio que necesitamos tener de tal manera que ellos se sientan integrados a la iglesia." (It represents a challenge to the church because we have to think about the ministry philosophy that we need to have so that they feel integrated into the church.)

Though the church's name included the word "bilingual," Pastor Pantoja asserted that it was not, and never had been, though that may have been the intention. Simultaneous interpretation in English was provided with headsets when monolingual English speakers were present, but the pastor indicated that to truly be a bilingual church, everything would need to be done in both English and Spanish, and it was not. The worship services and Sunday School classes were all in Spanish, even with the children. Youth group activities were in English because the leaders were monolingual English-speaking Anglos. At informal activities, the adults spoke Spanish, and the children and youth used English.

Grants Pass New Hope Mennonite Brethren Church was unusual in that the English and Spanish speakers met together at the same time in the same room for bilingual worship. The pastor was Anglo, all of the Spanish-speaking congregants were from Mexico, and the English-speaking congregants included three persons from two African nations. While there was not national diversity among the Latinos, the choice to meet together for worship had presented some "challenges with translation, worship songs and styles, and length of services." Pastor Stutzman replied emphatically, "Absolutely not!" when asked if he sensed that persons from one group of origin looked down on another. He recognized that his U.S. origins might impact whether or not Latinos choose to worship at this church, and indicated that the choice to meet jointly without segregation had caused difficulty in growing the congregation. During the site visit, the author observed that a Latino teen played the drums for worship music, and that the worship team was composed of four additional Latinos and two Anglos. Pastor Stutzman indicated that many of the young people left the area to attend college, so the church did not retain them, but he believed that they sought out another church to attend in their new town. About 5 percent had completed only elementary school, another 75 percent completed high school and about 20 percent had gone on to college. Nearly all of them were employed in "blue collar" jobs. Seven of the ten board members were U.S.-born Anglos and the remaining three Mexicans.

In this unique congregation, Sunday School, the sermon, and informal activities were all in English. The pastor indicated that all Hispanics currently attending had strong enough English listening skills to understand the sermon. Songs, announcements, prayer requests, scripture reading, and prayer happened in both English and Spanish during the worship service observed by the author. During one of the hymns, one of the younger Anglos sang out of the Spanish hymnal, while most Anglos chose to use the English hymnbook. The decision to have worship services this way was reached by consensus. Pastor Stutzman said that about 40 percent of the Hispanics in the congregation were first-generation immigrants, and observed that "second- and third-generation immigrants care little about hearing the message in Spanish. Many can understand Spanish but do not speak it."

Monmouth Christian Church's Spanish-speaking group was pastored by Ulysses Vela, whose mother was from Mexico but whose father traced his Mexican roots back to the period when Texas was part of Mexico. All of the congregation (excepting the several Anglos mentioned previously) was of Mexican origin at the time of the pastoral interview, though there had been Venezuelans and Guatemalans in the past. Only about 40 percent of this congregation was first-generation immigrants. Most were at least second-generation immigrants like the pastor. When asked how he thought this situation affected the congregation, the pastor replied, "I think it's been good that my wife is from Mexico, because I think you can bring a blend. I think we blend just perfectly into the culture that's coming up because it's English and Spanish and I think that . . . well, I don't spell as good as I should, I think I fit . . . most people confuse me from [*sic*] being from Mexico, my accent is a little bit off, but most people accept me as . . . being like them."

The pastor estimated that about 45 percent of the congregation attended only elementary school, some 50 percent finished high school, and 5 percent went on to attend college. Two of the congregation were teachers, while others worked in plant nurseries, canneries, factories or as janitors or caregivers. Over time, several from the Spanish-speaking congregation have served on the elder board of Monmouth Christian Church. All have been bilingual, and the representative at the time of the pastoral interview was a U.S.-born Hispanic. One previous Mexican-born board candidate was also bilingual but never was included on the board due to his lack of legal status.

Monmouth Christian Church's Hispanics used both English and Spanish for church activities. The author observed that announcements were made in Spanglish—fluid transfer between both languages even in the middle of sentences. The sermon was consecutively interpreted into English, and they used at least one English worship song per month. This decision to use English was made, "'Cause there's people that weren't getting any Word in. We've got to realize that most people don't read their Bibles. It's sad but it's true. And I was noticing that people spiritually weren't getting nothing on Sundays—the English speaking only, so that was why they did that. And like the high school, younger adults, I think they grasp better in English than they do in Spanish." The adult Sunday School program was taught in Spanish, and the children went to Sunday School with the Anglos and follow an English curriculum. This was a recent change, as the couple who had been teaching Spanish children's Sunday School moved away and no other teachers were found among the Spanish speakers. Pastor Vela also described a lack of available children's curricula in Spanish.

There were very few high school students attending the Spanish-speaking congregation at the time of the pastoral interview, although Pastor Vela said they used to have a strong Latino youth group in the past. He added, "We have four or five out of high school and working and going to college but they don't integrate well into the English, even though I'm invited to let them know, but they just . . . it's a different culture." At potlucks and other informal events, those thirty years of age and older used mostly Spanish, and the younger people English, but Pastor Vela indicated some fluidity in this situation.

Pastor Argueta of Rogue Valley Fellowship was the lone Salvadoran in a congregation of Mexicans, including his wife. He stated that he had never seen any problem in coming from a different country than all of those he ministers to. All of the adult members of the congregation were first-generation immigrants, while the youth and children were born in the U.S. Most had lived in the area for at least ten years. About 5 percent were of indigenous background and spoke a dialect in addition to Spanish.

Most of the congregation worked in service industries, such as hotels, restaurants, landscaping, and agricultural processing. Pastor Argueta estimated that 50 percent of the congregation had completed only elementary school, and was unable to provide further information on education for the rest. He indicated that those who make up the leadership board were not characterized by having more advanced education, but by having greater spiritual maturity.

The Latino youth participated actively in church activities up until the time they graduated from high school. The author observed several teenagers serving as musicians during the worship service she attended. The pastor indicated that when they became adults and could make their own decisions, they distanced themselves from the church, and many of them quit attending church altogether. The youth of the Spanish-speaking and English-speaking groups at this church did not interact.

The worship services and Saturday evening children's activities were in Spanish. On Sunday mornings, the children attended Sunday School in English with the Anglo children while the parents had a worship service in Spanish. The pastor described how this decision to do nearly everything in Spanish came about over time. At first, Spanish speakers attended the regular English worship service, and simultaneous interpretation to Spanish was provided with headsets. Growth was small until the Latinos moved into a different room and began to do everything entirely in Spanish. At social activities, only the youth used English. The author and her family were greeted prior to a Saturday evening service in fluent, unaccented English by several adult Latinos.

Nueva Esperanza in Hermiston also had only Mexicans attending at the time of the pastoral interview, including Pastor Loredo. He noted that Hondurans and Salvadorans had attended in the past. He asserted that sharing nationality with his congregation had a positive impact on his ministry: "[A]yuda en el sentido que por lo menos tenemos más cosas en común, cosas culturales. . . . comida, tradiciones, costumbres, aunque varía también de estado a estado. Pero pudiera decir yo que afecta en una manera positiva, más que negativa." ([I]t helps in the sense that we at least have more things in common, cultural things. . . . food, traditions, customs, even though it also varies from state to state. But I could say that it affects in a positive way, more than negative.)

Eighty percent of the attendees were first-generation immigrants, as was Pastor Loredo, who came to the U.S. as a youth. When asked how the presence of the two generations in the church affected it, the pastor responded that the second generation was more comfortable speaking English than Spanish, and that they have acquired some different habits as they have grown up in the U.S. The Mexican-American youth participated with the Spanish-speaking congregation but also the broader church's youth group. During the Spanish service attended by the author, there were five Hispanic teens providing worship music. Some of the second-generation churchgoers had graduated from high school and participated in "lower levels" of leadership such as working with the youth. They had not yet assumed leadership at the board level. There were also second- and third-generation immigrants who regularly attended the English worship service: "Ese es el punto de tener los servicios simultáneamente para haber la oportunidad para las personas a que vengan a cualquiera de los dos servicios, que se sientan a gusto en el que quieren participar." (That is the point of having the services simultaneously, to have the opportunity for people to come to either of the two services, that they feel comfortable in the one they want to participate in.) This schedule also allowed the youth and children to attend Sunday School with the Anglos, and the classes were in English. There was an adult Sunday School class and a class for new believers taught in Spanish.

About 10 percent of the congregation completed only elementary school, while about 70 percent completed high school and 10 percent had gone on to college. Most of the congregation worked in agriculture, although some were medical or educational assistants. Representatives from the Spanish-speaking congregation served on various all-church committees.

Washington County Churches

Vida Church in Aloha was pastored by an Argentine couple. There were mostly Mexicans in their congregation, but also persons from

Guatemala, Honduras, El Salvador, Venezuela, and Puerto Rico. There was one couple whose first language is an indigenous dialect. For many years there was a Cuban as well, but he was not attending at the time of the interview. Pastor Giménez observed that all these persons mixed socially regardless of their country of origin, and stated that having people from so many diverse backgrounds had been "[e]nriquecedora en términos de cultura, roce social de gente de otros paises, puedo convivir con personas diferentes. Rompe estructuras y prejuicios." ([e]nriching in terms of culture, social contact with people from other countries, I can interact with different people. It breaks down structures and prejudices.) He did note that breaking down prejudices had taken time, especially from the Puerto Ricans toward the Mexicans. His wife observed that among some, it had been difficult to replace deeply-held cultural beliefs or old wives' tales with "the truth of the Bible" and that teaching persons with very limited prior schooling was challenging. Pastor Giménez also admitted that his nationality might put some off from attending his church as some were prejudiced against Argentines or "whiter" Latinos.

Most of the adults in this congregation had finished high school, with about five continuing to college. One held a master's degree. Most worked in service professions and none in agriculture. Those in leadership on the ministry team were from a variety of nations and educational backgrounds, but all had had both practical training and some spiritual leadership courses. Two of these persons were bilingual and also attended the leadership meetings of the English-speaking church.

Around 80 percent of those attending Vida Church were first-generation immigrants. There were about fifteen people who were second-generation, and no third-generation immigrants in this congregation. Some of the Latino youth in this congregation participated in the English-speaking youth group of Life Church; others stayed with the Spanish speakers. Pastor Giménez said that many youth actively used their talents in the Spanish-speaking ministry. During the site visit, a teenager gave a report to the church in English on her participation in a mission trip, and it was interpreted into Spanish for the congregation. The pastor indicated that the young people seemed to be fine while they are adolescents, but when they left and went to college, they struggled with their identity, trying to decide which culture they would embrace. At this stage, many left and went to an English-speaking church because they understood the language better.

Taking this second generation into consideration, Vida Church had always purposed to be bilingual. The worship services were simultaneously interpreted into English with headsets, and most of the worship songs were done in both languages. At the site visit, English worship music was playing prior to the beginning of the service. Bible studies, children's classes and children's church were in Spanish, but discussions were underway to move to English in the latter. Language was entirely mixed at social events.

Village Baptist's Spanish-speaking congregation in Beaverton was pastored by a Salvadoran who was raised in Canada. The congregation was principally Mexican, and most of these were from the mostly indigenous State of Oaxaca and spoke Mixteco, not Spanish, as a first language. Others spoke the Tritri dialect. There were also Hondurans, other Salvadorans, Guatemalans, Nicaraguans, Colombians and Peruvians. Including the regular attenders who were U.S.-born Anglos, there were eight nationalities represented. Pastor Rivas commented about the diversity of his congregation at length, reflecting the very purposeful direction taken by Village Baptist as a whole:

> Mi problema cultural no es tanto con los anglos es con mi propia gente . . . en el sentido que cada persona, cada pueblo tiene una identidad cultural. Algunas culturas son más calladas, algunas culturas son más abiertas, algunas tienen una forma idiomática diferente a otros. Ciertas palabras para mí significan una cosa, para otros significan otra. . . . La iglesia . . . tiene que ser multicultural y tiene que tener las puertas abiertas para cualquier grupo étnico y trae prejuicios, problemas, pero funciona. O sea, en la iglesia todos estamos con la misma misión ya que eso es lo que queremos y eso es lo que estamos juntando; cada grupo étnico respetándonos las diferencias culturales. . . . Ha sido algo positivo que viene caminando. Una iglesia multicultural no nace de la noche a la mañana, sino es un proceso. . . ."

> [My cultural problem isn't so much with the Anglos, it is with my own people . . . in the sense that each person, each people has a cultural identity. Some cultures are quieter, some cultures are more open, some have an idiomatic style that is different from others. Some words mean one thing for me, for others they mean something else. . . . The church . . . has to be multicultural and it has to have the doors open for any ethnic group and that brings prejudices, problems, but it works. In other words, in the church we all have the same mission, since this is what we want and that

> is what we are putting together; each ethnic group respecting
> our cultural differences. . . . It has been something positive that
> is coming along. A multicultural church isn't born overnight,
> rather it is a process. . . .]

He added that having such a diverse body was a blessing that worshippers in some countries do not have, given the insularity of some communities. He indicated that contact with persons of different backgrounds was a culturally enriching experience that provided personal growth. To prevent groups of one nationality or ethnicity from staying separate, he has worked intentionally to create events in which people get to know one another as individuals with whom they have something in common. Rather than perceiving that one group looked down on another, he sensed that some cultures esteemed themselves less than others. He has seen progress in this area, as people begin to feel welcome and accept both themselves and others as valuable persons. He has been aware of the impact of his own cultural and linguistic background as a Salvadoran-Canadian, and makes an effort to use less Salvadoran idiomatic expressions that might not be understood by his congregation. Nonetheless, he did use *vos*[8] during the sermon when the author observed a worship service.

At Village Baptist, the Hispanic children and youth had bilingual Christian education classes, with English curriculum but discussion in both languages. Pastor Rivas observed that this decision was based on their need. Imitating the interlingual characteristics of the youth, he commented, "porque muchos de los jóvenes, segunda generación, ellos hablan muy bien . . . no muy bien . . . ellos hablan español, but they don't get it very well. Y en inglés, Spanish and English they connect." (because many of the young people, second generation, they speak very well . . . not very well . . . they speak Spanish, but they don't get it very well. And in English, Spanish and English they connect.) The Latino youth were included in the multicultural youth group and served by the youth pastor of Village Baptist. They also had a Friday night youth activity in Spanish. Pastor Rivas indicated that ministry to youth must respond to their unique needs, regardless of the language in which it is provided.

---

8. A third form of address in addition to *Ud.* and *tú,* meaning "you." Though used in several Central American nations, Argentina and Chile, each with different verbal inflections, it is not used by Mexicans.

During the site visit, the author observed that several teens participated on the worship music team.

The adult classes at Village Baptist were in Spanish. At informal activities, Spanish is the main language used, but there are also indigenous dialects and English. There was a regular multicultural service on Saturdays that was mostly in English with interpretation to Spanish, and songs were in both languages. Pastor Rivas strongly encouraged interaction of the Latinos with Anglos and English language acquisition, saying that in his opinion, the number one problem of Hispanic churches in the U.S. was pastors who did not speak English and thus inhibited their congregations' interactions with Anglo churches.

The Latinos at Village Baptist were approximately 50 percent first-generation immigrants, representing the adult population, and most youth and children were born in the U.S. Aside from the language accommodations made by the church, Pastor Rivas indicated that this situation created difficulties for the families, because the adults spoke Spanish or a dialect, and the youth and children spoke English better than their parents' language, creating communication problems in the home. He concluded by indicating that he sees it as the parents' responsibility to learn English so that they can communicate well with their children.

Most of the Spanish-speaking Village Baptist congregation was employed in agriculture or other service jobs such as house cleaning. The pastor indicated that very few of the congregation, perhaps 15 percent, had completed elementary school and that there were several who were illiterate, that only 5 percent had finished high school and even less had gone on to college. These latter were U.S.-born. The ministry leaders at Village were mostly first-generation immigrants with little formal education but a great love for God. Pastor Rivas claimed that the pattern of immigrants is for the first generation to dedicate themselves to work, so that their children can dedicate themselves to an education, and that his leaders follow this pattern. There were six persons in leadership at the time of the pastoral interview, four of whom were fully bilingual in Spanish and English. The other two had insufficient knowledge of English to carry on a conversation. Four of the leaders were from Oaxaca, Mexico, and the other two were not Mexican, reflecting the congregation's composition by place of origin.

Elim in Hillsboro-Aloha had mostly Guatemalans and a Guatemalan pastor. Mexican attendees came in second in number, making Elim one of only four churches in this study that did not have a Mexican majority. Salvadorans also attend. Pastor Diego stated that he has worked very hard with the congregation to focus on cooperation and love in the body of Christ, to train people to see the congregation as their new culture and family, and not allow distinctions based on country of origin. He did not believe that his Guatemalan nationality is a draw for the congregation; instead he felt a call to preach in a place where there happened to be many Guatemalans.

About two-thirds of the congregants at Elim were first-generation immigrants. Pastor Diego stated, "The youth are the future of the church. The adults are just passing through," and indicated that Elim provides many activities for the youth, both fun and educational. While Spanish was the language used for all organized activities, many of the adult churchgoers spoke an indigenous dialect as their first language. The youth used English at informal activities, and the church was aware that it might need to transition to a bilingual format or to English for some programs in the future.

The pastor indicated that about one-third of the congregation had completed only elementary school, another one third high school, and another one third college prior to immigrating. Most of the congregation worked in factories or plant nurseries.

Iglesia Evangélica Cristo Viene in Hillsboro was pastored by a Guatemalan married to a Venezuelan. The congregation was mostly Mexican, followed in number by Guatemalans and Salvadorans. Pastor Rodríguez described this mixture of backgrounds as a source of "gozo, riqueza, aprenden" (joy, richness, they learn), and said that they mingle with one another and do not look down on groups of different nationalities. He acknowledged that his Guatemalan background may affect people's decisions to attend this church.

About 60 percent of those who attend Iglesia Evangélica Cristo Viene were first-generation immigrants, and the remainder second-generation. Worship services and social activities were in Spanish, as were adult Christian education classes. The youth and children had bilingual programming, using a bilingual curriculum published by the Assemblies of God. This decision to use both languages was based on the linguistic needs of those in attendance. The author heard many bilingual conversations during her visit. The youth of this church stayed actively involved, not leaving for an English-speaking church or quitting altogether. During the site visit, the youth presented a skit as part of the worship service.

The pastor estimated that about 50 percent had completed only elementary school, another 15 percent finished high school and 10 percent college. They worked in a wide range of jobs, from nurses and small business owners to hotel maids and construction workers. The six deacons in this church were from Mexico and Guatemala and were chosen because of their "entrega" (dedication), not because of higher educational attainment or bilingualism. There were fifteen ministry coordinators in this congregation of 180–200 (including children), and they were from Venezuela, Mexico, and Guatemala.

Iglesia del Pueblo in Cornelius was pastored by a Mexican, and most of the congregation was of Mexican origin, although there were also Costa Ricans and Salvadorans, as well as several U.S.-born Anglos. Pastor Medina said that she didn't think her status as a long-time U.S. resident born in Mexico made "any difference, I think it's just the people that attend that attract other people." She said she hadn't seen any effect on the congregation due to the diverse national backgrounds.

Only four couples attending Iglesia del Pueblo, as well as the pastor herself, were first-generation immigrants. This high percentage of U.S.-born Latinos had influenced the church's vision of itself as a bilingual church, as "our kids that are growing up now, they would rather have English." Worship songs were in English and Spanish, and the sermon was bilingual. Pastor Medina's husband identified the need to transition to a bilingual church many years ago, and the board eventually saw the need and their ability to use both English and Spanish in the services. During the site visit, Pastor Medina was out of town, and a woman from California had been invited to preach. She asked if everyone in the audience understood Spanish, and since everyone indicated they did, she decided to dispense with interpretation and use only Spanish. The author observed that much of the music and instructions from leaders were in both languages, sometimes in the same sentence: "En la Iglesia del Pueblo edificamos gente and we build families." (At Iglesia del Pueblo we build up people and we build families.) There were English NIV Bibles in the pew racks, although the oral scripture reading was from the King James Version. According to Pastor Medina, some of the classes were all in Spanish and others in English. At informal activities, the language used varied, but tended mostly to Spanish. Church outreach activities in local parks have used literature in both languages.

The youth of this church were actively involved in various activities. While the middle schoolers attended services and listened, the high schoolers helped by doing yard work, playing instruments or singing on the worship team, and managing the sound booth. Many also participated in the denomination's Bible school extension called Los Angeles Bible Institute (LABI).

The pastor estimated that about one-fifth of the congregation had completed elementary school only, another fifth had gone on to college, and the remainder finished high school. There was a wide range of employment types, from engineers to janitors and assembly workers. The adults involved in leadership at this church tended to be those either enrolled in the Bible Institute or those with more formal education, but Pastor Medina did not identify a trend as far as their nationality or generation of immigration.

Iglesia de Jesucristo in Forest Grove was pastored by a Mexican-American born in California. The congregation was mostly Mexican, followed in number by Guatemalans. Pastor Ramírez said that having persons from different nations did not affect the life of the church: "We don't look at as ourselves as Guatemalan or Mexicans, we look at ourselves as the body of Christ." According to the pastor, 75 percent of his congregation was first-generation immigrants, though based on the author's observations during the site visit, most of them had been in the U.S. for many years. Pastor Ramírez stated that his being a second-generation immigrant made no difference "whatsoever" in his ability to pastor the congregation, nor does the diversity of nationalities and generations of immigration. "No. It's the Scriptures, the Word of God. We are one body, we are one mind, the mind of Christ and all decisions that are made are made based on the word of God, so we're all in one accord."

Most of the adult members had completed elementary school, with about 10 percent continuing on to high school and college. Most worked in factories and construction. Of the five board members, four were bilingual second-generation immigrants.

The youth of this church stayed involved in the life of the congregation, and they used mostly English at social events, though the adults preferred to use Spanish. During the mid-week service observed by the author, the "young people" were addressed twice from the pulpit, both times in English.[9] Worship services were bilingual. Sunday School for adults was in Spanish and in English for the children. According to Pastor Ramírez, this was a conscious decision on the part of the leadership, "Because it would be better for the children, we want them to understand, most of the children are growing up and going to the grade school, and learning English, and we want them to learn the English language, so we start them off early." The author observed fluent code-switching between English and Spanish during the service she visited, and the young man preaching (not the pastor) used many false cognates from English as he labored to preach in Spanish. After some time, he switched to English, gained fluidity, and used commonly recognized phrases of Scripture with ease. The sign outside the church is also in English.

The most diverse church in this study in terms of nationality was City Bible in Tigard. The pastor was an Anglo raised in Nicaragua by missionary parents, and was married to a woman from Central America. Most of the congregation was from Mexico, but there were Salvadorans, Guatemalans, Hondurans, Nicaraguans, Costa Ricans, Puerto Ricans, Cubans, Venezuelans, Peruvians, Argentines, Ecuadorians, and a Brazilian—fourteen nations in all. Pastor Trolese stated that they were very happy with this diversity of nationalities. He commented that where "there is diversity there are differences, and there are some differences that tend to make people group, and some people stand out more than others." He went on to comment that he has seen the greatest division between persons from the Caribbean and those from other Spanish-speaking nations, noting that because Puerto Ricans hold U.S. citizenship, they are not aware of some of the difficulties other Latino immigrants face. He also observed that soccer rivalries between nations can carry over into a general disrespect for that country, and that Mexico in particular seems to bear the brunt of scorn. However, he emphasized that overall, the variety of nationalities had been "a plus," and described a recent birthday party, a baby shower, and home groups in which persons

---

9. English was used frequently during the service observed by the author. Thinking that her presence might be influencing this, when the pastor welcomed her and asked her to introduce herself, she used Spanish so that they would be aware that she was comfortable in this language. Nevertheless, English continued to be interspersed throughout the service.

from many countries socialized and shared. He believed that his transnational background and marriage recommended pan-nationalism to the congregation.

Pastor Trolese noted that "the majority of our congregation does not necessarily represent the majority of Hispanics in our area. . . . I think part of it is that it is part of an English-speaking church and so it just, it appeals to those who are a little more established, who already have kids in school, who want both languages." The children in this church were mostly second- and a few third-generation immigrants. The children's programs were all in English. The leadership discussed this decision, as it had initially been in Spanish, and some of the teachers were monolingual Spanish speakers. However, "those are the ones who have come and said we should be doing most of this in English, that is what the kids are all talking amongst themselves," and the church had made the transition, using the same curriculum as the English-speaking body.

During the site visit, the author noted that the demographics included many young couples, many children, some of whom formed part of the worship team, and several elderly women. According to Pastor Trolese, there were few high-school aged students: "what some of the current high schoolers do is they are at the Spanish service but during the week they are at the English youth service. We don't have a separate Spanish youth service and we intentionally don't." While worship services and most informal activities were in Spanish, City Bible did not assume a stance of cultural preservation:

> But the church overall . . . sometimes I think we are fighting ourselves in a sense, in a good sense, in that we are always encouraging anyone who wants to, and encouraging parents to think of their kids as integrating more and more fully into life here. Yeah, we have our culture and our things, but we intentionally did not start a Spanish church, we really tried to [say], this is [just] one of the City Bible church services because we want it to be for second- and third-generation kids. We want them, that's why we don't have a separate youth ministry. We realize those kids, and their parents are realizing it . . . that these kids are as comfortable in English, many of them more, the entertainment they like, all these things and so we haven't wanted to create a separate youth ministry. So, we encourage that . . . and we see that a lot of these kids won't be, probably once they're twenty, won't be at a Spanish

service. Whether or not they'll marry someone else of a Latino background, we don't know. But they may be just integrated into church life, which for us is fine.

Over 90 percent of the adults attending City Bible's Spanish services were first-generation immigrants, but most had been in the U.S. for a long time, according to Pastor Trolese, who asserted that many had assimilated to life in the U.S. There were very few third-generation immigrants in this congregation. The pastor observed, "We have one right now from Texas, second- or third-generation Hispanic and to all of us it's odd. We don't have very many and we do realize that is a different culture. With the few that we've had we have realized that that is a whole different culture. Maybe that's part of why we don't have them, because I'm . . . even though I speak English and my parents are from the U.S., I can relate much better to a Latino than to a second- or third-generation, I just know I do in general."

The pastor estimated that 50–60 percent of the congregation had completed high school and that perhaps 5 percent had completed college and a few people graduate programs. The congregation had a wide variety of occupations, from business owners and store managers to construction and food-service workers. There was "a fair amount of variety" of backgrounds among those on the leadership team. It had been composed by Mexicans, Salvadorans, and Puerto Ricans.

Salvados para Servir, now meeting in West Portland, was also very diverse in terms of national origin, though 90 percent were first-generation immigrants. The majority was from Mexico, but Pastor Mateo indicated that people attend from all the nations of Central America, as well as Ecuador, Peru, and Puerto Rico. He was Guatemalan, and the senior pastor and his wife were Salvadoran. He indicated that this diversity had not negatively affected the church: "No hemos visto una diferencia. Creo que entre todos hay hermandad." (We haven't seen any difference. I think that there is brotherhood between everyone.) The family groups that met during the week in homes were made up of persons of various nationalities and educational backgrounds. The pastor stated that "atienden a cualquier persona que tienen necesidad de Dios" (they tend to any person that has need of God), with the group leader interpreting into English if a non-Spanish speaker attended the group meeting. He said that people from Puerto Rico, Mexico, and Central America freely mixed with one another and that "gracias a Dios" (thank God) he had not seen one group looking down on another. He indicated that people might come to hear a Salvadoran preach out of curiosity, but that Pastor Franco had lived in the U.S. for over twenty years and had lost many Salvadoran linguistic characteristics. He himself did not see any difficulty in his ministry due to his Guatemalan nationality, noting that he worked mostly with Mexicans.

Pastor Mateo calculated that around 70 percent of the congregants had completed only elementary school, another 20 percent high school and that only about 3 percent had attended college. The congregation had varied jobs, from nurses to electricians to other construction workers and managers. He indicated that the "city leaders" (those responsible for supervising cell groups in the various cities where they meet) were from many different countries and have varying levels of formal education. They had these roles because "son personas que Dios ha usado dentro de la iglesia" (they are people that God has used within the church).

The youth of Salvados para Servir remained involved in this congregation, for the most part, although Pastor Mateo acknowledged that a few had left to attend English-speaking churches, and a few others had quit attending any church. The youth might speak in English at informal activities, but the church services and Sunday School classes were in Spanish. For the children, if the teacher knew some English, he or she might use it, but the pastor calculated that 80 percent of children's classes were still in Spanish. During the site visit, the author observed that most of the congregation was under forty years of age or so, and that there were many children present in the worship service as well.

This church had a very high percentage of first-generation immigrants. Pastor Mateo offered an explanation:

> Sí, normalmente las personas que están empezando a echar raíces en este país tienden a poner, quizás, algo espiritual . . . una rutina. Pero las personas que piensan de sus países tienden a buscar más de Dios, tienden a asistir más a las iglesias. Quizás sienten más solas en sus casas, entonces buscan la iglesia como para encontrar compañerismo y más que todo lo espiritual de Dios."

> [Yes, normally the people that are starting to put down roots in this country tend to put, perhaps, something spiritual . . . a routine. But the people who think about their countries tend to seek more of God, they tend to attend the churches more. Maybe they feel more alone in their houses, so they look to the church as a

means to find companionship and more than anything else, the
spiritual aspect of God.]

Casa del Padre reported similar diversity in both its Beaverton and
Portland locations. The pastoral couple was born in Guatemala. The majority in both congregations was from Mexico, but there were many others from Guatemala, and a few from Honduras, El Salvador, Argentina,
Colombia, and Puerto Rico. Including the Anglos who attended the
Beaverton site, there were eight different nationalities. Regarding this
variety of backgrounds, Pastor and Mrs. Alvarizares commented,
"Spiritually it enriches it, but in practicality . . . at times the differences
in culture. . . . expressions and language, cause somewhat of a separation
in groups." They indicated "a conscious planning to make sure that everybody's involved with everybody" at potlucks and other social events,
and that they taught "the kingdom mentality. You know, in here you are
not Guatemalan, right here you are Christian. . . . but you know it takes
a while for people to catch on to that." They said that sometimes persons
from one country or region mutually disregarded one another in both
congregations, and recognized that "that's something that we as pastors
find a challenge because some people are very. . . . they love their country
so much, they are proud, *nacionalistas*, they show it at times, so I don't
know if it's so much looking down on them but feeling proud of where
they're from."

The pastors did not feel that their Guatemalan nationality affected
their ministry, since they had both immigrated at a very young age and
had experience in several different U.S. Latino churches with persons
from many backgrounds: "Having worked with so many different nationalities, you catch on to a little bit of everyone, you kind of tend to
adapt, so you talk to Mexicans, you talk to Guatemalans, you have to do
that in order so that it won't become an issue."

About 25 percent of the congregants had completed high school,
and about 5 percent had gone on to college. Most of the people in both
congregations worked in construction or service industries. Six families
made up the leadership board of Casa del Padre. Pastor Alvarizares did
not indicate that educational level or nationality were factors in board
makeup, rather,

> there's a process that everyone goes through in our church. We
> call it "the ladder of success. . . ." It consists of everybody going

to a retreat and encounter, going through school of leadership, and from there, their testimony pretty much defines how far they want to get. These are people that have been with us for a while in church, and have shown, first of all, a spiritual calling over their life for leadership, spiritual leadership, and then . . . we do not elect them, it's more of a . . . we as pastors bring them into the circle, and then everybody accepts them.

Seventy percent of both the Beaverton and Portland congregations were first-generation immigrants, as were the pastor and his wife, who arrived in California as children. Because most of the second generation was still relatively young, they had not been involved in decision-making for the church body yet. The church had long recognized the preference of the second generation for English, though according to the pastors, the youth of this church remained actively involved. Regarding the use of Spanish at church, the pastor's wife commented, "Kids from the United States, they're like . . . huh?"

Since the church's inception, it has been bilingual. According to Mrs. Alvarizares, "we were prophesied as being a multicultural church," and Pastor Alvarizares added, "so two things, it was divine calling over the church, and because we're bilingual, we saw both needs." The Beaverton location had a special ministry for children from three months to six and one half years of age called the Learning Center, and from that program on up, everything was done in English and Spanish. The pastor's wife added, "We accommodate everything for them to be bilingual—activities and everything, flyers and everything." The church did not use a bilingual Christian education curriculum, but translated English materials to Spanish. In Portland, the worship services were mostly in Spanish. When the author attended, an usher approached her near the beginning of the service to inquire if she needed interpretation to English. The pastor interspersed English words throughout his message. According to the pastors, in Beaverton services were bilingual with interpretation to English, either consecutively or simultaneously with headsets. Adults preferred to use Spanish at social events. The young people spoke English amongst themselves but switched to Spanish when speaking to the adults.

Multnomah County Churches

Ministerio Restauración, the Portland Mennonite congregation, was pastored by a Guatemalan. About half of the congregation was from Mexico, the other half from Guatemala, with a few Bolivians and Cubans. During the site visit, the author observed a child in a dress that appeared to be a traditional Guatemalan weave (but it could also have been from one of the many indigenous cultures of Mexico). Pastor Morán stated that the diverse nationalities in the church body had presented many cross-cultural moments in which one had to make an extra effort to understand the other's culture. He stated that times of fellowship such as shared meals after Sunday services or games in the park had both helped understand other cultures and brought personal enrichment. He joked that his church practiced Paul's statement in Romans 8:39 that "Neither height nor depth, nor anything else in all creation, will be able to separate us from the love of God that is in Christ Jesus our Lord" with a twist, saying "nosotros decimos 'ni los tacos ni tamales, nos va a separar del amor de que Jesucristo nos da.'" (we say "neither tacos nor tamales are going to separate us from the love that Jesus Christ gives us.") He added that he taught specifically about unity in the body of Christ and that the church's vision was multicultural, though he had sensed at times that persons from one nation had looked down on those from another country. During the sermon observed during the site visit, the pastor used several languages to emphasize one word: "In English, lazy. En mexicano, flojo." (In English, lazy. In Mexican, lazy), but he did not identify a term used in Guatemala.

The pastor estimated that about 85 percent of the adults had completed high school, with the remainder having completed some portion of elementary education but none going on to college. Most of the congregation worked in factories or service occupations. The leadership team was made up of both Guatemalans and Mexicans, and changed regularly. Current members gave input on those they thought should rotate in and assume leadership during the next period. There was an active youth ministry for the teens from Ministerio Restauración, separate from the English-speaking Mennonite congregation. Pastor Morán observed that the teens participated in the youth programs and did not leave the congregation for an English-speaking church or quit attending church. During the site visit, there were youth on the worship team, and teen Sunday School classes and activities were mentioned from the pulpit.

Approximately 60 percent of the congregation at Ministerio Restauración was first-generation immigrants, as was Pastor Morán. When asked how the mix of both first- and second-generation immigrants affected the church, the pastor indicated some cultural differences, especially the preference by the second generation for English. Sunday School classes for children and youth were bilingual, according to the language needs of the students and abilities of the teachers. The pastor's daughter, Ana, director of Sunday School activities, indicated that they tried to maintain Spanish because the parents felt it was important, but when they saw that children didn't understand something in Spanish, they used English. Some of the classes used Spanish curricular materials, while other teachers had English materials that they translated to Spanish as needed. The pastor reported that worship services and social activities were done entirely in Spanish.

Though no longer meeting, the author was able to make several observations about background, youth involvement, and language use during her site visit to Iglesia de Jesucristo, Ministerio de Vida Eterna. In the parking lot before the service, there were several younger Hispanics who spoke English as a first language. The author and the pastor's wife were the only two Anglos. Two of the three musicians were children. Eight of the nineteen people present near the beginning of the service were children or teens. References were made in the sermon to Mexico, Honduras, Nicaragua, and Guatemala, suggesting that some of the congregants were from these nations. At the altar call, the pastor's wife asked the author in English, "Do you want to pass up front?"—a linguistic transfer from the Spanish verb *pasar,* meaning to go or go by, which indicates that she frequently uses Spanish, perhaps more than English. Other than this, no English was used in the service.

Iglesia Luz del Pueblo in East Portland had mostly Mexicans and a Mexican pastor married to an Anglo. This Southern Baptist congregation also had Guatemalans, Hondurans, Salvadorans, three additional Anglos, one Chilean and one Cuban. Pastor González stated that in informal activities people from all nationalities mingled and that he had not seen one group disregarding another in this congregation, though he had observed this in previous settings as a church planter. He claimed that the multiplicity of countries of origin "la hace más fuerte, nosotros no hemos tenido ninguna división en cuestión de cultura, porque ya son cristianos. Hemos tenido más división en cuestión de comidas, del habla, pero espiritualmente, hay gente muy fuerte." (It makes it stronger, we haven't had any division in matters of culture, because they are already Christians. We have had more division in matters of foods, of speech, but spiritually, there are very strong people.) He indicated that he taught specifically about the kingdom of God superseding national differences, and did not believe that his own nationality had any impact on people's decision to participate in this church body. During the site visit, the sermon was replete with Mexican idiomatic expressions, used to illustrate a point.

The pastor estimated very few of the adults in the congregation had attended school beyond the primary level in their home countries, but that about 50 percent of them had gone on to obtain a GED in the U.S. and four individuals had obtained college degrees. Many of the congregation worked in factories, but others were electricians, teachers, administrators and mechanics. The leaders of this church varied in nationality and background. According to Pastor González, their educational background or length of time in the church was not important in qualifying them for leadership: "Su fidelidad al Señor nada más. No importa si tienen estudios o no, él que es fiel, es fiel; es lo más importante." (Their faithfulness to the Lord is all. It doesn't matter if they have schooling or not, the one who is faithful is faithful; that is the most important thing.)

Iglesia Luz del Pueblo had its own youth group, separate from the English- and Russian-speaking congregations that met in the same building. Pastor González observed that many of the second generation preferred English and left for other, well-established churches:

> Es que los jóvenes, la segunda generación, muchos de ellos no entienden los inicios de la Iglesia. Y muchos . . . es por consecuencia de los papás, y muchos, porque se sienten más cómodos en el inglés, entonces se van al inglés, y yo pienso que ahorita no, pero en unos 20–30 años, se van a reducir las iglesias hispanas, porque yo lo he visto en los matrimonios ahorita, se van a la mejor comodidad con los anglos . . . no les gusta trabajar. Les gusta que ya, lo que hicieron ya es hecho.

> [It is because the youth, the second generation, many of them don't understand the beginnings of the Church. And many of them . . . as a consequence of their parents, and many, because

they feel more comfortable in English, so they leave for the English, and I think that, not now, but in some 20–30 years, the Hispanic churches are going to be reduced, because I have seen it now in the married couples, they leave for greater ease with the Anglos . . . they don't like to work. They like to have everything already done for them.]

He restated his belief that the second generation and beyond will leave for English-speaking churches, and added that another possibility might be the development of bilingual churches, citing Texas as an example of a place where many bilingual churches exist.

Though 75 percent of the congregation of Luz del Pueblo was first-generation immigrants, many had lived in the U.S. for over twenty years. When asked how having a blend of first- and second-generation congregants affected decision-making and the vision for ministry, Pastor González again responded,

Afecta mucho. Primeramente, afecta en lo espiritual porque los niños están más confortables en el idioma inglés. Y los papás, como no tienen comunicación del inglés al español, ahí vienen los problemas. Ahora, la otra que afecta es, no les gusta trabajar, son más confortables. Ya quieren agarrar un templo hecho con todos los ministerios. No les gusta . . . han perdido la visión de empezar desde abajo. Digo, casi el 90 por ciento, no todos. Y afecta económicamente, en el sentido de que muchos de los jóvenes, como hablan dos idiomas, tienen buenos trabajos. Y aportan a las iglesias americanas, en lugar de aportar a la iglesia que necesita, que es la hispana o la iglesia local donde están ellos. Afecta.

[It affects things a lot. First, it affects it spiritually because the children are more comfortable in the English language. And the parents, since they don't have communication from English to Spanish, there come the problems. And, the other thing it affects is, they don't like to work. They are more comfortable. They want to get a church building already made with all the ministries. They don't like . . . they have lost the vision of starting from the ground up. I mean, nearly 90 percent, not all of them. And it affects economically, in the sense that many of the young people, since they speak two languages, have good jobs. And they contribute to the American churches, instead of contributing to the church that needs it, the Hispanic church or the local church where they are. It does affect things.]

The youngest children had Sunday School in Spanish, as their parents spoke only Spanish, and they hadn't started to learn English in school yet. The older children had bilingual classes, and the teens studied in English. The need for the children to understand their teachers had driven the language choices. Sunday School materials were from Lifeway, in both Spanish and English. Worship services were entirely in Spanish, and both languages were heard at potlucks and other informal gatherings. During the site visit, at the end of the service, a young Latino made a marriage proposal in English to a young Latina on the platform.

Pastor Mario Macías of Reedwood Friends in Portland was from Mexico. Most of the congregation was from Cuba, with others from Mexico, El Salvador, and Guatemala. When asked how this diversity affected the life of the church body, he said that it had a positive impact: "Pero también aunque algunos lo ven negativo por las diferentes culturas, en mi experiencia como pastor, no lo veo negativo porque es el momento a través de la manifestación de Dios, integrarnos en un solo sentir." (But also even though some see it negatively due to the different cultures, in my experience as a pastor, I don't see it negatively because it is the moment, through God's manifestation, to integrate us into a single viewpoint.) He added that having persons from several countries might represent a challenge to some pastors, but that since he conceived of himself as a missionary, it was not a problem (implying that missionaries are prepared for cross-cultural ministry). He did not believe that his Mexican nationality influenced people's decision to attend this church, and indicated a lifelong interest in and ministry to Cubans.

All of those attending Spanish services at Reedwood Friends were first-generation immigrants, and everything was done in Spanish, with the exception of children's activities. For these, the Latino children attended the programs of the English-speaking congregation. There were no speakers of indigenous dialects attending at the time of the pastoral interview. The majority of the congregation had at least a high school education. Many worked in factories. This group was relatively new at the time of the interview and did not yet have a leadership team or board.

Manantiales de Vida Eterna in Gresham had a Salvadoran pastor and pastoral family. Most of the congregation was from Mexico, but there were also Guatemalans and one Chilean. Pastor Nelson Reyes said that there were many cultural differences in his congregation, including food, customs, and beliefs, specifying the latter as "the way they give themselves to the Lord." Though he said that all the nationalities mingled at church fellowship events, he said that he "always" observed that Mexican youth "looked very differently" at youth from other countries, postulating that this is due to Mexico's proud and influential national heritage. When asked if he thought his Salvadoran nationality impacted the composition of the congregation, he responded,

> No, porque en Cristo ya no hay fronteras y [por] el aprecio y el amor que Dios ha puesto en mi corazón, no veo la diferencia entre una nación a otra. He tratado de expresarle en veces a la gente, que soy mexicano aunque soy salvadoreño. Quizás es el amor de Cristo en uno.

> [No, because in Christ there are no longer borders and [due to] the appreciation and love that God has put in my heart, I don't see the difference between one nation and another. I have tried to express this at times to the people, that I am Mexican even though I am Salvadoran. Perhaps it is the love of Christ in oneself.]

This attitude of acceptance of all by the pastor was voluntarily confirmed by the Chilean congregant during the site visit.

The pastor estimated that 60 percent were first-generation immigrants and that about half of the adults had completed only elementary school, while the other half were high school graduates. They were employed in plant nurseries, restaurants, factories, and as nannies or maids. The seven people who made up the board of Manantiales de Vida Eterna were mostly Mexicans, as was the congregation. They varied in their educational backgrounds. The teens at this church continued to participate in the body, and did not share a youth group with either the Anglo or Philippine congregations who also were using the building.

Pastor Reyes estimated that 80 percent of those in attendance were first-generation immigrants. When asked about how this affected the congregation, he indicated that sometimes he perceived a desire on the part of the Hispanic youth to have more contact with the Anglos and to adopt their way of life.

Spanish was used for worship services and informal events. The children's Sunday School was bilingual, for they used *Senda de vida* (Path of Life) curriculum that was bilingual. The teachers used Spanish, but the children could read the lesson in English.

Pastor Ortiz of Roca de Salvación Assembly of God in North Portland was from Mexico, as were the majority of those who attend.

There were also Salvadorans and Guatemalans. Pastor Ortiz observed that the previous pastor had been Salvadoran, and that when he first came, he often heard comments like, "Well, he is from Mexico." Since that time, new people had started to attend the church.

> [C]on nuevos hermanos unidos en la fe, lo que nos enfocamos es en el amor de Cristo. En el hecho de que nuestra diferencia de cultura en lugar de separarnos nos une más, nos da más fortaleza para ser una iglesia donde no hay diferencias; sea raza o nacionalidad. Entonces nos hace más fuertes.

> [With new brothers and sisters united in the faith, what we focus on is the love of Christ. On the fact that our cultural difference instead of separating us unites us more, it gives us more strength to be a church where there are no differences; be they race or nationality. So it makes us stronger.]

He indicated that his greatest desire was to build a church in which the love of God was a reality, preaching and teaching "que Cristo sigue teniendo sus brazos abiertos—no importa si somos guatemaltecos, salvadoreños o mexicanos." (that Christ continues to have his arms open—it doesn't matter if we are Guatemalans, Salvadorans, or Mexicans.)

The adult Sunday School teacher during the site visit was a Salvadoran who freely switched between English and Spanish as she taught. She apologized for "hablando como salvadoreña" (speaking like a Salvadoran), making reference to her use of *vos* instead of *tú* (both meaning the informal "you"). In her lesson, she mentioned that there were different cultures represented, including Mexicans and Salvadorans, and that these created cultural differences, but asserted that for Christians there are no cultural barriers as Christ overcame them.

Pastor Ortiz recognized that his nationality might affect whether or not people choose to congregate there. He told of two different Guatemalan families who had visited recently. The first attended a service and immediately observed that the pastor was Mexican. They did not return or give the church and pastor a chance to welcome them into fellowship. The second family attended a potluck, where they were warmly welcomed and introduced to others, and the pastor's wife served them *flan*. They felt very comfortable and continued attending the church.

Pastor Ortiz also indicated that disdain or prejudice was "always" going to exist from one nationality towards another, except among children, who seemed to accept one another and get along. He believed that it was important to provide a friendly atmosphere for cross-cultural dialogue and described situations where people interacted and got to know one another, making comments such as "¿Qué comida comen? Oh . . . a ver cuando nos invitan a probar las pupusas." (What food do you eat? Oh . . . let's see when you invite us to try *pupusas*.[10]) The church purposefully planned this type of activities for interaction, and Pastor Ortiz says, "Something beautiful happens" when people were given the opportunity to get to know one another.

Pastor Ortiz stated that the number of youth was growing, and that several of them had previously attended another church. He indicated that he felt the youth who did leave the church, in general terms, not speaking of his congregation specifically, did so because they were expected to behave as adults and follow many rules, instead of being accepted as adolescents with different questions, needs, and behaviors than adults. Half of the youth and about eight adults in this congregation were born in the U.S. There were also a few babies who were third-generation immigrants. The pastor most noted the impact of this multigenerational congregation in terms of language use. In recognition of the children who learned English in school and felt more comfortable using this language, there were two Sunday School classes taught in English, and the youth had bilingual programs. However, "Algo que también hacemos énfasis es que no olviden el español. Yo a cada rato les digo a los padres que en Europa la gente por lo menos habla tres idiomas, así que no me digan que no se puede." (Something that we also emphasize is that they not forget Spanish. I am always telling the parents that in Europe people speak at least three languages, so don't tell me that it can't be done.) The worship services were in Spanish, with an occasional song in English. Adult classes were in Spanish, and "la mayoría no tienen problema en que todo sea en español aunque varios de ellos manejan el inglés." (most don't have any problem with having everything in Spanish even though several of them use English.) Informal activities had a mix of both languages, and sometimes English was used even with the adults because several were born in the U.S. During the site visit, a sermon was broadcast over the sound system in English with consecutive interpretation into Spanish prior to the beginning of adult Sunday School. The author heard several conversations between family members in the pews in

10. A typical Salvadoran dish.

English, and the pastor used one English sentence in his message, which otherwise was replete with Mexican sayings.

Approximately 50 percent of the adults in this congregation had completed elementary school, some 20 percent high school, and less than 5 percent held a college degree. Most of the adults worked in manufacturing. When the pastoral interview was held, Roca de Salvación was considered a "mission" church of the Assemblies of God, and as such, was not self-governing with a church board. Nevertheless, Pastor Ortiz worked with a group of "counselors" who got together to plan activities. He indicated that maturity was the main characteristic rather than seeking persons of a specific nationality, gender, or educational background: "más que nada son las personas maduras espiritualmente y también que se puede decir aparte del espiritual se necesita madurez como persona. Más que nada son personas maduras." (more than anything they are spiritually mature people and also one could say that aside from the spiritual aspect, one needs to be mature as a person. More than anything they are mature persons.)

The final Multnomah County churches in this study were the two Foursquare churches pastored by Alfonso Rodríguez, who was from Mexico. Most of the congregation was also from Mexico, with a few Guatemalans. In the Rosa de Sarón congregation, about 70 percent were indigenous people of Mayan descent from the Yucatán peninsula. During the site visit, the author observed a woman and little girl wearing embroidered indigenous-style dresses, though she was unable to identify which culture they represented. Pastor Rodríguez indicated that there had been some difficulties between Guatemalans and Mexicans in the past, but that most of the Guatemalans had left for a more conservative church, and those who remained got along well with the Mexicans. He did not believe that his own nationality impacted the congregations.

A majority of the members of these congregations had completed high school, but none had attended college. Many worked in service industries such as restaurants and hotels. A few were small business owners while others worked in construction or factories. The seven board members of this church were all from Mexico and had taken classes at the Bible Institute led by Felix Rosales. Pastor Rodríguez estimated that only 20–25 percent of the congregation in the SE Portland church were first-generation immigrants, and said the youth stay actively involved in the Hispanic congregation. The large majority of the congregation speaks

English. At Rosa de Sarón in NE Portland, most spoke a Mayan dialect and were more recent immigrants. At potlucks and social events, one heard at least three languages. The church had made a conscious decision for youth classes to be taught in English, while all other Christian education programs were in Spanish, as were worship services. Interpretation was provided for special services. Prior to the beginning of the service at the site visit of Rosa de Sarón, a slide projected up front in both English and Spanish indicated that this was a Foursquare church.

DISCUSSION AND ANALYSIS

The following sections examine the data gathered in Oregon in light of other information. The first sub-section includes observations from studies on immigrant churches in general, and U.S. Latino churches in particular, regarding the many variations of race, ethnicity, national origin, and social class represented in the churches. These elements, as observed in the churches in this study, are summed up, and the sub-section concludes with a summary of the pastors' statements regarding their approach in dealing with these factors. The second sub-section singles out one debate in the literature on immigrant churches—their impact on social mobility—and examines the data in this study regarding it. The third sub-section focuses on multiple generations of immigrants and their language use within the church, summarizing both previous studies' findings and information from the present study.

Heterogeneity

The relationship of religion and immigrant populations has been the subject of debate by scholars. Researchers have long observed that immigrant groups are more heterogeneous than they may appear: "Immigrant communities. . . . were far from the homogenous bodies so often envisioned by outsiders, but rather were replete with various 'subethnic' divisions based upon distinctions of class, religion, ideology, and local culture."[11]

Stout claimed that early immigrant churches in New England served to divide, not unite, immigrants of various ethnic backgrounds: "Among every major immigrant group the central institution was the

---

11. Pozzetta, *The Immigrant Religious Experience*, vol. 19, *American Immigration and Ethnicity* (Hamden, Conn: Garland Publishing, 1991), vii.

church, which served the function of organizing allegiance around the ethnic group. Characteristic of all such immigrant churches was the functioning of the church as a community, the centrality of the pastor in affirming group solidarity, and the replacement of the evangelical vision by ethnic insularity. The failure to transcend ethnic boundaries was . . . apparent between diverse nationalities. . . . "[12]

Regarding Latino churches specifically, Orozco Hawkins noted, "within the churches our Hispanics are divided along class, social and economic lines."[13] Aponte challenges researchers to do better work on this aspect: "At present however, most studies of Hispanic religion in the United States use interpretive models that do not allow us to see the complexity which actually exists within the Latino/a community. This needs to be rectified so that the full spectrum of Hispanic faith can be considered. . . ."[14]

On the other hand, Smith observed that European "[e]migrants to the United States regrouped on this side of the Atlantic into larger aggregations that both preserved and revised inherited patterns of language, religion, and regional culture."[15] Pozzetta claimed, "Immigrants did not succumb passively to pressures for conformity, but rather followed patterns of resistance and accommodation to the new land by which they turned themselves into something new—ethnic Americans."[16]

Regarding Latino immigrants specifically, García-Treto asserted that a pan-Latino identity is emerging in the U.S.: "a transnational Hispanic/Latino consciousness of being a people is emerging and setting a sociocultural agenda in the United States."[17] González agreed, stating, "[O]ne could say that a new form of being Hispanic—a form that includes traits from all Latino subgroups—is slowly emerging in the United States."[18] These statements indicate that immigrants of various backgrounds band together after immigration and create something new—a new community, a new sense of identity and purpose.

12. "Ethnicity: The Vital Center of Religion in America," 380.

13. "Hispanic/Latina Women," 118.

14. "Hispanic/Latino Protestantism," 381.

15. "Religion and Ethnicity," 1158.

16. *The Immigrant Religious Experience*, vi.

17. "Reading the Hyphens: An Emerging Biblical Hermeneutics for Latino/Hispanic US Protestants," 164.

18. "Hispanic Worship," 9.

The following paragraphs evaluate the heterogeneity of congregations in this study in terms of national origin of the congregations in relation to that of the pastor; social class as indicated by educational attainment and type of employment; and racial and ethnic background. Generational differences are discussed in a separate section that also deals with language preferences, assimilation, and cultural preservation.

As described in chapter 2, most of the Protestant Hispanic churches in this study reflect the state's Latino population in terms of country of origin. Most are Mexican, followed by Guatemalans. The churches with high percentages of Guatemalans are in the counties with the largest Guatemalan populations. Several rural churches have only Mexicans, and the percentage of Mexicans living in Oregon is higher in the counties outside the Portland metropolitan area. Reedwood Friends was unusual in that it had a majority of Cubans attending. Sixteen of the congregations had persons from at least three nations (and most several more). All of the pastors that had more than one nationality in their congregation reported that this diversity had been a positive element, though sometimes it had represented momentary or practical challenges.

The pastors in this study were representative of the general Oregon Hispanic population in terms of country of origin, for the most part. Seven of the pastors in this study were born in Mexico, and two others' parents were born in Mexico. (In one case only the mother was Mexican-born, while the father was Texan, tracing his Mexican heritage back to when Texas was part of Mexico.) The number of Mexican pastors in Oregon is proportionate, given that the largest group of Latinos in Oregon is Mexican. There were three Anglo pastors, two of whom were married to Latinas; four Guatemalans, four Salvadorans, and one each from Costa Rica, Perú, and Argentina.

It is a commonly-held belief that a pastor will attract congregants that share his or her nationality, or at the very least, get along better with those from the same country.[19] The impact of the nationality of the pastor on the composition of the congregation is difficult to determine. Twelve of the pastors interviewed denied that their country of origin made any difference to the congregation, and two more said that it had

19. The Co-Executive Presbyter of the Cascades attributed a failed attempt of this denomination to establish a Spanish-speaking congregation partly to the fact that the pastor was not Mexican, though the majority of the initial small group was. Aleida Jernigan, in e-mail message to author, Sept. 28, 2011.

in the past, but no longer did. The remaining pastors indicated that their nationality made some difference to those who attended; five of these indicated it was a plus, and three thought it was a detracting factor.

In addition to the mixed responses by the pastors, the national composition of the churches themselves paints a blurry picture. Most of the churches that had only Mexicans had pastors from other countries. The pastor of Newport Nueva Esperanza was Peruvian, Grants Pass Mennonite Brethren had a U.S.-born Anglo pastor, and Medford Rogue Valley Fellowship had a Salvadoran pastor married to a Mexican.

Elim, which is mostly Guatemalan, and Ministerio Restauración Mennonite (evenly divided between Guatemalans and Mexicans) had Guatemalan pastors. They were also in areas where many Guatemalans have settled. However, both Iglesia Evangélica Cristo Viene and Salvados para Servir had a Guatemalan pastor or associate pastor and were in Washington County, where there are many Guatemalans, but had a majority of Mexicans in attendance.

Reedwood Friends had mostly Cubans and a Mexican pastor. Although the Cubans in this congregation arrived after the 2000 census, over 60 percent of Oregon's small Cuban population were living in Multnomah County (where Reedwood Friends is located) in 2000.[20] The pastor of Reedwood Friends described a long-time call to minister to Cubans, and he had made multiple mission trips to the island before moving to Portland. Undoubtedly his special desire to minister to Cubans was a deciding factor in the composition of the congregation.

The Woodburn church had a majority of Mexicans but a significant percentage of Costa Ricans. In the 2000 census, there were only ten persons from Costa Rica living in Marion County where the church is located.[21] This aligns with the pastor's indication that most of the congregants were commuting from other communities. It appears that in this case, the desire to have a leader from the same nation drew these families to this church.

The U.S.-born Anglos, Hondurans, and South American pastors were all ministering to congregations of mostly Mexicans. Thus, the evi-

20. U.S. Census Bureau, American Fact-Finder, "Region and Country or Area of Birth of the Foreign-Born Population: 2000." SF 3, Oregon All Counties.

21. U.S. Census Bureau, American Fact-Finder, "Place of Birth for the Foreign-Born Population." Census 2000 SF4, Oregon.

dence indicates that the pastor's nationality is not the only determining factor for those choosing a church body.

In addition to national origin, social class is another factor that could potentially cause division within churches. The tendency for people of similar socioeconomic status to cluster together for worship is not unique to Latino churches; this is also found among various denominations in Anglo and Black American churches.[22] Some pastors showed awareness of these distinctions. The pastor of City Bible recognized that his congregation had unintentionally attracted a more assimilated and more established congregation that was not representative of most of Oregon's Latino population. During the announcements at the site visit to Iglesia de Jesucristo, Ministerio de Vida Eterna, the pastor stated that the vision for an upcoming evangelistic event was "to go beyond field-workers to reach professionals." As mentioned in chapter 2, Manantiales de Vida Eterna seemed to be a church of persons on the lowest rungs of the class ladder, described by the pastor as those who had tried attending other churches but had not found acceptance in them.

The ranges of educational achievement among the congregants of the Hispanic Protestant churches in this study are mixed, but tend toward completing elementary school and high school. Though the cut-off points are different, this is generally in line with other observations about the educational level of Latino immigrants to Oregon.[23] Most churches have few who have attended college—Elim had the highest ratio at 33 percent. City Bible and Vida Church each had representatives who had attended graduate school. These three churches are all in Washington County, where higher education is readily accessible. The churches in Grants Pass, Hermiston, Cornelius, and Reedwood Friends, Ministerios Restauración, and the two Foursquare congregations in Portland all indicated that 70 percent or more of their con-

---

22. A study by Warren summarized several research projects on this topic spanning much of the twentieth century. It identified Presbyterians, Episcopalians and Congregationalists as having above-average socioeconomic status, Methodists and Lutherans in the middle, and Baptists on the lower end. "Socioeconomic Achievement and Religion," 130, 137–39. Vasquez, "Pentecostalism," 617–36, makes the case that Pentecostals both in Latin America and Latino Pentecostals in the U.S. draw from the lower socioeconomic echelons, and this is the author's observation regarding non-Latino Pentecostals in the U.S. as well.

23. Martinez Jr. and Eddy state that most have a ninth grade education or less in "Latino Youth," 841–51.

gregation had completed high school, higher than that of the general Hispanic population in the state.

On the opposite end of the spectrum, Village Baptist had persons with the lowest levels of education. The pastor calculated that only 15 percent of the congregation had completed elementary school and that 5 percent had graduated from high school, with a few individuals attending college. The pastor of Esperanza y Vida en Jesucristo in Hood River estimated that 80 percent of his congregation had completed only a sixth-grade education, with Casa del Padre and Woodburn's Iglesia Pentecostés reporting 75 percent and Salvados para Servir, 70 percent completing only through sixth grade. The pastor of Iglesia de Jesucristo in Forest Grove also indicated that perhaps 60 percent of his congregation had only an elementary school education. The other churches had greater balance between those who had completed elementary school only and those who had finished high school, and most mentioned at least a few persons with college studies. In sum, approximately two-thirds of the churches in this study showed clustering of persons of similar levels of education, and most of the churchgoers had levels of education similar to those of the state's overall Latino population.

One often considers educational attainment a key factor in type of employment. This is clearly the case for Village Baptist and Woodburn Iglesia Pentecostés participants, as most of them were employed in agriculture, which is at the lowest level of the occupational scale due to its difficulty, low pay, health risks, and seasonal nature. Many of the congregants from Hood River also worked in the local fruit industry, though some were employed in hotels and restaurants. Other than these three congregations where lower levels of education strongly correlated with work in agriculture, the relationship between education and type of employment was much less clear. This is likely due to other factors such as their location, fluency in English, whether their education was before or after immigration, and legal status. For example, most of the congregation in Hermiston worked in agriculture, though the pastor estimated that 70 percent had finished high school. This entire area is geographically isolated and heavily dependent on agriculture, so location may be more important than education for employment.

The pastors of the majority of the churches in this study indicated that most of their congregation worked in trades a step up from seasonal agriculture: plant nurseries, food processing plants and other factories, restaurants and hotels, cleaning houses and construction. Most of these jobs pay minimum wage. These claims are in accord with a 2008 study that estimated the annual income of Mexican immigrants to Oregon at $15,918, with a majority of Mexican immigrants working in production, agriculture and service industries although there is an increasing number of small business owners.[24] Again, the types of employment for the majority of churchgoers in this study closely align to those of the state's Hispanic population.

Several pastors in each county, however, indicated a broad range of employment for their congregants. The churches in Madras, Monmouth, and Hermiston, along with Iglesia Evangélica Cristo Viene in Hillsboro, Iglesia del Pueblo in Cornelius, City Bible in Tigard, Salvados para Servir in Beaverton/West Portland, and the Foursquare churches had persons in the service and manufacturing roles mentioned above, as well as jobs like educational assistant, social service agency employee, teacher, small business owner, manager, engineer, nurse, electrician, administrator, and mechanic.

There were very few types of employment that require advanced degrees, such as professor or medical doctor. It is the author's impression that there are very few Latinos in Oregon working in these types of jobs, and that the churches reflect the Latino population. It is also possible that such highly-educated and necessarily bilingual persons do not attend Protestant churches, or choose to worship in English.

The two congregations that found employment mostly in agriculture are not Pentecostal—one is Mennonite and the other Conservative Baptist. Two of the three congregations with the highest ratio of college attendance were of Pentecostal background: Elim and Vida Church. It appears that the tendency of the lesser-educated Latin American population to be Pentecostal has not transferred to the U.S.

Nine of the churches had a mixture of types of employment, indicating that many lower-level professionals and small business owners choose to remain in their Spanish-speaking congregations. The majority of churches, however, were made up of people of similar job status. Thus, the Protestant Hispanics of Oregon do tend to worship with others of similar educational and employment backgrounds, for the most part, as do Anglo and African-American Protestants.

---

24. Aguilera, et al., "Work and Employment," 69–73.

Another important divisor for Latin Americans is racial background. There is strong discrimination against indigenous groups in Mexico and profound division between the multiple native peoples of Guatemala and those of mixed blood known as *ladinos*. Those from the southern-most countries of South America take pride in tracing their heritage to European immigrants of the nineteenth and twentieth centuries.

In the churches of Oregon, many indigenous persons clustered together for worship. Village Baptist had a high percentage of native peoples from Oaxaca but also families from other areas of Mexico and several other nations. Rosa de Sarón had approximately 70 percent indigenous persons from the Yucatán Peninsula.[25] Guatemala's population is mostly indigenous, and the pastor of Elim, which has a Guatemalan majority, indicated that there were speakers of many dialects in his congregation, though he did not specify which, and that Spanish was used as a *lingua franca*.

However, there were some churches in which there was only one family that spoke an indigenous dialect (Vida Church, Newport Nueva Esperanza). In the latter case, in Lincoln County, the Guatemalan family was part of a tiny minority in the general Hispanic population, as the 2000 census indicated only 18 persons born in Guatemala living in that county.[26] If the population has not dramatically changed in composition since the 2000 census, this family had few other Guatemalans nearby with whom they could associate, let alone join for worship. The pastor of Rogue Valley Fellowship indicated that approximately 5 percent of the adults in his congregation spoke an indigenous dialect. While there may have been persons of indigenous background in the remaining churches, either they did not use a dialect or the pastor did not indicate their presence. This includes Ministerios Restauración, the Portland Mennonite congregation that had approximately 50 percent Guatemalans in the congregation.

25. It is interesting to compare these two mostly-indigenous congregations in light of the prior discussion of educational attainment. The mainly Oaxacan church had the lowest level of schooling, with only 15 percent completing elementary school and 5 percent high school, while the pastor of the mostly Yucateco church indicated that the majority of them had finished high school

26. U.S. Census Bureau, American Fact-Finder, "Place of Birth for the Foreign-Born Population by Year of Entry by Citizenship Status." Census 2000 SF4, Oregon.

Racially, Argentina is a nation of *criollos*, persons born in the Americas of European ancestry. Pastor Giménez alluded to his status when commenting that some Oregon Hispanics might choose not to attend Vida Church because he is a "whiter" Latino. Argentines also have a very distinctive accent, but Pastor Giménez has lost nearly all of it due to his many years in the U.S. working with non-Argentine Latinos.

Pastor Jiroo Kuroda of Nueva Esperanza was the other South American pastor among the churches studied. He is quite representative of the Peruvian population, which has a strong indigenous presence, many *mestizos*, as well as many of mixed Japanese heritage, like former president Alberto Fujimori. Nevertheless, the pastor's non-Spanish name and South American nationality have not put off the many Mexicans in his congregation. He acknowledged an initial period of cultural negotiation and adjustment but indicates he has been accepted in the community as he has become known and trusted.

In sum, based on the pastors' comments and congregational make-up in terms of nationality and race, Oregon Latino Protestant churches appear to be places where Latinos of many backgrounds overlook such distinctions, gathering not only for worship but to socialize. The majority of congregations extend their church family to include Anglos, both Spanish-speaking and monolingual English speakers. A few churches are mostly indigenous but not to the exclusion of other Latinos. Some indigenous immigrants attend churches that have a majority of *mestizos*. The nationality and ethnicity of the pastor seems to be a draw or detractor for some, but there is broad evidence of acceptance of pastors of different nationalities by their congregations. Most congregations were made up of persons of similar economic status based on employment and educational attainment. However, about one-third of the congregations had diverse types of employment, though very few reached up into the most prestigious or highest-paying professions. In broadest terms, the Protestant Hispanic churches of Oregon were inclusive rather than divided by race or ethnicity, nationality, or class.

Pastors recognize the potential for division based on nationality, as exemplified by Pastor Diego's comments that he works very hard to focus on cooperation and love in the body of Christ, to consider the congregation as one's culture and family, and not to allow country of origin differences. Christianity has within its teachings an emphasis on religious identity superseding nationality or ethnic background, and this may pave the way for lessening these distinctions, as observed by Pastor Ramírez: "We don't look at ourselves as Guatemalan or Mexicans, we look at ourselves as the body of Christ. . . . That's biblical." Pastor Alvarizares's remarks concur: "There's a conscious planning to make sure that everybody's involved with everybody. . . . By ministering to them the kingdom mentality. You know, in here you are not Guatemalan, right here you are Christian."

Several pastors in this study observed that their congregations are in the process of becoming something new in terms of identity. For example, Pastor Kuroda commented, "we ourselves are making a different culture." Pastor Diego of Elim said that the church specifically trains the congregation to see the church as their new culture and family. This coincides with the findings of Smith, Pozzetta, García-Treto, and González cited at the beginning of this section.

Social Mobility

Studies suggest that Pentecostal churches in Central America and the U.S. are associated with upward mobility[27]—but there is debate in the literature on immigrant churches as to whether they serve to enable immigrants' assimilation and upward mobility in their new society or hold them back from effective participation.[28]

The ability to participate in leadership within the church is a measure of some social mobility. Nueva Esperanza in Hermiston, Grants Pass New Hope Bible, Nueva Esperanza in Newport, Vida Church, and Monmouth Christian all had Latinos participating in leadership roles for the broader (English-speaking) church, and the pastors of Village Baptist and Reedwood Friends indicated that they had been invited to

---

27. Freston states that neo-Pentecostals (as opposed to classic Pentecostal churches like the Assemblies of God) are "middle-class and elite charismatic churches. . . . privileged city dwellers." "Contours," 238; Soliván, citing Costas regarding Latino Pentecostal churches in the U.S., comments: "The church reaches out to those who have few resources for responding to the daily challenges of life. It is the church that stands in the midst of life's storms and reaches out to those in need of refuge. It is the church of the Galileans, the Samaritans of our times, a church of the poor, as Costas argues. This is in contrast to the upwardly mobile, quickly growing middle-class composition of Anglo Pentecostalism, as in the case of the Assemblies of God." "Hispanic Pentecostal Worship," 47.

28. Hurh and Kim give a helpful summary of these views in "Religious Participation," 23.

send representatives in the future. Filling these positions could be considered a form of social mobility beyond the ethnic group.

Decision-making and leadership roles require skills and provide experiences that transfer well to greater responsibilities and higher positions outside the church, such as prioritizing, public speaking, planning, delegating, and participating in educational opportunities. Three pastors in this study mentioned leadership development or personal initiative to obtain further education or skills as the strong points of their congregations. The following section summarizes information about the leadership boards of the churches in this study and the requirements for laity to participate in them, albeit this represents mobility within the confines of the Latino population and specifically within the Protestant churches.

All the church boards were representative of the nationalities of their congregations, with the possible exception of Hood River CMA Esperanza y Vida en Jesucristo Church, where all the board members were from Mexico, and while this church had mostly Mexican members, it also had congregants from seven other nations. Four pastors indicated that their board members had slightly higher educational levels than the majority of the congregation. A majority of the board members were bilingual in six of the churches in the study. These were all churches that perceived themselves as an integral part of the larger church body, as described in chapter 3, except Iglesia de Jesucristo in Forest Grove. Five church boards were made up of persons who had participated in some type of biblical, theological, or ministerial training.

Seven pastors (representing eight congregations) indicated that the principal characteristic of their board members was spiritual maturity or dedication, and four of these stated that this was the only qualifying factor. Five of the congregations that identified spiritual maturity as a main component could be classified as Pentecostal congregations: Rogue Valley Fellowship, Salvados para Servir, Casa del Padre in both sites (though they also required leaders to have completed the "Ladder of Success" internal training program), and Roca de Salvación. Given the anti-intellectual bent of Pentecostalism described in chapter 3, this is not a surprising finding. Only Roca de Salvación (an AOG mission at the time of the pastoral interview) is considered a "classic Pentecostal" church; the other three are neo-Pentecostal groups. The ability for any believer attending these churches to move into leadership through spiritual growth and faithful service indicates that there is space for upward mobility, at least within the context of the church body. The other three congregations in which spiritual maturity was a key requirement for leadership had Baptist ties: Village Baptist, Iglesia Evangélica Cristo Viene in Hillsboro, and Luz del Pueblo Southern Baptist.

These findings indicate that individuals attending the Protestant Hispanic churches of Oregon have the opportunity to assume leadership roles regardless of national origin. While a higher-than-average formal education and bilingualism were characteristics of some boards, the pastors did not indicate them as requisites, but hinted that these elements gave people confidence to serve in those positions. Training within the church, however, was a requirement for leadership in several congregations, as was spiritual maturity in many congregations. Latino churches provide their members opportunity for further education and skill development through service that can lead to roles of increasing responsibility.

Second-generation Immigrants and Language Use

The impact of multiple generations in an immigrant church is complex. The most obvious challenge is language use, as children born in the U.S. are likely to attend English-speaking schools and may be much more competent in English than in Spanish. Closely related to language are issues of cultural identification and assimilation. The following section presents points of view expressed in previous studies, then synthesizes the information presented earlier in this chapter on second-generation immigrants, language use, conscious assimilation or cultural preservation efforts by the churches in this study, as well as ongoing religious participation of younger generations.

Many assume that language preference will trump other cultural considerations when choosing a church, or that language is the only barrier to worshiping in a majority (English-speaking) church. The Protestant Council of New York so asserted in 1960: "A major problem to which it seems Spanish speaking churches might profitably turn their attention is the problem of youth and the second generation. Data from this study . . . suggest that Spanish speaking churches may be able to reach young people less effectively than English-Spanish or English churches."[29]

---

29. Department of Church, 88.

Some immigrant churches begin using English in order to avoid losing the second-generation and their contributions. Regarding European immigrants in the early twentieth century, Mohl and Betten observed, "The churches themselves often took on American ways in order to retain the interest and eventual support of parish children growing up in an American environment. . . . Thus English was slowly introduced in Greek, Serbian, and Russian services."[30]

Chávez Sauceda has commented at length on the pervasiveness of the language issue. She wrote, "the cultural hegemony of the English language guarantees that every Latino congregation struggles with the question of how to include a younger generation that speaks little or no Spanish."[31] In a previous article focused on Latino Presbyterian churches, she observed, "the conflict around language is a product of the congregation's commitment to be fully inclusive, to enable each and every member of the family to participate in worship. As the dialogue about language continues, it has raised important questions about identity and mission for Hispanic congregations. In choosing to be both a church for the Spanish speaker and for the English-dominant Hispanics, Hispanic congregations have rejected a negative, limiting definition of themselves. Hispanic congregations see themselves as something more than a non-English-speaking Presbyterian church, more than being merely a means to an end, a way station for the culturally unassimilated."[32]

Some authors have described the immigrant church as a place of linguistic and cultural preservation. Mohl and Betten observed that some European-immigrant churches had language classes for the second generation and that "[t]he various church language programs served to lessen the communication gap between generations. . . . a small but growing minority from the Christian Orthodox communities . . . viewed the [native language] folk schools as delaying integration into society."[33] Chávez Sauceda concurred regarding Latino churches: "What Hispanic congregations want to pass on to their children is both their religious

---

30. "The Immigrant Church in Gary, Indiana," 281 in Pozzetta, ed. *The Immigrant Religious Experience*, vol. 19, *American Immigration and Ethnicity*. Many other chapters in this volume detail the linguistic decisions of Catholic, Protestant, and Orthodox immigrant congregations.

31. "Race, Religion and La Raza," 191.

32. "Becoming a Mestizo Church," 93.

33. "The Immigrant Church in Gary, Indiana," 279.

tradition and their cultural identity. Thus, worshiping in Spanish is as important for the children, for whom Spanish is a second language, as it is for the grandparents, for whom Spanish is their primary language."[34] This comment indicates how important language is in cultural identity. Indeed, church may be the only place where younger generations read a written text in Spanish.

In addition to matters of language and the possibility that second-generation immigrants may choose to worship with English speakers instead of in a Spanish-speaking congregation, some researchers have observed that second-generation immigrants are less religious, overall. According to Hernández, ". . . second generation Latinos, those who have experienced greater levels of acculturation, will be more likely to limit their religious commitment."[35]

Again, the debate in the literature on immigrant churches is whether they serve to enable immigrants' assimilation and upward mobility in their new society or hold them back from effective participation,[36] particularly through language proficiency and preference.

All pastors were asked what percentage of their congregation was born abroad and what percentage was second-generation immigrants. In some cases, their responses did not clarify if they were including all members of their congregation or only adults, making analysis difficult. Nevertheless, Iglesia del Pueblo in Cornelius had around 75 percent second-generation immigrants and Pastor Rodríguez reported a similar percentage for the Southeast Portland Foursquare congregation La Cosecha. Monmouth Christian and Grants Pass New Hope Bible had approximately 60 percent second-generation immigrants, while Hood River CMA Esperanza y Vida en Jesucristo had 50 percent, as did Village Baptist.

Census statistics from 2000 indicated that 51 percent of the Mexican or Mexican-heritage population in the state were U.S. born. This statistic varied somewhat for the counties where there are churches with high percentages of second-generation immigrants: Washington County (Iglesia del Pueblo and Village Baptist) had 43 percent, Hood River County had 41 percent, Multnomah County (SE Rim-La Cosecha Foursquare) had 48 percent, Josephine County (Grants Pass New Hope

---

34. "Becoming a Mestizo Church," 93.

35. Hernández, "Cathedral to Storefront," 224.

36. Hurh and Kim, "Religious Participation," 23.

Bible) 79 percent and Polk County (Monmouth Christian) had 52 percent U.S.-born persons among those claiming Mexican heritage.[37]

This data, though outdated, places the percentage of second-generation (or beyond) immigrants from Mexico in the Hood River and Village Baptist congregations on a par with the general state population, though higher than the percentage in their specific counties. The remaining congregations with a majority of second-generation immigrants have a percentage that is significantly higher than the counties where they meet, except for the Grants Pass church. The following paragraphs explore the pastor's generation of immigration and language practices of the church as possible factors for attracting or maintaining the participation of younger generations of Latinos.

The pastor in Monmouth is a second-generation immigrant on one side and *tejano* on the other. The Cornelius pastor has lived in the U.S. for most of her life. Both these pastors chose to use English for the pastoral interview. The Foursquare pastor immigrated as a young person. The Village Baptist pastor has lived in North America all of his adult life. The pastors in Hood River and Grants Pass are Anglos. It would appear that being born in the U.S. or having lived here for decades is a factor in attracting second-generation immigrants to the churches in this study, but there are several cases that indicate the contrary. The same Foursquare pastor also leads a congregation in another part of the Portland that has a very high percentage of first-generation immigrants; one individual ministers to two very different congregations in terms of cultural identity. Pastor Ramírez of Iglesia de Jesucristo in Forest Grove was born in California and preferred to speak English during the pastoral interview, and the worship services are bilingual, but he indicated that 75 percent of his congregation are first-generation immigrants.

As previously mentioned, language is an important issue for younger generations. The Hood River and Monmouth churches and Iglesia del Pueblo describe themselves as bilingual churches and have interpretation of worship services regularly. Village Baptist is part of a large church with multiple languages and ethnic groups. Grants Pass New Hope Bible has joint worship with Anglos and Hispanics in English and Spanish, although the sermon is entirely in English. In sum, most

---

37. U.S. Census Bureau, American Fact-Finder, "Fact Sheet for a Race, Ethnic, or Heritage Group: Mexican." Census 2000, Oregon.

churches with high percentages of second-generation immigrants from Mexico use both English and Spanish in their programming.

Most of the children and teens in the churches in this study were born in the U.S. The great majority of pastors said that the teenagers in their church stay actively involved with their congregation. The author observed many young people participating in congregations in various ways during the site visits. The Newport, Madras, Hermiston, Vida, Village Baptist, and City Bible youth could also participate with the English-speaking youth groups associated with their churches. The pastors of Woodburn's Iglesia Pentecostés, Salvados Para Servir, Luz del Pueblo, and New Hope Bible Church in Grants Pass indicated that some may leave and attend English-speaking churches,[38] and the pastors of Iglesia Pentecostés and Salvados para Servir acknowledged that a few leave the church altogether. It is important to observe that all formal activities at these latter two churches were in Spanish, while Luz del Pueblo and New Hope had English options.

Several pastors indicated that graduation from high school was a critical point in the attendance of the youth—many were forced to leave rural communities for higher education or employment opportunities, while others no longer were bound by their parents' expectations of church attendance.

Half of the congregations in this study provided programs for children or youth that were either in English or are bilingual English-Spanish. Eight other congregations indicated that everything was bilingual, including the worship services. Three churches (Woodburn's Iglesia Pentecostés, Elim, and Salvados para Servir) used only Spanish for all official church activities.

Several pastors mentioned communication difficulties in families between the generations, as observed by Mohl and Betten in their studies of European immigrant churches in Indiana.[39] Pastor González observed that ". . . los niños están más confortables en el idioma inglés. Y los papás, como no tienen comunicación del inglés al español, ahí vienen los problemas." (. . . the children are more comfortable in the English language. And the parents, since they don't have communication from English to Spanish, there come the problems.) Pastor Ortiz

---

38. Pastor Stutzman of New Hope indicated that when young people from his church leave to attend college, they seek a church in their new community.

39. "The Immigrant Church in Gary, Indiana," 279.

said, "... los padres dicen '¡ya les hablé y no me entienden!' Y los hijos se sienten incomprendidos, que los padres no los escuchan. Es falta de una comunicación efectiva." (... the parents say, "I already spoke to them and they don't understand me!" And the children don't feel understood, that the parents don't listen to them. It is a lack of effective communication.) Pastor Rivas remarked,

> Es un problema porque los padres no hablan inglés y los hijos crecieron en una sociedad donde el inglés es su idioma primario. Y hay un problema de comunicación entre padres y los hijos. ... el problema grande es la comunicación, el lenguaje es una barrera entre padres e hijos y segunda generación comunicándose con primera generación. Eso es el problema pero si un padre aprende el inglés se comunica perfectamente con sus hijos en ambos idiomas.

> [It's a problem because the parents don't speak English and the children grew up in a society where English is the primary language. And there is a communication problem between the parents and the children. ... the great problem is communication, the language is a barrier between parents and children and second generation communicating with first generation. That is the problem but if a father learns English he communicates perfectly with his children in both languages.]

Pastor Rivas's comments indicate that he favored cultural assimilation, or at least accomodation, by urging his churchgoers to learn English. His congregation's frequent interaction with the English-speaking congregation and his statement that the number one problem of Latino churches in the U.S. was non-English-speaking pastors, support this view.

Pastor Ramírez of Iglesia de Jesucristo in Forest Grove explained his church's decision to use English with the children in terms of linguistic assimilation: "Because it would be better for the children, we want them to understand, most of the children are growing up and going to the grade school and learning English, and we want them to learn the English language, so we start them off early."

City Bible also clearly supported those who would prefer to participate with the majority culture: "we are always encouraging anyone who wants to, and encouraging parents to think of their kids as integrating more and more fully into life here ... we see that a lot of these kids won't be, probably once they're 20, won't be at a Spanish service ... they may be just integrated into [English-speaking] church life, which for us is fine." Hermiston Nueva Esperanza had a similar approach to integration, choosing to hold Spanish worship services at the same time English services are held, so that the Latinos could attend the service in which they felt most comfortable.

On the other end of the spectrum, several churches indicated a tendency toward linguistic and cultural preservation. Pastor Vargas of Woodburn Mennonite Iglesia Pentecostés stated that the youth in his church

> les gusta buscar identidad con los hispanos aunque ellos tam- bién entren en grupos de relación con anglos . . . pero . . . ellos ven la iglesia como la casa. . . . está bien que aprecien las raíces. Personalmente he hecho énfasis hacia ellos no pierdan las raíces, que no se avergüencen de su origen.

> [like to seek their identity with the Hispanics though they may also enter into relationships with Anglos . . . but . . . they see the church as their home . . . it is good that they appreciate their roots. Personally I have made an emphasis toward them not los- ing their roots, that they not be ashamed of their origin.]

The Woodburn church's programming was entirely in Spanish, strengthening their linguistic heritage.

The Portland Mennonite congregation Ministerios Restauración noted that the children's Sunday School teachers tried to use Spanish "because it is important to the parents" but they struggled with the issue of making sure the children understood the content. The parents' desire for the children to learn and maintain Spanish conflicted with the church's goal of Christian education. The practice of using Spanish only for worship, education, and events at Salvados para Servir and Elim indicated a preference for maintaining the linguistic heritage of the second generation, though the pastors did not specifically indicate this as a goal of the church.

Cultural assimilation goes beyond language. Pastor Vela's comments about the Latino high school graduates in his church continuing to participate with the Hispanics, though they spoke fluent English and were invited to join the Anglo congregation's activities, indicate that some simply prefer to worship with those of a similar background.

Two other pastors commented on the cultural struggles of Hispanic youth. Pastor Reyes of Manantiales de Vida Eterna showed a clear preference for maintaining his cultural values and even disapproved of some the values of Anglo churches in the U.S.:

> . . . es que la juventud que se está desarrollando en nuestra congregación . . . hay momentos que se le siente o desmida el deseo de mejor relacionarse, más que todo con gente americana. O tener más manera de vida, de vivir como el americano. La iglesia americana lo desarrolla especialmente cuando chocan los diferentes puntos doctrinales.

> [. . . It's that the youth that are developing in our congregation . . . there are moments in which one feels or underestimates the desire to relate better, more than anything with American people. Or to have more of a lifestyle, to live like the Americans. The American church develops this especially when the different doctrinal beliefs collide.]

Pastor Giménez of Vida Church observed that cultural identity conflicts occurred among the youth in his church when they left for college and had to decide which culture they would identify with more. He did not express a preference for assimilation to the Anglo culture, preservation of Latino heritage, or some blend of the two.

In summary, some Hispanic churches in Oregon see their role as transient, a place that second- and third-generation Latinos will leave in preference for an English-speaking church. Other Hispanic churches envision themselves as a place where those born to first-generation immigrants can learn about their parents' culture, partially through strengthening their Spanish skills. The bulk of the churches in this study have opted for a middle road, providing some or all of their activities in English or in both languages. All of the pastors indicated that they and their leadership have wrestled with the issue, confirming Chávez Sauceda's statement that "every Latino congregation struggles with the question of how to include a younger generation that speaks little or no Spanish."[40]

Several pastors made specific comments regarding the lack of commitment by younger generations, along the lines of the observations by Hernández regarding Latino churches.[41] Pastor González of Luz del Pueblo was critical of this characteristic in the second generation: ". . . se van a la mejor comodidad con los anglos . . . no les gusta trabajar. Les

---

40. "Race, Religion and La Raza," 191.

41. Hernández, "Cathedral to Storefront," 224.

gusta que ya, lo que hicieron ya es hecho." (. . . they leave for greater ease with the Anglos . . . they don't like to work. They like to have everything already done for them.) He predicted that this preference for the "comfort" of well-established English-speaking churches would cause the demise of Latino churches in Oregon in twenty to thirty years, although he also suggested that becoming a fully bilingual church might retain some of the younger generations.

Pastor Vela of Monmouth Christian, a mostly second-generation immigrant congregation, commented that his congregation's lack of commitment had left them without enough Sunday School teachers when one couple moved away: "'Cause we have such a hard time getting teachers, our congregation's not big enough, or we don't have people committed to being teachers. . . . [the teachers' move] kind of left us—we didn't prepare nobody else, we got comfortable." At the same time, however, there were five churches in this study, including Pastor Vela's, with at least half second-generation immigrants in their congregations, and they were located in counties with a smaller proportion of second-generation immigrants. These churches refute the theory that subsequent generations participate less in religious life.

Pastor Argueta of Medford also indicated reduced participation among the young adults: "El problema que tenemos . . . aquí en las iglesias cuando ya entran en la edad adulta y ya toman decisiones, es cuando deciden alejarse de la iglesia." (The problem that we have . . . here in the churches when they enter into adulthood and they can make their own decisions, that is when they decide to distance themselves from the church.)

Pastor Mateo remarked that first-generation immigrants are more committed to their churches due to emotional needs caused by the separation from the homeland: "Pero las personas que piensan de sus países tienden a buscar más de Dios, tienden a asistir más a las iglesias. Quizás sienten más solas en sus casas, entonces buscan la iglesia como para encontrar compañerismo y más que todo lo espiritual de Dios." (But the people who think about their countries tend to seek more of God, they tend to attend the churches more. Maybe they feel more alone in their houses, so they look to the church as a means to find companionship and more than anything else, the spiritual aspect of God.) These comments closely align with what some sociologists provide as an explanation for increased religiosity among first-generation immigrants and what

Hurh and Kim summarize as "the comfort theory,"[42] citing, for example, Smith: "Separation from both personal and physical associations of one's childhood community drew emotional strings taut. Friendships, however, were often fleeting; and the lonely vigils—when sickness, unemployment, or personal rejection set individuals apart—produced deep cries of the spirit."[43] As mentioned in chapter 2, ten pastors indicated that caring fellowship and mutual support were strengths of their congregations. These same churches had more than 50 percent of first-generation immigrants in attendance, except for La Cosecha Foursquare.

CONCLUSION

Country of origin did not appear to be an excluding factor for participation in the Protestant Hispanic churches in this study. A few Anglos were included, even accepted as pastors. The nationality of a pastor did not have a demonstrable effect in attracting persons from that same country, except possibly in the case of Costa Ricans to Woodburn Iglesia Menonita Pentecostés. Several churches had very high percentages of persons of indigenous background with a smattering of *mestizos*; many other churches were majority *mestizos* with a few indigenous people. National background, race, and ethnicity, then, appear to be porous rather than absolute divisors in church participation. Like other U.S. congregations, persons of similar educational levels and occupations types tended to worship together. In general terms, the Protestant Hispanic churches of Oregon were inclusive rather than divided by race or ethnicity, nationality, or class. Additionally, many of the pastors specifically teach unity rather than division, using biblical admonitions as their authority.

Latino churches provide their members opportunity for further education and skill development through service that can lead to roles of increasing responsibility. Persons attending the Protestant Hispanic churches of Oregon have the opportunity to assume leadership roles regardless of national origin. While some boards had bilingual members with a higher-than-average formal education, the pastors did not indicate bilingualism and schooling as requisites, but implied that these characteristics provided the necessary self-confidence to assume those

42. "Religious Participation," 22.
43. "Religion and Ethnicity," 1174.

positions. Training within the church, however, was a requirement for leadership in several congregations, as was spiritual maturity in many congregations. In addition to this limited type of social mobility within the Hispanic congregations, nearly one third of the churches indicated that their Spanish-speaking members had also served in leadership roles in the English-speaking church of which they formed a part.

Due to relative physical proximity, economic disparities, and an up-swing in violence in Mexico, ongoing immigration by Latinos is likely to continue, especially from Mexico. The continuing arrival of first-gener-ation immigrants makes the Hispanic churches of Oregon (and indeed, across the nation) significantly different from the European-immigrant churches of the Midwest, which in large part closed a generation or so after the wave of immigration ended.

The bulk of the Latino population of Oregon is relatively new, with most immigration occurring in the late 1980s. For many in this first gen-eration of immigration, church attendance appears to provide important emotional support through fellowship. The U.S.-born children of these immigrants are just now coming of age. These young people prefer to use English, and all the churches in this study indicated that they have given consideration as to which language to use and how to include the younger generations. Most congregations in this study that had high percentages of second-generation immigrants from Mexico used both English and Spanish in their programming. Four of the churches indi-cated a clear preference for cultural preservation, in particular through a greater use of Spanish, and an equal number indicated a tendency to en-courage assimilation, especially through the use of English. Though five of the churches in this study had at least 50 percent second-generation immigrants, the upcoming decade could bring about dramatic changes in the Latino churches as more Hispanic young people come of age and are able to make choices for themselves about religious participation and begin to participate in leadership in the churches.

5

Worship Services

INTRODUCTION

THE CONTENT OF THIS chapter has provided the author with several challenges, both in methodology and in analysis. First, the method of participant observation was used. The author attended, unannounced, the main worship service of twenty-five Latino Protestant churches in Washington and Multnomah counties as well as outside of the Portland metropolitan area, over the course of three years. In each service, she took notes about the participants, order and elements of the service, including music, announcements, and sermon.

This method, though potentially providing rich description, is not without its problems. First, due to scheduling issues, in a few instances the service she attended was not the main service, and in several cases, the person preaching was not the pastor. This provides rather uneven data for comparison purposes. All such instances are noted in the descriptions of the services that follow, which are presented in general chronological order—the Washington County observations were done mostly in 2008, Multnomah County in 2009, and the rural churches in 2010.

Second, as these church visits were done over the course of three years, the author's method of observation evolved over time. Specifically, she began taking more detailed notes about the lyrics of the worship music after hearing the chorus "El rubio de Galilea pasando va" (The Blond Man of Galilee is passing by), in reference to Jesus. Thus, the descriptions of worship music that follow are finer-grained for the latter counties.

Third, and more importantly, participant observation is a dual task: one participates and one observes. Thus the author, a fellow believer in Christ, found herself both participating in worship as a visitor at the churches and striving to take detailed notes at the same time, no easy feat. Complicating the entire process was the fact that the author is not Hispanic, and her presence in the services never went unnoticed. This was ameliorated in many cases by being accompanied by her Latino husband. In other cases she had attended the churches occasionally and was known to the pastor and congregation, but there was always the possibility that her presence affected the service in some way, especially in the smaller congregations.[1]

Beyond the author's racial and linguistic background, she is shaped by cultural and religious norms and preferences. Worship is an experiential activity, and during each service, she found herself experiencing it on several levels. On the personal cultural level, she felt that some services were too hot, too loud, too long, and/or too disorganized, that the sermon was too rambling, the music lacked musicality, and that the pastor used terms that were not "politically correct." On the religious level, she found some statements heretical and battled her skepticism of charismata, as she does not come from a Pentecostal background. Despite this inner commentary, she strove to document what she heard and observed in an objective manner, but recognizes that one never fully escapes one's personal prism, which has undoubtedly colored her observations.

Other challenges arise for the analysis of the information gathered for this chapter. The author originally planned to present a comparison of liturgies. However, scholars of Protestant Hispanic churches agree that trying to categorize Hispanic worship is a nearly impossible task. This observation can be made for churches in Latin America: "Las vastas diferencias geográficas, étnicas, culturales, sociales, económicas, educativas y políticas del continente en general y del pueblo evangélico en particular impiden una apreciación completa de la realidad [de la Iglesia evangélica latinoamericana]." (The vast geographic, ethnic, cultural, social, economic, educational and political differences of the continent in

---

1. This seemed especially to be the case at Iglesia de Jesucristo in Forest Grove, where the author sensed that English was used more than usual during the service due to her presence.

general and of the evangelical[2] people in particular impede a complete appreciation of the reality [of the Latin American evangelical church]).[3] The same principle holds regarding U.S. Latino worship: "There is no such thing as . . . a typical form of Hispanic worship."[4] Even focusing on one denomination (albeit a very large one with multiple divisions) does not simplify the task: "It is impossible to speak of a Baptist theology of worship. Not that there is not one, but rather that there has never been to this day, a comprehensive liturgy that is common to all Baptists—or one common to all Hispanic Baptists."[5]

There were no mainline churches in this study, and none of the churches were from a liturgical tradition,[6] although a standard order of service was observed in most cases. Indeed, González claims that there are common threads discernible in Hispanic worship services: "As one travels throughout the nation and worships . . . in a wide variety of Latino contexts, one senses a commonality that somehow holds these various strands together. Latino churches, whether Catholic or Protestant, whether mostly Mexican, Cuban, or Salvadoran, have their own particular flavor in worship."[7]

Finally, the author's own frame of reference for worship services is limited: she has most often attended services in the Church of the Nazarene, with occasional visits to Church of God (Anderson, Indiana), Baptist, Mennonite, Assemblies of God, and Christian Church services, and Quaker, Presbyterian, United Methodist, and Lutheran churches very few times. Thus, when drawing conclusions about an Apostolic service, for example, she is uncertain what to attribute to Latino culture and what is standard denominational tradition.

Music was an especially complicated area for analysis. The past decades have seen dramatic changes in worship music, both in English- and Spanish-speaking churches. Much of the information now available

2. Again, in Latin America the term "evangelical" is used synonymously with "Protestant," unlike its usage in the U.S. ,which identifies a sub-group of Protestants.

3. Costas, "La realidad de la iglesia evangélica latinoamericana," 35.

4. González, "Hispanic Worship: An Introduction," 9.

5. Darino, "What is Different about Hispanic Baptist Worship?," 75.

6. Though researcher Santillán Baert was describing Hispanic United Methodists, a mainline denomination, her comments are also descriptive of many elements of the non-mainline worship services observed in Oregon, and are included in the discussion area when pertinent. See "Hispanic United Methodist Church," 57–71.

7. González, "Hispanic Worship: An Introduction," 13.

on lyrics, authors and composers, and copyright holders is only available electronically, and conflicting information abounds. Further, the use of hymnals or written songbooks has all but been abandoned, making such identification during the site visit difficult. In many churches, the use of printed material has been replaced by words projected on a screen. While the author wrote down as much of the lyrics as possible during the latter site visits, she was unable to annotate the melody line. In many cases, the songs are textually lifted from Scripture, and several versions with the same text but different melody and rhythm exist. On the other hand, multiple versions of lyrics exist for the same worship choruses. The author made note when she recognized a song that is also sung in English, and though she has a broad general knowledge of hymns and popular Christian music from the 1970s forward, it is possible that some of the songs sung in Spanish also exist in English, and she simply did not recognize them.

Why, the reader may ask, bother to write this chapter that has presented so many challenges? Because a church's worship service is an important indicator of the life of that church. Meeting together for worship has been a mark of Christianity since its beginnings. Darino observes, "Baptists consider the maintenance of public worship, based on scriptural patterns of carefully studied worship, to be a vital part of church life . . ."[8] Speaking in much broader terms, Costas claims, "que el culto es un índice de la realidad de la Iglesia. . . ." (that the worship service is an indicator of the reality of the Church . . .).[9] Thus, a careful description of the worship services of these twenty-five Oregon Protestant Latino churches will give a picture of their recent state and may identify trends or commonalities.

The author hopes that her detailed description of each service will honor the nuances of variety in each congregation. As González states, "there are many faces to Hispanic worship, and any attempt to describe that worship without taking that [national, regional, denomination, and generational] variety into consideration would be false."[10] The faithful representation of the services will also allow readers to draw conclusions beyond, or different from, those offered by the author at the end of the chapter.

8. "Hispanic Baptist Worship," 78.

9. "La realidad de la iglesia evangélica latinoamericana," 65.

10. "Hispanic Worship: An Introduction," 13.

DESCRIPTION OF WORSHIP SERVICES

Many aspects of the Latino worship services will be described in the following section, but an explanatory word about one type of music is needed at the outset. Many churches sang *coritos* (little choruses). Soliván defines *coritos* as "short and repetitive spiritual songs that often tell a story, but always include praise—usually a psalm or other portion of scripture. The *corito* is an indigenous Hispanic Pentecostal singing style. . . ."[11] Aponte, in his article on *coritos,* adds that, "Often the exact origin of specific songs is unknown, but they are seen to have risen from the *pueblo.*"[12] Many times, these songs are sung in a *cadena de coritos*—a chain of repetitive worship songs done mostly in the same key and with a similar rhythm.[13]

Washington County Churches

Hillsboro's Iglesia Evangélica Cristo Viene had only a guitarist and a vocalist leading worship music. No words were provided for the songs, which lasted around five minutes. During the service a dozen teens presented a skit that dealt with youth in gangs, drug use, a violent fight, and the story of the prodigal son. It was Mother's Day, and many elements of the service reflected this. There were many children present in the service. Two different primary classes went forward with their teachers and sang songs. Eleven preschoolers and their three teachers made a presentation as well. Twin babies were dedicated. In addition to the opening Scripture reading of 1 John 1:1—2:6, Prov 31 was read, extolling the virtuous woman. A special prayer was offered for the mothers in the congregation and all received a gift. The pastor indicated that the children normally left the service for their own activities earlier in the service, but on this day they stayed until just before the sermon. The tithes and offerings were collected, and then the pastor preached. Although a bulletin was provided, he had chosen to change topics from what was

11. "Hispanic Pentecostal Worship," 52–53.

12. "*Coritos* as Active Symbol," 60–61.

13. For an example of a *cadena de coritos* done professionally, see "Cristo es la peña" by Ricardo Rodríguez: http://www.youtube.com/watch?v=GxSNQQdJAjc. Rodríguez recorded five volumes of *Alabanzas del pueblo* "Praises of the People," from 1999–2005, which he describes as collections of "aquellos coros antiguos que fueron de tanta bendición para tu vida" (those old choruses that were such blessings for your life). Rodríguez, Liner Notes, *Alabanzas del pueblo,* Vol. 1, ©Parael Producciones, 1999.

printed there. The message he preached was entitled "A Mother's Prayer." He mentioned the suffering of various mothers in the Bible, including Eve, the two mothers claiming one baby who brought the case to King Solomon, and the prophet Elisha and the childless Shunammite woman, finally focusing on the prayers of Hannah as found in 1 Samuel. The sermon emphasized the role of a mother as providing emotional support to her children. The pastor made several other comments that revealed cultural values or were specifically geared to his audience. He stated that children should be conceived within the confines of marriage, but "Si se dan, ¡qué va! ¿verdad?, pero no es el plan de Dios." (If they come along, what are you going do about it, right?, but that's not God's plan). He went on to tell a story of children as coffee plantation workers in his native Guatemala, and then described a mother's expectations of her children as "you go to college, get a good, job, support your mother and give her gifts." He relayed Hannah's promise to return her child Samuel to the temple for service to God as "palabra de hombre" (a man's word), making a comment that this was a *machista* phrase and that women keep their word, too. He went on to make several more references to Guatemala, including persons who live by scavenging in a garbage dump, saying that God lifts "garbage dump people" out of their circumstances. The sermon was about forty-five minutes long, and the entire service lasted about two hours, ending with a pastoral prayer.

The City Bible service had many young couples present and was held in a sanctuary decorated with flags of many nations (not just Spanish-speaking ones) all around the perimeter. Men and women ushers guided people to seating. Before the service started, the congregation was reminded to turn off its cell phones. The worship team was made up of nine adults and several small children. The worship music lasted nearly forty minutes. It was followed by a time of greeting visitors, who were asked to raise their hands in order to receive an informational packet from the ushers, and who were invited to a visitor reception after the service. The announcements included information on a special activity with Mexican Christian musician Marco Barrientos and a six-week series on spiritual gifts. The tithes and offerings were collected, and the congregation was reminded that City Bible was opening another satellite site in Vancouver and that they could join in giving a special offering to support this project. 1 Kings 17:7–16 was read, the story of the widow of Zarephath who collected containers from her neighbors and whose oil lasted until she had filled all of them. At this point, a few small children had wandered up to the front of the sanctuary, and the pastor asked their parents to keep them off the platform. The pastor noted that the teens were meeting with the English-speaking youth group and invited any teens present to join in. The sermon, entitled "Abrir las ventanas de los cielos" (Opening the Windows of Heaven) began fifty-five minutes after the beginning of the service. It included scriptures on tithing (Malachi 3:10), and God's care and provision for his people (Matthew 6:26–34 and Deuteronomy 32:9–10). The pastor indicated that people often interpret more money or possessions as a sign of God's blessing, but that actually these things can serve to separate one from God or make one quit trusting God. The sermon included comments about trusting God for immigration status situations and mentioned Joseph as an immigrant in the Bible. The service ended with prayer and an invitation for anyone in the audience who had not accepted Christ as savior to do so. The service lasted one hour and thirty-five minutes, and the sermon occupied forty minutes of this time.

The author and her husband attended a regular Sunday afternoon service of Iglesia del Pueblo Assembly of God in Cornelius. In the foyer there was a selection of literature in Spanish about the Assemblies of God and AOG activities. There were five young adults leading worship music and one woman in the audience filming the service. The two vocalists were females and men played a guitar, a bass guitar and the drums. The song leader, using both English and Spanish, admonished the church to clap loudly. The congregation was welcomed after two songs, and after the third song, a keyboard was added to the music. The opening song in this service was "Open the Eyes of My Heart, Lord." The lyrics were projected first in Spanish, then in English. The next two songs were also sung first in Spanish then in English: "Señor, eres fiel" and "Jesús, amante de mi alma," the Spanish translations of "Lord, You Are Good" and "Jesus, Lover of my Soul," respectively. The last two songs focused on God's love and faithfulness as a motive for worship. The next song was sung in Spanish only: "Algo en mí necesita de Dios" (Something in Me Needs God). During the offering, the congregation sang the bilingual song "Ven, es tiempo de adorarle" (Come, Now is the Time to Worship).

A bilingual prayer was offered by a woman, then 2 Cor 8:13 was read as a prelude to the offering. The leader read it in English from the King James Version, but the pew racks had English Bibles in the New

International Version. Congregants left their pew and went forward to deposit their tithes and offerings in a container at the front of the sanctuary. After the offering the congregation was told to "Give a hand to the King." A different person began to direct the service, also speaking in both English and Spanish. He stated that "this is a bilingual church" and that they had an interpreter.[14] A visitor card was handed out, and the leader announced that Pastor Rose Medina was not present that day, but that a special guest would be sharing in song and preaching. The leader very informally asked whether or not the children would be leaving to children's church, and learned that they would be staying in the service that day.

The guest speaker and a female interpreter went to the platform, but after asking if everyone spoke Spanish and learning that they did, they decided to use only Spanish, and the interpreter returned to her seat. The guest speaker began approximately forty minutes into the service. She stated, "I bring a word from God," and then sang two *tejano*-style songs with Christian lyrics.[15] When the congregation began to applaud, she said, "Denle un aplauso a Dios." (Give God an applause). Applause was, in fact, offered throughout the sermon by various members of the audience. She introduced the topic of her sermon as "Your joy and peace depend on Christ, not on external circumstances." She spoke in a very active, dynamic way with many gestures. She spoke very quickly, then slowly, alternately shouting, pausing, and whispering. She deviated from the sermon topic for a few minutes to talk about salvation by grace, then returned to the theme, seemingly addressing

14. The author was one of two Anglos in the audience (the other one was obviously a regular attender), and she felt that this comment was made for her benefit.

15. Tejano literally means Texan. According to Encyclopædia Britannica, "Tejano [is] popular music style fusing Mexican, European, and U.S. influences. Its evolution began in northern Mexico (a variation known as norteño) and Texas in the mid-19th century with the introduction of the accordion by German, Polish, and Czech immigrants. Distinguished primarily by instrumentation and orchestration, three forms of Tejano (Spanish: "Texan") music developed." "Tejano." Encyclopædia Britannica. Encyclopædia Britannica Online Academic Edition. http://0-www.britannica.com .catalog.georgefox.edu/EBchecked/topic/1163291/Tejano. Accessed Oct. 17, 2011. This style is very different from mariachi music, but the author does not trust her ability to make distinctions among the three styles of tejano music, so what she might erroneously term ranchero or norteño are more generally classified throughout this chapter as tejano.

second-generation immigrants, that in spite of "todo tu título, todo tu dinero, necesitas a Cristo." (all your degree, all your money, you need Christ). She shared some of her life circumstances, narrating that she had been in full-time ministry in Selma, California, for three years and had come up to a denominational conference in Eugene the previous week, representing the Fresno Section of the Latin Assemblies of God. She told of the three services at her home church (Spanish, English, and Bilingual) and her television program called "The Truth Sets You Free." She mentioned her humble beginnings on a remote Mexican *ranchería* where "there was no school," saying that she herself could barely read when she started out in ministry. She then spoke of ways in which the world occupies itself—"parties with carnitas, cervezas y pleitos" (parties with Mexican-style spicy braised pork, beer, and fights). She urged the parents in the audience to "Get involved for the sake of your children. Do it now, so later you're not paying for rehab, getting them out of jail or gangs." She said that kids were living in dangerous times, with the "Internet Diablo, droga, prostitución, rebelión" (Devil Internet, drugs, prostitution, rebellion). She urged parents to invest in their children: "Go without tortillas if you have to." She went on to speak of ways to see if one is being disobedient to God, saying that sometimes it seems God "casi nos trajo con un mecate" (almost dragged us in with a rope), using a term for rope readily understood by Mexicans and Central Americans, derived from Nahuatl.[16] Fifty minutes after beginning, she turned to the Scripture for the message, based on Matthew 14:22–27, the story of Jesus walking on the water to his disciples in a boat. She continued to pepper her message with cultural sayings that she termed "dichos de la abuelita" (Grandma's sayings), such as "ven la tempestad y no se hincan" (they see the storm coming and they don't get down). The sermon touched on topics such as salvation, surrender, and grace. After one hour and ten minutes in the pulpit, she brought the service to a close by calling various groups to the front of the church to pray for them. She started with the "head of the family," the men, then the youth, then the worship team and finally the women. Some of those who went forward prayed out loud, and some spoke in tongues as they prayed. A "catcher" was present to ease those who were "slain in the Spirit" down gently to the floor. She

16. Native language used as a *lingua franca* in what is now Mexico and Central America, prior to and at the time of the Spanish conquest. There are still many Nahuatl speakers today.

prayed out loud individually for each person at the front, saying "I'm going to give you a blessing in Jesus's name." She admonished the men that they were chosen as priest of their homes, and that their children should see them praying. She passed her hands over the arms, stomachs, heads, and chests of the women who went forward, giving them a little push backwards after praying for them. When the prayers were done, the worship leader guided the congregation in an offering for the guest speaker and made announcements, mentioning that the service had been longer than normal. A family retreat was announced, as well as a letter from the pastor regarding the church's building program. The service ended about two and one half hours after it started.

The site visit to Iglesia de Jesucristo in Forest Grove was for a Wednesday evening worship service. This congregation owns its building, and the sanctuary had a U.S. and Jewish flag on the stage, a Star of David on the pulpit, and a pie plate, wooden box, basket, and two crystal decanters on the altar. The women present were wearing skirts and no earrings. Women with short hair wore black lace head coverings. The congregation was a mix of young families, teens, and older people. The service began with prayers that were offered by various persons in the pews, both in English and Spanish. There were five male musicians, playing a drumset, a conga drum, a guitar and an accordion. Though the sanctuary was equipped with an LCD projector, it was not used, nor were there any hymnals or songbooks; the songs were sung from memory. The song leader exhorted the people in both English and Spanish to worship God. An audience member played a tambourine during the singing. Several songs were followed by testimony time, during which a woman stood to speak. As she spoke, many congregation members murmured in agreement. The leader made several comments addressed to the "young people" in English. Scripture was read, followed by another congregational song, "Me fortalecerá" (He Will Strengthen Me). More testimonies were given, and there were several more exhortations in English to praise God, including, "Young people, bless the Lord!" The author was the only visitor present, and she was greeted in English.[17] A children's choir went forward and sang a song in Spanish. Two more

17. Sensing that the leader's extensive use of English might be due to her presence, the author responded to the greeting, addressing the congregation in Spanish. The leader continued to switch back and forth between English and Spanish, sometimes mid-sentence.

musicians went forward, adding a keyboard and electric guitar to the accompaniments. A smaller group of children (five girls and two boys) sang the chorus "As the Deer Panteth for the Water" in Spanish. The congregation sang "Con Cristo en la familia, que feliz hogar" (With Christ in the Family, What a Happy Home) and then the leader gave a testimony. This was followed by a soloist who sang a *tejano*-style song about the prodigal son. The leader then inquired if others wanted to sing a special, but no one did.

The tithes and offerings were collected as the congregation sang "Caminando" (Walking), a *corito* about going joyfully to heaven, and walked forward to deposit their offerings in the basket on the altar. Several announcements were made, including one in English about a teen carwash to raise money for them to attend camp. Several other extended announcements followed, then a child came forward to the leader with a slip of paper with another announcement on it about needing to raise money for cleaning supplies and that the person in charge was suggesting a ten dollar donation each. At that point, several people went forward and gave money, stating the amount they gave as they did so. The leader encouraged the congregation to serve and give faithfully, making a cultural reference, "Here we can get money even if we're not working, not like in our countries." Further announcements included an exhortation to punctuality, a monthly raffle drawing, a meeting Sunday at seven a.m., an encouragement to support the pastor's leadership and the burrito sale, and to pray and be in unity. This was followed by a story regarding income requirements for members at an Apostolic church, implying that the congregation should be grateful they were not subject to such rules. The twenty minutes of announcements concluded with the leader's request that the congregation pray for him.

The pastor went to the pulpit and led the congregation in reading Ps 119:1–16. He then invited a younger man to the stage to preach. He based his sermon on Rom 6:12–14, focusing on the believer's freedom from sin and indicating that the purpose of redemption is to be instruments of righteousness. He started out preaching in Spanish, but was obviously uncomfortable and struggled to do so. He used several false cognates from English and made only half-references to several scriptures in Spanish. He switched to English and his speech became more fluent, and he was able to use proper, well-known scriptural terms. The sermon lasted fifty minutes. The congregation stood, and the pastor spoke a blessing in Hebrew over them, concluding a nearly two and one half hour service. When the author asked the pastor about the Hebrew blessing and Jewish symbols later during the interview, he said that the founder of this group of churches, Brother Efraín, had taught them that their salvation came from the Jews and that they should have a love for the Jewish people. The blessing meant "The Lord is with you."

The regular Sunday evening worship service for the Spanish-speakers at Village Baptist was held in the large sanctuary. The foyer had a candle burning and a sign saying, "Our service is in progress, quiet please." Prior to the service, a Christian music video of Jesús Adrián Romero was projected. There was a cross at the front of the sanctuary, a small altar where one person was kneeling in prayer, and a small table with candles and what appeared from a distance to be a picture of a saint. The service was being videotaped. Following the music video, a slide welcomed the audience to the church. The young adults from the English-speaking Village congregation had been invited to this service, so there were many Anglos. The service was scheduled to begin at 6 p.m. and early on, a high percentage of the audience was Anglo, but many more Latinos came during the first thirty minutes. The monolingual English-speakers sat in one area, and an interpreter stood near them and interpreted the service. Beyond these visitors, the congregation was made up of many children, youth, and families, but no older people.

The worship team was made up of musicians playing the piano, bass, trumpet, guitar, electric guitar, and two female vocalists, as well as a teen playing drums. The service began with prayer about fifteen minutes after its scheduled start time. Several persons in the audience prayed out loud as the pastor prayed with the microphone. During the songs, the leader encouraged the audience to clap. A woman greeted the visitors from the platform and asked them to stand. One couple had been invited by another family. They had arrived early to the service, and it was announced that they had accepted Christ as savior prior to the service. Following the introduction of all visitors, the congregation was told to greet one another. Many people left their seats and extended handshakes, hugs, and kisses on the cheek with many others. After people returned to their pews, announcements were made, including plans for a Thanksgiving service, a discipleship class, a membership class, the Purpose Driven Church class, an upcoming Luis Palau event in Portland, Family Camp, and a deacons' meeting. The leader reminded the congregation that they were eligible for membership in Village Baptist Church, as the Spanish-speakers were part of the broader congregation. He also stated that no one should miss family camp due to finances.

The offering was taken, and the offertory was a *tejano*-style song. The leader then announced that children from two years to eight years of age should go out for their activities and admonished the parents to keep those who stayed in the service quiet. This was followed by more worship songs and prayer for healing for a congregation member.

The sermon began precisely one hour after the announced start time for the service. It was based on Luke 18:9–14, which contrasts the self-righteous prayer of the Pharisee with the humble prayer of the tax collector. The sermon focused on humility as a requirement for drawing near to God, and the pastor used several other scripture passages to support this theme. At the beginning of the sermon, he addressed the audience formally, using *Ud.*, then changed to *tú*, and ended up using the least formal form of address, *vos*, typical of his native El Salvador. He also made references to the humble situation of immigrants in their lives before immigrating. The sermon lasted fifty minutes, and the service ended with a pastoral prayer, which included a prayer for salvation.

The congregation that is now Vida Church was not yet meeting with Life Church at the time of the site visit. The author attended a regular Saturday evening service when this congregation was independent and meeting in a modified commercial building that they rented from another congregation. Prior to the service, the congregation gathered to share coffee, cookies, and conversation. English worship music was playing in the background. There was one monolingual English speaker in the audience, for whom simultaneous interpretation was provided with a headset. The service started promptly at the announced time, with the reading of Psalm 121 and an opening prayer. The congregation sang a few worship songs in English first, then the same songs in Spanish. The words were projected using an overhead projector. There were four on the worship team; two of these were instrumentalists.

Visitors were welcomed and invited to speak. This was followed by announcements, which included the weekly prayer meeting and the ladies' bi-monthly gathering. It was the pastor's birthday, and a special prayer was said for him. The offering was collected; then a female teenager went forward to give a report on her recent mission trip. She spoke in English, and her words were consecutively interpreted into Spanish.

The congregation sang "Happy Birthday" to the pastor. Then the congregation was given the opportunity to share testimonies specifically about miracles. One did so. The worship leader encouraged the audience to say "Amen," and twenty minutes of worship singing followed. At this time, the youth and children left for activities in another part of the building.

The sermon began about forty-five minutes into the service, after a pastoral prayer. It contrasted Isa 5:1–7 with Luke 19:41–42, which both describe a vineyard and its owner. The pastor used these and several other passages from both Testaments to explore the question "Is my life producing fruit?" The sermon was very exegetical and did not include any specific references to Latino culture. The service ended with prayer, having lasted one and one half hours. The author had attended several services with this congregation over a period of several years, and noted that this particular service was unusual in that there were no prophecies made nor was anyone slain in the Spirit, events she had observed on nearly every other occasion.

The Sunday evening service of Salvados para Servir was held in the sanctuary of a building rented from a Korean congregation. The visit happened in July, and the sanctuary was sweltering. There were many children present. The women all wore dresses, and the men had neckties. No one greeted the researcher and her family as they entered the sanctuary. Several people went directly to kneel at the altar before finding a place to sit. Others knelt briefly in the pew before being seated. There was a video playing before the service started, showing people worshipping, then the projection of a countdown to the start time of the "Pentecostal Worship Service." The service started precisely at the announced time.

A woman led a responsive reading of Prov 16:1–21 and prayed to open the service. The worship team was made up of nine people, all wearing white shirts. The instruments included two keyboards, three guitars, and two young teens playing trumpets. The music was excruciatingly loud, as was the microphone used by the leader and later the pastor. During the entire service, ushers with nametags stood in the side and center aisles as well as along the front of the sanctuary facing the congregation. Information on a children's ministry project was projected with an LCD projector. Then the worship team led the congregation in singing "Abre mis ojos," the Spanish translation of "Open the Eyes of my Heart." This was followed by a song about praise destroying strongholds and a song making reference to God as a strong tower. These were both sung multiple times, after which the leader encouraged the people to worship out loud on their own.

The visitors were welcomed, and the deacons handed out cards entitled "To help you as we can." An additional card was handed out on which to write prayer requests. These cards were collected along with the tithes and offerings. As the offering plates were being passed, a leader said, "God will duplicate your tithe." The collection was followed by announcements, which included a Bible institute, a children's outing to the zoo, and an invitation for congregants to get involved working in a ministry of the church and take the first step by attending a meeting the following week. Just before the sermon, the leader admonished the audience to listen quietly and respectfully to it.

The sermon was part of a series on "The mysteries of God." This particular message was entitled "The mysteries of the kingdom of heaven" and was based on Matt 13:10–12. The pastor asked for two volunteers from the audience with dollar bills and two men went forward. He offered to exchange their dollars for Mexican pesos. Both men refused. After they were seated, the pastor went on to expound on the parable of the talents, saying that the church doesn't do many things out of a fear of loss. He said that if people don't use what is given them, they may lose it, and used practicing English as an example, or the children in the church using Spanish, which they might forget. The pastor then cited John 3:1–3, when Jesus told Nicodemus that he needed to be born again, saying that this rebirth is in the future and is another of the mysteries of the kingdom. He asked for a female volunteer to come forward and asked her if she remembered being an embryo. The message then diverged into human child development, along with a story of how children in the womb taste what their mothers eat, thus explaining why Mexican children like chile peppers from an early age. The pastor directed the congregation to read John 14:1–3 which speaks of Jesus's preparation of "many rooms" in heaven.

Though neither the sermon nor service was finished, the author left after one and one half hours due to a headache from the heat and volume in the sanctuary. Two deacons ran out after her and her family, stopping their car and asking why they had left.

The worship service for Restauración Elim Internacional that the author observed was held in an adapted commercial building in

Hillsboro, though the congregation has since moved and now shares a church building with an English-speaking congregation in neighboring Aloha. The author and her family were greeted by several male and female ushers. The men were wearing white shirts, and dark suits and ties, and the women were wearing skirts and white head coverings. The seating for the worship service was divided down the middle with stanchions, and the ushers deftly separated the author's husband from her and her daughter and seated him with the men, while the females were seated on the opposite side. All the worship team were males, wearing matching red shirts and neckties. The instruments used were two keyboards, a drum set, a bass, an electric guitar, and a trumpet. The worship leader himself was a vocalist only. There was also a cameraman filming the service. There were approximately 160 men at the beginning of the service and only about 40 women. (The author believes the women were in other areas of the building with children and youth, and preparing food for a sale that was to follow the service.) The only children in the service were babies. Most of the men in the congregation were wearing ties, but others wore jeans and polo shirts. About one third of the women were wearing headscarves. Most wore long dresses or skirts, although there were some teen girls wearing jeans.

The service started promptly at the announced hour. The leader welcomed everyone then led a congregational reading of Psalm 113. The leader stopped and made special note of verse 7, indicating that the congregation, too, was poor and was nothing, but that God had made them princes. After the Scripture reading, the leader prayed and the congregation also prayed out loud in their seats.

This time was followed by very loud worship songs. No words were provided for the congregation, and the congregation did not stand but remained seated during all the songs. The theme of the first song, "Los enemigos de Jehová están derrotados" (The Enemies of Jehovah Are Defeated), was spiritual warfare. The two next songs, "Es el Rey de los cielos" (He is the King of the Heavens) and "Maravilloso es" (He Is Wonderful) focused on the majesty, sovereignty and power of God, and the latter included a stanza about dancing in God's house. All the congregation clapped in rhythm with the music. The fourth song spoke of freedom to worship in God's presence: "En la presencia del Señor hay libertad" (In the Presence of the Lord there is Freedom). The last song in this group was about God's glory: "Su gloria cubrió los cielos" (His Glory Covered the Heavens). All of the songs were repeated multiple times.

At this point, the congregation greeted one another, and several women hugged the author and other women, saying "God bless you." This was followed by another group of songs. The first was the well-known *corito* "Los que esperan en Jehová" (They that Wait upon the Lord), which promises renewed strength from God. The second was "En el principio el Espíritu de Dios," (In the beginning, the Spirit of God), which describes the Spirit of God moving in the present time and place. The worship leader gave a loud call to pray and sing while seated, in recognition that the Holy Spirit was present and moving among the worshipers. This was followed by singing "Ven, Espíritu, ven," (Come, Spirit, Come), many times. Though still seated, many men lifted their hands while singing this song. The keyboard was not in the same key as the other musicians during this song. Many in the congregation called out to God while this song was being repeated. The final song in this set was "Aleluya, Dios es Rey" (Aleluya, God is King). It was repeated numerous times. The congregation sang it very reverently, with their heads bowed while in their seats. The leader mentioned Psalm 113:7 again. While the chorus continued, a man began to speak in tongues then interpret what he called a prophetic word, "dice el Señor" (the Lord says). He was given a microphone, but the author was unable to understand him because he spoke in singsong sobs. Many in the congregation responded with tears and sniffles. This portion of the service had lasted approximately forty-five minutes.

A different leader began speaking from the platform, leading the congregation in a responsive saying "Y a su nombre . . ." (And to His name . . .) for which the expected response is "¡Gloria!" (Glory!). He then led the congregation in singing three more songs. The first described God as provider, and the leader exhorted the congregation to pray with raised hands and tell God he's good. This was followed by the song "Dios ha sido bueno" (God has been good), and then the chorus "Aleluya" which was repeated around twenty times while the audience was urged to clap, to use their freedom to worship.

The singing ended and all the visitors were welcomed with applause and a wave, and given a card which asked for basic contact information, as well as whether the visitor had accepted Christ and/or attended a cell group. There was space to indicate where the group met and the leader's name as well. A second card was distributed for requesting a pastoral call for specific needs, and offering envelopes were handed out as well. The leader announced that they were planning on holding two services in this location so everyone could fit, but that the congregation should be praying that they could find and purchase their own building. Plans to reinitiate a radio ministry were announced. The leader indicated that the rent and radio ministry were pressing financial needs. He spent some time clarifying that there were different envelopes for tithes and for offerings and that preprinted tithe envelopes were available. Prayer was said for the offering, and it was collected. One hour and twenty minutes after the service started, a young man went to the platform to preach, after it was announced that the pastor was absent due to illness. His sermon was about faith and was based on Heb 11.

Multnomah County Churches

Pastor Victor Alvarizarez leads two Casa del Padre congregations. The author visited the Portland location, which they share with a Russian congregation in a remodeled commercial building, for a Sunday afternoon service. Before the service, the members of the Russian congregation were cleaning up after a meal in the foyer area, and the Latino congregation had a table selling Christian books and Bibles. The author observed someone purchase a hefty hardbound copy of *Matthew Henry's Commentary*. Before the service, one could hear loud prayer coming out of the sanctuary area. The volume and intonation were similar to those of a Latino soccer sportscaster. The doors to the sanctuary were kept closed until the group inside finished praying. The congregation was allowed in twenty minutes after the announced start time of the service. The atmosphere in the sanctuary was as if the service had already started, although the pastor was nowhere to be seen. There was a female greeter at the door, and both male and female ushers with nametags. One approached the author and asked if she would need interpretation, and noted basic contact information on a visitor card. Five of these ushers stood in the aisles during the first half of the service. The women in this church were dressed casually; none had head coverings or floor-length skirts.

There were seven men and two women on the worship team, referred to by this church as *salmistas* (psalmists). The men wore dress shirts and ties. The lead vocal was male, and the two women were vocalists as well. They were accompanied by two keyboards, acoustic and electronic drums, other percussion instruments, and a bass guitar. The group was very melodic and musical. Words for the worship songs were projected with an LCD projector, and there was also a video camera filming during the service, with a live feed to the large screen occasionally. There was a banner across the back of the platform with the words "Ministerio internacional Casa del Padre."

The worship leader exhorted the people during the first song to "Tell God your pain, how you feel the disdain of people, now is the time to get that out, to rid yourself of everything that is bothering you." This song was entitled, "Dame de beber" (Give Me to Drink) and focused on one's need to sense God's presence. At about forty-five minutes after the announced start time, there were approximately 120 people present, including children. The next song was "El poderoso de Israel" (The Mighty One of Israel), which spoke of the power of God. The third song was "Pon aceite en mi vida" (Put Oil in My Life). The theme of this song was the joy of salvation. At this point in the service, the author could see a woman standing in the front row, waving her arms back and forth ecstatically. The next two songs both centered on spiritual warfare: "Jehová es mi guerrero" (Jehovah is My Warrior) and "Le llaman guerrero" (They Call Him Warrior). Many people in the congregation were dancing in place as they sang these songs. The following song was "Así como María hermana de Moisés" (Like Miriam Moses's Sister), which spoke of singing and dancing before the Lord. This was followed by another spiritual warfare song, "Los muros caen" (The Walls Fall Down).

One hour after the service started, the pastor danced his way up front, leading the song "El río de Dios" (The River of God). This song described deeply experiencing God's presence. Many of the congregation made their way up toward the front and danced and sang. The author saw an usher run quickly across the front area, and based on previous experiences, believes he was running to catch someone who was falling backwards after being slain in the Spirit, but she could not see to verify her hunch. The dancing and singing continued with "Has cambiado mi lamento en baile" (You Have Changed My Mourning into Dancing). This song's theme was joy, and it was followed by "Libre, Tú me hiciste libre" (Free, You Made Me Free) which was about freedom in Christ. At this time, both men and women were dancing across the front and in place, while others were jumping up and down. Many applauded or whistled. The next song was also about freedom found in God's Spirit: "Donde está el Espíritu de Dios hay libertad" (Where the Spirit of God is There is Freedom). It was followed by a repetitive *corito* about giving God glory through various movements in worship: "Y si yo danzo/giro/ etc. la gloria es para Él" (And if I Dance/Whirl/etc. the Glory is for Him). The pastor and a few others spoke in tongues. The glosalalia was very brief, and the author couldn't hear if the pastor interpreted what he said or not. The last song was "No hay nadie como Tú" (There is No one Like You). After this slower adoration song and a pastoral prayer, lights were turned on in the sanctuary. The congregation was exhorted to clap for the Lord.

The pastor used English for a few moments, then switched back to Spanish. For the offering, people were instructed to get an envelope from the ushers who were towards the back of the sanctuary. The musicians left the platform, and an offertory was sung with a background tape. Those with offerings to give walked forward and placed them in a large basket, and "rebuking the devourer" was mentioned. After the offering, visitors were welcomed. The ushers were no longer standing in the aisles, the children had gone out to their own activities, and the message began, one hour and forty minutes after the announced start time.

The sermon dealt with spiritual maturity and was based on Eph 4:11–16. The pastor made mention of the five roles in verse eleven, stating that they were spiritual mentors, teachers, trainers, or spiritual parents. He emphasized the phrase "so that" in verse twelve, noting its connotation of purpose. He read verse twelve slowly out loud and asked the congregation to repeat aloud several words from the verse. He then told of a dream he had had the previous Saturday and Sunday nights about a beautiful blond, blue-eyed baby that was somehow related to the church's need to purchase land for a building. He stated that new Christians were "babies held in the arms of the church" and described several stages of human child development, occasionally using English, or mixing Spanish and English in a single phrase, such as "bien nice" (really nice). He reminded the congregation of three babies in the Bible: Moses, a child "preserved" to be a liberator, Samuel, a child "presented" to God as promised by his mother Hannah, and Jesus, the "prophesied" one. He compared spiritual birth to human conception, saying that one may hear a lot about God or salvation (like the many sperm) but one day, the light comes on (a single sperm penetrates) and one says "Oh, my God, I am a sinner." The pastor briefly shared the plan of salvation at this point. He went on to describe how Christians need to mature gradually, as do human children, and that no one expects babies to walk immediately, but neither should the child drink Enfamil forever without going on to solid food. He stated that if a Christian isn't growing into maturity, there is a problem.

Due to difficulty finding the meeting place, the author arrived at Manantiales de Vida Eterna twenty-five minutes after the announced beginning of the service. However, it had not started. The congregation was sharing a meal of tostadas in a small kitchen adjacent to their meeting room, and warmly welcomed the author's family and invited them to join in. They did not tell the guests that this was a fund-raising activity or invite them to purchase the food; rather they served them plates as honored guests. The pastor was not in the kitchen; he was down the hall in the large room used as a sanctuary, prostrate in prayer.

Shortly after the author and her family had eaten, the congregation went to the meeting room. After kneeling at the altar for a few minutes, the worshippers were seated; the men on one side and the women on the other. Most of the women wore white head coverings with Bible verses machine-embroidered on them. The men were wearing dress slacks. There were two older couples, children and teens, and several single women in the congregation, and less than thirty were present.

Though there was a bass guitar, drums, and a keyboard on the platform, the male leader announced that all the musicians were gone today, and that singing would be acapella. After opening in prayer, he led in music using a songsheet, but there were none for the congregation, and there was no projector in the room. Several in the congregation kept rhythm with tambourines and others clapped along. One older woman had a clapping device that she used frequently. The lack of written words and a clear melody line from either the leader or audience made identifying these songs very challenging. The first song was an old *corito*. The next was entitled "He guardado la fe" (I've kept the faith). It was followed by "No puede el mundo ser mi hogar," a Spanish translation of "This World Is not my Home." The theme of this song is separation from the world. The next song was "Por una senda estrecha" (Down a Narrow Path), which spoke of salvation and taking up one's cross. This was followed by a *cadena de coritos*, mostly older ones that the author learned more than twenty years ago. The leader guided the congregation in a long prayer, during which some babbled out loud while others played the tambourine, and the lady used her clapping machine. The more recent chorus "Amén, amén" which focuses on God's faithfulness to his promises and the believer's surrender, was sung several times. This was followed by a *corito* "El rubio de Galilea pasando va" (The Blond Man from Galilee is Passing By), which encourages one to recognize Jesus's presence and seek his salvation and healing touch.[18]

The congregation knelt at their chairs in a prayer for the offering. The offering was taken, and the congregation read Ezekiel 37 responsively, led by a woman. The pastor took the pulpit, and his sermon, based on the Scripture reading, was a continuation of the day's Sunday School lesson. Photocopies of the lesson were provided to the audience, and the pastor read much of it, stumbling over words, and with assistance from the congregation, who seemed accustomed to doing so.[19] The pastor's style was not loud or dynamic, but it was replete with cultural references. The scripture passage referred to the valley of dry bones, which the pastor related to "walking through the desert" while crossing the border. He used phrases such as "hasta la marimba," (lit. 'up to the marimba,' fig. '[I've had it] up to here') and made reference to *machismo*, imitating a husband: "Soy el señor, cocíname, limpia, etc." (I'm the man, cook for me, clean, etc). He also made a play on words, saying that some Christians care more about soccer than attending church: "Su AL-ma se encuentra en el Mundi-AL" (His soul is found at the World Cup). He also made a comment about politics, saying that the congregation should hope the Democrats gained power, "Otherwise they'll send our kids to war" but countered this remark with "The U.S. is a missionary-sending country and we should be thankful for that." The overall theme of the message was the restoration of God's kingdom and lordship.

The Rosa de Sarón Foursquare congregation was meeting for worship on Sunday evenings in a rented Presbyterian building. Five minutes before the service was scheduled to begin, worship music in Spanish was broadcast in the sanctuary, and the pastor was dancing to it. A greeter met the author's family at the door and welcomed them. The church had

18. The origin of this chorus is unknown, but the author has found that those most familiar with it are all Puerto Rican. The author plans to explore its astonishing racial and colonial implications in a future conference presentation.

19. The author learned during the pastoral interview that Pastor Reyes had suffered a long-distance fall on a construction site and was still undergoing rehabilitation from it. His memory and reading ability were affected.

an LCD projector in use; the first slide announced that Rosa de Sarón is a Foursquare Church; the second slide had a Bible verse. A woman came and took contact information from the author after she was seated. Before the service started, one woman knelt in prayer in her pew. One woman and one little girl were wearing embroidered cotton dresses, and all the other congregants were wearing casual clothing. The congregation was mostly middle-aged adults, with a few women who appeared to be in their late fifties or older. Later in the service, there were around eighty people present; about half of them were children.

The service started with prayer about fifteen minutes after its scheduled start time. The worship leader then exhorted the congregation to worship God. The worship team had a keyboard, a drum set, an electric bass guitar, three female vocalists, and one male vocalist who was the worship leader. Before beginning to lead singing, he instructed the congregation on the difference between "alabanza" (praise) and "adoración" (adoration/worship). The first song had a theme of praise, and was "Rey de gloria" (King of Glory). The second song spoke of God's friendship and was "Eres mi amigo fiel," a translation of "Friend of God." This was followed by "A ti sea la gloria" (To You Be the Glory) with a rock rhythm, and then "Damos honor a ti" (We Give You Honor). Both of these songs focused on giving God glory and honor, as did the following hymn "Cuán grande es Él" "How Great Thou Art."

At this time, thirty-five minutes after the service began, the pastor welcomed everyone present and asked the author to go forward to bring a word of greeting to the congregation. Following this, the offering was taken. An usher admonished some unruly children. The offertory was "Eres Señor" (You Are Lord), again with a rock rhythm. Following the offering, the pastor made several announcements, including an invitation to participate in the upcoming Luis Palau Festival. The pastor made some culture-specific comments. When indicating where the festival was held, he said, "It's where they do Cinco de Mayo," indicating the Portland Waterfront. When trying to determine how many would participate, he said, "Telling people to raise their hands doesn't work with Hispanics."

About one hour after the service began, the children were dismissed to their activities, and a young man whom the pastor called "Felipín" went forward to preach. His message was entitled "The Most Wanted Man" and was about Paul's conversion as told in Acts 10. The preacher obviously had little experience and the sermon was short.

When the researcher did the site visit at the Spanish-speaking service at Reedwood Friends, the pastor first assumed that she had come for the Spanish language classes that he offers to the church and told her to come back later in the day. After clarifying that her purpose was to attend the worship service, he spent twenty minutes sharing about the nascent Spanish-speaking congregation there. Five minutes after the announced start time, there were four Cuban men present; thirty minutes after the announced start time several families arrived. The pastor opened the service with prayer. A Mexican woman played an acoustic guitar and led the audience in singing two *coritos*, and several in the congregation kept rhythm with tambourines. The children went out to classes with the English-speaking congregation. The pastor then named those who were not there and asked for testimonies from those present. Several shared about what they were experiencing or learning. There wasn't really a sermon, per se, more of a commentary on the testimonies.

At Roca de Salvación Assembly of God in North Portland, the researcher and her family were very warmly welcomed. At this church, the author participated in and observed both adult Sunday School and a worship service. There was a hubbub of children's activity (Royal Rangers) before Sunday School began. Along with the children, there were two elderly women seated in the sanctuary very early. There was a sermon in English with consecutive interpretation to Spanish on the speakers, and an LCD projector providing a short rotating program with a welcome slide, a Bible verse, and announcements. Sunday School started a few minutes before the announced start time, with a word of welcome and opening prayer. The pastor then exhorted the class to praise God by applauding. After they did so, he said, "If that applause were for George Bush, it would be OK," and asked the class to do better in applauding. He welcomed the author and her family as visitors, then turned the time over to a female Sunday School teacher from El Salvador. She prayed, then reminded the class members that their participation in Sunday School was a valuable part of the class. The topic of the class was the purpose of the church. The congregation had been working on a mission and vision statement, and this was projected for all to see. The teacher observed that she was "talking like a Salvadoran," using *vos* instead of *tú* as the familiar form of address. She went on to mention the different cultures represented in the class, including Mexicans and Salvadorans, and that they have some cultural differences, but that stated that "for

Christians there are no cultural barriers, Christ overcame them." She also mentioned differences between living in the U.S. and in the members' countries of origin: "Our churches in our home countries are bigger." She concluded by stating that a church's success was not measured by the number that attend, but by whether or not it is fulfilling its purpose, using 2 Cor 13:5 as a key verse.

Shortly before the service, Spanish worship music was played in the background, and the pews filled with families, approximately ninety people including children. People were dressed casually, and the author heard lots of conversation in English in the pews. The worship team was made up of one boy, two young men, two adult males (one on keyboard), and one female vocalist. One person in the back of the congregation participated with a tambourine. The first song was "Siempre fiel," (Always Faithful), which speaks of coming before the Lord seeking forgiveness. This song was followed by "Que sería de mí" (What Would Become of Me), which expressed gratitude to God. After this, the congregation sang several songs of worship: "Declaramos tu majestad," the Spanish version of "We Declare Your Majesty"; a *cadena de coritos* including "Jehová está en su templo" (Jehovah Is in His Temple) and "Alábale quien vive" (Anyone Who Is Alive Worship Him); "Pues Tú glorioso eres Señor" (For You Are Glorious Lord) and "Cantaré a Jehová por siempre" (I Will Sing to Jehovah Forever—based on the song of Miriam and Moses in Exodus 15), and "Hosana al Rey" (Hosanna to the King).

This set of fast-paced music was followed by a report on missions fundraising, given by a woman, a welcome to everyone, and then a man went forward to encourage giving a special offering for an anonymous member of the church in need. He read a scripture on tithing, and then prayed for the tithes and offerings, which were collected immediately after.

More worship music followed, including "Libre, yo soy libre" (Free, I Am Free) with the theme of freedom in Christ; a *cadena de coritos* which included the song "Cristo no está muerto" (Christ Isn't Dead), focusing on Christ's resurrection and life in the believer; "Dios, el más grande y digno de alabar," the Spanish version of "Great Is the Lord and Most Worthy of Praise" which was a slower song of praise to God.

After these songs, the children under five were excused, and the sermon began. The message was on David's mighty men, based on 2 Samuel 15. The pastor made many cultural references, including saying that the Philistines had stolen what rightly belonged to God, "comieron el mandado" (they ate up what they had been sent on an errand to get). There were many other Mexican sayings in the message, such as "Órale, 'mano" (That's it, bro');[20] the play on words "sus Dodge (dos) pies" (lit. 'his two feet' fig. 'he doesn't have a car, so he walks'); "a trancazos" (by blows), "mangonear" (to boss around or to henpeck) and "bonitas horas de llegar" (this is a fine time to arrive/it's about time you got here). He said it is easy to criticize the warriors in the Bible who left the battle from the comfort of today, which is like "toreando desde su asiento" (bullfighting from your seat).[21] He made reference to the Spanish language television channel Univision as "carnevisión" (fleshvision) for its many shows with scantily clad women and carnal viewpoint. He focused on Shammah, as described in verses eleven and twelve, who did not back down against the enemy even though all the other troops of Israel abandoned him to fight alone in the middle of a lentil field. The pastor said the lentils in the Old Testament are a symbol of God's blessing, and that like Shammah, believers need to stand their ground and defend the territory God has given them, using the sword of the word of God to both defend themselves and attack the enemy. At this point, there was audience participation in the form of applause, and the preacher urged the congregation to turn to one another and repeat his words. He then cited James 1:15–18, mentioning the devil's schemes. He finished the sermon by naming several members of the congregation and telling of how they had withstood great difficulties, that they too were mighty men and women of God. His love for the congregation was evident as he told these stories. The service concluded with the pastor describing the struggles of the young keyboardist as a single father who had just lost his job, and then delivering him the offering that had been taken earlier in the service.

The author visited a regular Sunday afternoon service at the short-lived Ministerio de Vida Eterna, which was a combination of an Assembly of God congregation and an Apostolic congregation. It met in the rear of a kitchen/fellowship hall in an English-speaking Apostolic

20. A colloquial Mexican expression with various meanings, according to the thread of discussion "Orale, andale, hijole, ejele, quihubole, ecole, epale, ujule, uchale" at http://forum.wordreference.com/showthread.php?t= 291264&langid=5. Accessed Oct. 25, 2011.

21. Similar to the English expression "armchair quarterback."

congregation's building. Prior to the service there were Spanish worship choruses being played on the speakers. There was a Christian flag at the front of the meeting area, and folding chairs for the congregation. People were kneeling at chairs in prayer before service, and one man was leaning against an outside door, crouched down, reading his Bible. Nearly everyone greeted the author and her family.

Most of the women present were wearing head coverings, except the Assembly of God pastor's wife, who was an Anglo. All the women were wearing dresses or skirts. The men and boys were wearing suits, ties, and dress shoes. There were approximately twenty people present aside from the researcher's family, and about half of these were teens or children. The men and women did not sit in separate areas to worship. The worship team had three males: an adult who led the singing and played the electric guitar, a boy playing the drums, and a boy playing the keyboard. There were no hymnals or songsheets, nor were the words of the songs projected.

The worship leader talked on top of the music, exhorting "Denle un fuerte aplauso al Señor" (Give the Lord a loud hand of applause). At first the music was painfully loud, but later it was adjusted to a volume more appropriate to the room size. The first set of songs all focused on worshiping God and included "Quiero llenar tu trono de alabanza" (I Want to Fill Your Throne with Praise), "Tu fidelidad" (Your Faithfulness), "Dios está aquí" (God Is Here), "Santo, Santo" translated from the English "Holy, Holy," a version of "Te alabo, Señor" (I Praise You, Lord), and "Mi pensamiento eres Tú Señor" (You Are My Thinking, Lord). This set was followed by another group of songs. "Entrad por sus puertas con acción de gracias" (Enter Through His Gates With Thanksgiving) urged the congregation to focus on worshipping joyfully. "El sacrificio" (The Sacrifice) described Jesus's death on a cross, and the following *corito* his resurrection: "Cristo no está muerto, Él está vivo" (Christ Isn't Dead, He Is Alive). This led into a series or *cadena de coritos* during which one of the pastors danced, and several children also were dancing at the back of the meeting room. It included "Alabaré" (I Will Praise), which refers to John's vision in Revelation; "Hay poder," the Spanish translation of the hymn "Power in the Blood," "Solamente en Cristo" (Only in Christ), "Déjale que se sienta" (Let it [the Holy Spirit] Be Felt), a variation of "Déjalo que se mueva" (Let it [the Holy Spirit] Move), and "Prepárate para que sientas" (Get Ready to Feel). Some of these focused on Christ's power while the latter two were about the Holy Spirit's moving. A woman in the congregation played the tambourine. There was a transition to another set of choruses, which included "El río de Dios" (The River of God), "Va bajando ya" (It's Already Coming Down), "Que no se acabe" (Don't let it stop), and "En el principio, el Espíritu de Dios" (In the Beginning, the Spirit of God). All of these choruses had the movement and presence of the Holy Spirit as their theme. They were followed by a song focused on joy called "No puede estar triste el corazón que alaba a Dios" (The Heart that Praises God Can't Be Sad), and "Hosana al rey, Aleluya, Bendito el que viene en el Nombre" (Hosanna to the King, Aleluya, Blessed is He Who Comes in the Name of the Lord), which recounts Jesus's triumphal entry. This was followed by a chorus that appeared to teach the unitarian doctrine of Oneness Apostolics: "No son dos, no son tres, El es uno" (They're not Two, They're not Three, He is One). The last song in this group was "Cristo es el supremo rey" (Christ is the Supreme King), proclaiming Christ's sovereignty.

This set of songs was followed by a traditional greeting *corito* "Mi hermano serás" (You'll Be my Brother), which speaks of Christian brotherhood and during which everyone present shakes the hand of everyone else, while singing. The Apostolic pastor then went forward, proclaiming "Estamos en los últimos días" (We are in the last days) and speaking of events in the Middle East during the preceding several weeks. He urged people not to put off doing things that needed to be done. This was followed by announcements, given by the other pastor, including a special service by a pastor from out of town, and an upcoming evangelistic campaign. He mentioned those who were missing in the service by name, and then asked if anyone wanted to share a testimony or a special song. No one chose to do so. The pastor read Proverbs 3:9, then prayed for the offering, and the tithes and offerings were collected. The pastor's wife sang "Tu fidelidad" (Your Faithfulness).

After this song, the congregation read Col 1:27, and the former AOG pastor prayed before preaching the message. The children did not leave to another area but stayed in the meeting room to hear the message. The sermon was titled "Your Hope is Not Dead" and was based on the Colossians passage as well as the miraculous catch of fish as narrated in John 21. The pastor stated that non-believers have their hope set on the visible, but Christians' eyes are set on what is unseen. He made reference to the large families in many Hispanic cultures, saying that some parents place their hope in their twelve kids to provide for them in the future. He mentioned social position (and hope to change it or frustration with it) twice. He recalled several disasters as reasons that people give up hope, the '85 earthquake in Mexico, Hurricane Mitch in Honduras and Nicaragua, the attacks on the twin towers in New York, and tied them to the hopelessness of godless as described in Job 27:8.

The pastor indicated the Hebrew word for hope, and stated that it implies waiting. He then turned to the passage in John 21, after Jesus's resurrection. He stated that the disciples thought their hope had died with Jesus and that Peter, discouraged by Satan, had decided to go back to fishing. The pastor stated that if the disciples, who had seen all Jesus's miracles, got discouraged, how much more the present day believer?

The sermon continued noting that Peter's all night work fishing rendered nothing. Just as there was an empty tomb, Peter had an empty net and an empty boat, but Jesus came to Peter in midst of his discouragement. Peter still didn't recognize him, but John did. The sermon ended with an admonition to not lose hope.

The preacher had a very loud, dynamic preaching style. People in the congregation responded to various statements with applause. The pastor used several cultural references, including the play on words "En vez de ir a Guatemala, vas a Guatepeor" (Instead of going to Guatemala (Guate-bad), you go to Guateworse). When he spoke of Christ's empty tomb, he added, "La Virgen Maria todavía está en la tumba" (The Virgin Mary is still in tomb). He also made reference to the "bigote de Cantiflas," the moustache of a popular Mexican comedic film star.

The service at Ministerios Restauración Mennonite Church in Portland was held on a Sunday afternoon in the sanctuary belonging to the English-speaking congregation. Many people greeted the researcher, one in English. At the announced start time there were about twenty-six people, including five elementary-age children, and two seniors. Thirty minutes later there were about forty people, including children. Most of men in the congregation wore dress shirts or suits and ties, and the women wore dresses or dress slacks. One little girl had on an embroidered indigenous-style dress. The worship team was made up of an Anglo male playing an acoustic guitar, 2 young women on vocals, a boy playing the drums, and an adult male playing an electric bass and singing. They opened with a song representing a call to worship in which only the worship team participated and for which there no words projected. The pastor's wife went forward to welcome the congregation. She then prayed and read Scripture.

The music leader exhorted the congregation to clap during worship songs. The words for the songs were projected with an LCD projector. The first song was "Creo en ti," a Spanish translation of "I Believe." The next spoke of God´s strength: "Con mi Dios asaltaré los muros," (With My God I Will Scale the Walls). "Amor sin condición" (Unconditional Love) was the next song, which had a theme of Christ's sacrifice and love. During and between these songs, the worship leader verbally exhorted the congregation to worship and spoke his own praises using melodic speaking. The author found the volume of the music appropriate for the space.

After these songs, the pastor's wife announced that the offering would be taken, and an usher prayed before taking the offering. After the offering, the congregation was told to welcome each other, which they did by shaking hands with or hugging those nearby. The author was the only visitor, and she was recognized and welcomed with applause. During this time, the song "Renuévame" (Renew Me) was playing in the background. The children were excused to go to their activities, and the pastor took the microphone. The congregation sang "Dios tiene cuidado de mí" (God Cares for Me). The pastor led the congregation in a special prayer for a couple in the congregation who had learned that their unborn child had some malformations and would need a series of operations. Two women from the congregation went up to pray for the couple, one laid hands on the mother while praying for her.

Approximately one hour after the service started, the youth went out to their class, and the sermon, based on Heb 5:11–14, began. The pastor read the Scripture out loud. His sermon focused on Christian maturity. He preached very actively, not yelling, but moving around the platform and using different vocal inflections. He made cultural references to "our countries" and used several languages to make his point that some had become inactive in their service: "In English they say 'lazy.' En mexicano, 'flojo'" (In Mexican, "lazy"). He encouraged the audience to repeat certain phrases, saying, "Digan conmigo . . ." (Say it with me . . .). He said that his church of origin had so many teachers attending it that it was known as "the teachers' church" then asked, "Where are the teachers now?" He asked the audience to name some of the many resources available to them to study God's word, and many in the congregation called out suggestions. He referred the audience to Acts 17:11 and the diligent scriptural study of the Berean Jews. The pastor continued to develop his theme of studying Scriptures to grow into Christian maturity, using a phrase popularized by Raul Velasco, a Mexican variety show host: "Aun hay más" (And there's still more). He closed the message with prayer after approximately thirty-five minutes.

Before dismissal, there were announcements, which included a request from the teachers of the teen Sunday School class for parental involvement to prepare for classes, and the need to choose an alternate delegate to the general assembly of the denomination. A woman in the congregation expressed appreciation to the youth group who had visited her daughter while she was undergoing surgery and asked for prayer for bringing the young woman's grandmother from Mexico. Another testimony was shared, and the service ended with thanks to the men for the Mothers' Day barbecue and a reminder to keep commitments to pay for sound equipment.

The Sunday service at Luz del Pueblo Southern Baptist had a worship team with three women vocalists, a man playing the bongos, another man playing a drum set, and males playing the keyboard, bass guitar, and piano. The lyrics to the songs were projected with an LCD projector. The three opening songs were Spanish translations of English worship songs, including "Breathe." There were approximately 110 people, including youth and children. Some women wore pants, others sundresses. Some had short hair while others wore long hair. Some had gang or other tattoos.

A woman led a responsive Scripture reading. The pastor prayed for the children before sending them to their classes. Church planters from the denomination's regional division were in the audience and were recognized.

The message began approximately forty minutes after the announced start time for the service. A bulletin insert was provided for the congregation to follow the message, and fill in the blanks. The pastor emphasized the need for order and reverence in the service, and spoke against emotionalism and Pentecostalism. His message was replete with Mexican cultural references or sayings, including "Mi cuate Pedro, le doy una mordida" (My buddy Peter, I'll bribe him); "Me quieren dar chicharron" (They want to kill me); "Este vato" (This dude); "No hay fijón—son mis camaradas" (Don't worry—they're my buddies); and "chamuco," "chanclas," both meaning the devil; "cotorreo" (chatter or smooth talk). He referred to a Mexican commercial for a chile and salsa company: "Herdez, la auténtica" (Herdez, the authentic one) and commented that people say to him "Pastor, échese una fría" (Pastor, have a cold one [beer]) when he is out visiting.

The pastor explained that he was teaching people how to read Scripture and find scripture references. During the message he asked three different women to read Scripture out loud to the congregation, and a man to re-read one verse. The sermon was focused around the question, "Are you really God's child?" and used John 8:31–47 as the text. He told how his brothers bother him about his conversion by saying, "Te lavaron el coco en los Estados Unidos." (They brainwashed you [lit. washed the coconut] in the United States.) The message finished with a reference to the final judgment as described in Revelations, with the pastor urging people to make sure they truly are children of God while "ahorita tiene chanza" (you have the chance right now) and speaking of death's inevitability. He mentioned someone who "colgó los zapatos" (died [lit. Hung up his shoes]). An invitation to accept Christ as savior was given, followed by a pastoral prayer. The sermon lasted nearly one hour.

The message was followed by communion, and the pastor mentioned Roman Catholic beliefs regarding the communion elements. The author was intrigued to see that the communion bread was oyster crackers. After communion was served by several men, a prayer was said for the tithes and offerings, and they were collected by the same people who served communion. This was followed by announcements, which included a financial management class in conjunction with another area church, and the opportunity to participate in a membership class. At the very end of the service a young Hispanic man proposed marriage to a young Latina in front of the church, going down on one knee on the platform, and speaking in English. The congregation sang "Si tuvieras fe como un grano de mostaza" (If You Have Faith Like a Mustard Seed) and the service was dismissed.

Churches outside the Portland Metropolitan Area

The Hood River Christian and Missionary Alliance Esperanza y Vida en Jesucristo Church met on a Saturday evening for their regular worship service. About seventy adults and many youth and children were present. The evening the author visited it was over 100 degrees outside, but despite the heat, some of the men were wearing suits and ties, though the pastor wore a cotton *guayabera*. Some of the women were wearing skirts, but others wore jeans. Many people greeted the author and her family before the service, in English and Spanish. Before the service began, a video of Marcos Witt in concert was running. There were two tables at the front of the sanctuary with many lit candles of different types and sizes and the elements of communion.

This church used an LCD projector and two screens to project images and song lyrics for the congregation at the front of the sanctuary and for the worship team at the rear of the sanctuary. The worship team was made up of five musicians: a woman playing the keyboard, a man on electric guitar and lead vocals, the pastor on bass guitar, a woman vocalist, and a man playing the drums.

The service started at the announced time with a scripture reading from Isaiah 40:28 and prayer. The pastor's wife welcomed the congregation and encouraged everyone to greet one another, which they did by hugging or shaking hands with those nearby and saying "Dios le bendiga" (God bless you).

Several worship songs followed. The first was "Oh, gracias, encontré la vida" (Oh, Thank You, I Found Life), which was a song of gratitude. It was followed by a jazzed-up version of the hymn "Sólo de Jesús la sangre" ("Nothing but the Blood of Jesus" in English), that focused on the salvific work of Christ on the cross. The next song was rock style: "Oh celebraré, me alegraré," (Oh, I Will Celebrate, I Will Be Glad), speaking of celebrating the benefits of salvation. The next two songs had themes of spiritual warfare: "Ganaremos la batalla de las tinieblas" (We Will Win the Battle of Darkness), and "Debajo de mis pies Satanás está," (Satan is Under my Feet). This was followed by "Tu palabra" (Your Word), which had an English translation at the bottom of the slide and extolled the virtues of the Bible.

The pastor prayed, and then a young Anglo man gave his testimony in Spanish and led a slower worship song, "Señor mi vida te necesita" (Lord My Life Needs You), a song of dedication. The first worship leader quoted some psalms bilingually and encouraged the congregation to cry out to God during this prayer time. Some people knelt at their pews and others went to the altar at the front.

The prayer time was followed by more songs of worship such as "Mi primer amor" (My First Love), a song of re-commitment to Christ; "Sólo Tú" (Only You) which highlighted the uniqueness of Christ; and "Dulce refugio" (Sweet Refuge), focusing on Christ as a refuge. This song also had a translation to English on the slide. The last song in this group was "Te quiero ver" (I Want to See You), a quiet song expressing longing for God's presence.

Another prayer was said, and a different man went up front and talked about tithing, while the pastor's wife provided consecutive interpretation to English standing behind him. He cited several scriptures, including 1 Sam 15:22. There was music in the background while he spoke. He prayed for the tithes and offerings, which were then collected. During this time, an image of the Last Supper was projected, and a recording of the song "Pedro ¿me amas?" (Peter, Do You Love Me) played in the background.

The pastor's wife commented that Jon Montalbán (the artist singing the recorded offertory) had visited the radio station that she and her husband manage, and went on to give various announcements. These were also projected on the screen. They included the need for volunteers to evangelize at the upcoming county fair, an outing for girls to Kahneetah resort in Central Oregon, a pool party for all children, a baby shower, a boys' youth camp (only for those who regularly attended a cell group), the availability of a CD and notes for the evening's sermon, prayer meeting, discipleship and cell groups in different communities, as well as a meeting for teen parents. She then welcomed the author and her husband and the congregation applauded for them. An audience member stood up and invited everyone to his daughter's thirteenth birthday party to be held in a local park. The pastor's wife prayed and the children were dismissed to their activities.

The sermon began nearly ninety minutes after the service started. The pastor explained the reason for the candles—he was trying to recreate the atmosphere of the upper room where Jesus celebrated the Passover meal with his disciples. A series of artwork portraying Jesus's last days rotated on the screen as the pastor preached. It included pictures of Jesus washing his disciples' feet and Judas Iscariot's betrayal. He indicated that this sermon, based on John 13 and 14, was part of a series on the Gospel of John.

He described Jerusalem 2,000 years ago as a place of many diverse and divisive ideas, saying that the great variety of views expressed on bumper stickers today indicates that the present has a similar diversity of ideas. The Jews were subject to the Roman Empire, and in these chapters Jesus was comforting the disciples as he prepared them for his death. The pastor paused to pray. He continued, describing how Jesus explained God's plan to the disciples and encouraged them to trust in him and not despair, saying it was not the end but the beginning. The preacher cited John 10:18, emphasizing Jesus's humility in submitting to his Father's plan. The Israelites didn't know where they were going either, but God faithfully led them. The pastor read most of John 14 out loud. When describing the Last Supper, the pastor noted that, in the tradition of those days, the first person to be served was the most honored guest, and Jesus served Judas Iscariot first. According to the pastor, Jesus was offering another chance to Judas. It was a moment of pride for Judas to be honored in this way. However, Judas made a decision not to follow Jesus, as no one can serve two masters. The pastor then stressed that each decision people make is an invitation to either follow Jesus or not. He told the congregation that Jesus was also offering them honor, holding out the bread to them, offering an open door to fellowship with him and that each person needed to make their own decision about how to respond. He referred to Luke's description of the Last Supper in chapter 22, and also to the wedding feast of the Lamb in Revelation 19:9.

The pastor went on to describe how Jesus would "poner el mandil y servirnos" (put on an apron and serve us.) He stated that people don't like to do menial jobs like washing someone's dirty feet or waiting tables, but that Jesus's humility was to be imitated. At this point, the pastor read from 1 Cor 11 regarding taking communion with an appropriate attitude, and communion was served. The pastor reminded the congregation that God should be their priority, as sovereign, the center of the universe. He said that believers are pilgrims, passing through, who will soon be with God, standing before him. He asked the congregation to consider their unique giftings and how they are using them. He stated that there will be crowns in heaven, products of lasting fruit, for the saved. The pastor had the congregation stand and prayed to dismiss them.

The author attended a Sunday morning service at Madras Iglesia Bautista Conservadora Bilingüe. The author and her family were greeted warmly as they entered, as they have known many people in this church for over twenty years. In the foyer there were several posters about up-coming Conservative Baptist Northwest events, and a bulletin board with photos of youth group activities. Most of the women were wearing dresses or skirts or dress pants. The men wore button-down shirts and a few wore suits. This congregation also had two projection screens for the LCD projector, one on the back wall for the worship team and another in front for the congregation. The worship team had an adult male lead vocalist, two keyboardists—one female, one male—an adult female vo-calist, an adult male on bass guitar, a teen male playing another bass, an adult male playing acoustic guitar, and a teen male on drums.

The service started at the announced time, by singing "Cuando suene la trompeta la iglesia subirá" (When the Trumpet Sounds the Church Will Rise) in a Latin rhythm. This song points to Christ's second coming. The pastor then greeted the visitors, who included two former pastors of this congregation—one from the Dominican Republic, and the other a Chilean (the author's husband). The congregation welcomed the visitors with applause. The wife of the Dominican pastor took the microphone and greeted the congregation. This was followed by many announcements, including several CBNW events, a report on an evange-listic concert the previous day in a nearby town, and a word of testimony from the pastor that his son had accepted Christ as savior at this event. The pastor expressed gratitude for the for faith promises for future giv-ing. He informed the congregation of the events planned to celebrate the church's thirtieth anniversary the following month, including a Saturday seminar on "luchas y pruebas del cristiano" (the Christian's struggles and trials) to be led by yet another former pastor, and a special worship service Saturday evening. The worship leader made an announcement about a children's festival and outreach event, and a woman informed the couples in the congregation of a special dinner planned for them. Both of these events were still two months in the future. The worship leader, who was also the adult Sunday School teacher, said that the visit-ing pastor had brought a gift of the teacher's guide and thirty copies of the adult Sunday School curriculum, and encouraged the adults in the congregation to attend Sunday School.

At this point, the congregation was told to stand and greet each other, which they did by hugging or shaking hands with several oth-ers, many adding "Dios le bendiga" (God bless you). The worship team led in singing "Señor eres fiel," the Spanish translation of "Lord, You

Are Good," which focused on God's faithfulness. Another announcement was made by the same woman for a ladies' activity, then the congregation sang "Amor sin condición" (Unconditional Love), which had themes of Christ's sacrifice and love. The tithes and offerings were collected by ushers as the congregation sang a song focused on God's glory, "Al alto y sublime" (To the High and Sublime One), as an offertory. During the following praise time, the worship leader exhorted people to worship out loud on their own as the musicians continued to play. The pastor played a tambourine from his seat in the congregation. The next song was "Siento tu Gloria" (I Sense Your Glory), which spoke of God's healing presence.

The worship leader asked the Dominican pastor to go forward and speak to the children as he always used to. He took the microphone and invited all the kids to go to the front of the sanctuary. He asked them where their family was, and they pointed to the audience. He then asked, "Cómo se llama este lugar? (What is this placed called?) and the children responded, "El templo" (the church building), and the pastor confirmed this and added "y la gente es la iglesia" (and the people are the church). He asked them why they came to church, and answered his own question by saying, "to learn about the Lord, not to play! You can play at home! You worship and learn about God at church." After praying for the children, he sent them out to their classes.

The visiting Dominican pastor was the guest preacher. He began by greeting the author's husband as well as the current pastor, and noted how much the children had grown since he had left. He encouraged the congregation to praise God from their seats. After praying, he began speaking on Isaiah 58. This passage referred to God's provision in dry places. The pastor made a cultural reference, saying, "Algunos saben lo que es vivir en el desierto—es seco, hay víboras, insectos, cascabeles, y aparecen hombres malos, pero no estoy hablando de ese tipo de desierto." (Some know what it is to live in the desert—it's dry, there are snakes, insects, rattlesnakes, and bad men appear [referring to border agents or *coyotes*], but I'm not talking about that kind of desert). There was a ripple of laughter as he mentioned the "bad men." He went on to describe times of spiritual dryness, citing several scriptures to affirm that God does not abandon his people in any circumstance. He named the many pastors that had served this congregation during its thirty years, saying that though all those pastors had left, God will not leave his people. He asserted that because God does not leave his people, if there is a separation, it must have been caused by the person and not God, and urged repentance, a turn-around. He stated that God keeps his promises regardless of human emotions, and cited Deut 7:9, which speaks of God's faithfulness to a thousand generations, and said that since he was the first generation in his family to follow Christ, he had hope for many future generations.

Returning to Isaiah, the pastor said that God promised abundant spiritual food, and that Christians shouldn't allow their spiritual drought to make them unproductive. He indicated two options for those in spiritual drought. The first was to continue as they were and be food for spiritual buzzards, using the Mexican word "zopilote." The other option was to rise up in faith, like an eagle, and say, "Lord, here I am, send me." He emphasized that this decision was a personal responsibility, not that of the pastor or one's spouse. He encouraged the congregation to close their eyes in prayer and speak with God about this for a few moments. He then continued through the chapter in Isaiah, saying there were four things that God did. The first was open rivers from rock. The pastor told of a large rock with a spring coming out of it in his native Dominican Republic, and compared the flow of water to an open fire hydrant that he had seen in California, asking the audience how Mexicans said "fire hydrant." He said the second thing God does is bring vigor to the believers' bones. He named one of the elderly ladies in the congregation and said that she and he both felt old sometimes. He made reference to this congregations' places of employment, saying that it appeared that God gives strength to work ten to fifteen hours in the sawmill or field, but not to go to church! He admonished the congregation that the strength given by God is for his service. He went on to say that everyone goes through a desert time in their lives at some time or other, and referred colloquially to Elijah, who fled to the desert after successfully trumping the prophets of Baal, saying, "Elijah se dijo, 'Patita, pa' que te tengo'" (Elijah said to himself, "Little paw, what are you good for?"), meaning "Let's get out of here!"

The third promise the pastor spoke of was being like a well-watered garden. Here again, he made reference to both Mexican terms and tastes, as well as a member of the congregation: "Serás como . . . como un jardín limpio, con jitomates, chiles, bien regado, como el de la Ha Maria con sus flores" (You will be . . . like a tidy garden, with tomatoes, chiles, well-watered, like Sister María's garden with her flowers). The final point was that believers will be like a spring that never runs dry. The preacher asked the current pastor to lead in a final prayer. The worship team went forward and the congregation sang "Señor eres fiel" again to dismiss the service.

The author and her husband attended a Sunday morning worship service at Nueva Esperanza Conservative Baptist in Hermiston. There were greeters at the door to the fellowship hall where the service is held, who provided bulletins. There were about forty people, including children, shortly after the service started. An LCD projector was used to project both song lyrics and visuals for the sermon. The worship team was made up of a male leader who played the guitar and sang, the pastor's wife and 2 female teens on vocals, a teen male on drums, another teen male on bass guitar and a third male teen on another guitar.

The service started at the announced start time with the song "Ven, es hora de adorarle," a Spanish translation of "Come, Now is the Time to Worship." This was followed by "Queremos ver" a translation of "We Want to See," a song calling to lift Christ up for others to see. The congregation stood while singing these songs, then was seated for the pastoral welcome, which specifically included the author and other visitors. Announcements followed, which were brief, and included a special service the following month to celebrate the congregation's seventh anniversary. The pastor then directed the congregation to greet one another, which they did, shaking hands or hugging those around them and saying, "Dios le bendiga" (God bless you). He then asked the author's husband to pray. The pastor gave a report of a recent trip to a migrant camp a few hours away where a group of musicians had ministered to cherry pickers.

This was followed by two more songs. The first was the hymn "Hay poder, poder," the Spanish translation of "Power in the Blood." It was followed by a song with a Jewish-style melody and rhythm, "Grande es el Señor" (Great is the Lord). The first song was Christocentric, while the latter focused on God's sovereignty and creative power. The pastor prayed for the tithes and offerings, which were collected while singing "Porque para siempre Dios tu misericordia es" (For Your Mercies are Forever, God). The congregation sang "Canta al Señor toda la creación," a Spanish version of "Shout to the Lord," the children were dismissed to their classes, and the pastor began to preach.

The sermon was entitled "Señales antes de la venida de Cristo" (Signs Before the Coming of Christ), based on Matt 24:1–8 and Matt 16:1–4. An outline was provided in the bulletin. The pastor provided some historic information about the destruction of the Jewish temple in Jerusalem. He then said that one type of signs would be religious signs and false teachers. He projected a slide with a collage of a picture of David Koresh, several images of Christ perceived by people in California and Latin America on different buildings or in plants, a Hollywood image of an extraterrestrial being, and a photo of Puerto Rican pastor José Luis de Jesús Miranda who has 666 tattooed on his arm. He remarked that people see visions of Christ everywhere: "se apareció en un comal, en una tortilla" (he appeared on a [tortilla] griddle, in a tortilla). He told of a statue of a saint in the Mexican state of Michoacán that cried tears of blood and how the owner was found to have rigged up a hose to the inside of the statue. He stated that it was easy to believe in religion because this requires little commitment but that believing in a living God is harder. He said many people "A cualquier santo se le van a inclinar" (will be inclined toward/bow to any saint).

The second signs mentioned by the pastor were political signs. He said these signs were evident, and that one didn't have to ask "Walter Pecado" (Walter Sin—making a play on words with the name of Walter Mercado, an exotically-dressed man who appears on Spanish television to announce the day's horoscope). He projected another slide with a collage of photos and drawings of various political leaders and events, including Muamar Gadafi, Hugo Chávez, Evo Morales, and Sun Yat Sen. He stated that political strife is not just something that happens far away in other countries, but could be found close to home in the history of Mexico and Spain. He gave several examples, including Hernán Cortés, the battle of Puebla, and the Pastry War. He said, "Mexico también tiene colita que le pisen," a colloquial expression meaning roughly "Mexico also has its own dirty laundry." He went on to comment that the U.S. government spends millions of dollars on war while people in the U.S. need food. He added that Israel is the only country whose "blueprint" is in the Bible, switching briefly to English.

He went on to describe natural signs, citing deterioration of the environment and waste. He also used English to mimic children saying, "I don't like it," saying that in the U.S. much food is thrown away. He said that those in this country who complain that they are suffering are sinning against God's faithful provision, reminding the congregation that in their country of origin they most likely had much less. He added in English that children "throw a fit," and their parents don't want them to suffer want like they did in their home country. The pastor recalled, "A los seis, siete, ocho años, andaba con mi papá en el campo cosechando azúcar y maíz. Con cien dólares comía toda la familia y tenían como seis hijos" (When I was six, seven, eight years old, I was out with my father in the field harvesting corn and sugar. With one hundred dollars the whole family ate and they had like six children). The pastor wrapped up the sermon by returning to Matt 24:32–36 and used these verses describing the suddenness of Jesus's return to urge the congregation to seek Christ's forgiveness, presenting the plan of salvation. The service ended with the congregation singing the hymn "Yo me rindo a Él," the Spanish version of the well-known invitational "I Surrender All."

The author and her husband visited a regular Sunday service of Iglesia Menonita Pentecostés in Woodburn. This church's worship team was made up of a man playing keyboard and two females singing. Many people in the congregation played tambourines. They had a projector screen but didn't use it, and no song lyrics were made available. Shortly before the announced start time there were about forty-eight people including children present; by end of the service there were 155 including children. About eight of these were elderly people.

At the announced start time, the male leader opened in prayer and then read Psalm 8. This was followed by three sets of music, which lasted about twenty-five minutes. The first two sets were *cadenas de coritos* and the last group was more contemporary worship songs. The first *cadena* included "¡Qué bueno es el Señor!" (How Good the Lord Is!); "Eso es lo que me hace cantar" (That is What Makes Me Sing); "Todo lo que respira" (All That Has Breath); "Esta obra no va a parar" (This Work Isn't Going to Stop); and "El cielo cae, cae" (Heaven Falls, Falls). This first chain of choruses focused on joy, praise, and the work of the Holy Spirit. The second chain included the songs "Ven, ven, ven, Espíritu divino" (Come, Come, Come, Divine Spirit); "Ho- ho- hosana al Hijo de David" (Ho- ho- hosanna to the Son of David); "Quien, quien, quien como Jehová" (Who, Who, Who Like Jehovah); "Su gloria cubrió los cielos y la tierra se llenó" (His Glory Covered the Heavens and the Earth Was Filled); "Para ti, O Jehová" (For You, Oh Jehovah); and "Satúrame Señor con tu Espíritu" (Saturate Me, Lord, with your Spirit). These praise songs focused on worshipping God and asking the Holy Spirit to be present. The last set of songs included "Cuán Bello es el Señor" (How Beautiful is the Lord); "Te amo" (I Love You); "Hay una fuente en mí" (There Is a Fountain in Me); and "Bendito sea el Señor, Dios poderoso," the Spanish translation of "Blessed Be the Lord God Almighty." The theme of these last songs was adoration and love for God.

After singing these songs, congregation members walked up front to give their tithes and offerings, and children helped with this collection. The pastor spoke briefly, saying "Dios es la fuente de todo" (God is the source of everything). He then prayed over the offerings. His prayer included several calques from English that referred to the employment of some of the congregation: "en el fil, la tierra, la norsería" (in the field, the ground, the nursery). Visitors were greeted after offering time. The pastor then read Psalm 3 and prayed again before beginning to preach.

The sermon was based on Psalm 3, which the pastor entitled "Crying Out to God." He said that believers can identify with David, the author of the Psalm, when facing physical and spiritual battles. The pastor identified an internal struggle in David as many were naysaying him and his faith in God. He described David's response, declaring God to be his shield, as a positive confession in the midst of his circumstances. He added that some people need "un escudo chaparrito" (a short shield)— using both a Mexican colloquial term for 'short' and identifying the smaller stature of many in his congregation. He said that as a soldier, David knew that when he lay down out in the field, he might not awaken and recounted that "En nuestros países se metían ladrones a las casas . . . me pasó tres veces en Costa Rica. Aquí no pasa eso pero aquí hay cosas que no nos dejan dormir." (In our countries thieves would break into the houses . . . this happened to me three times in Costa Rica. Here that doesn't happen but there are things that keep us from sleeping). He continued talking about attacks, relating the story of a small town in Guatemala where a group of armed men came in with machine guns, killing everyone they saw and pillaging their belongings. They came upon three pastors, and one said, "Vete, Diablo" (Get out of here, Devil), and the invaders left. The pastor concluded his message on God as reliable protector with prayer.

The author attended a regular Sunday evening service at Nueva Esperanza Conservative Baptist Church in Newport with her husband. The sanctuary was decorated with flags along the sides from many nations, including Peru, Ecuador, the U.S., Italy, Japan, and Mexico. The worship team was made up of the pastor on a keyboard, a female vocalist who also played a tambourine, a male on bass guitar, and a male on drums. This congregation used an LCD projector to show song lyrics and background images. A bulletin was provided. The women in this congregation wore casual clothes and did not use head coverings. At the beginning of the service, there were about twelve adults present, and the number grew to twenty by end of the service.

The service started about fifteen minutes after the announced start time with a pastoral prayer. The pastor announced that one of the church families was moving to Washington State, and then read Psalm 107:1–15. This was followed by a group of songs that the congregation stood to sing. The first was "A ti cantaré" (I Will Sing to You), followed by "Al que me ciñe de poder" (To the One who Girds Me with Strength). Both of these songs spoke of singing to praise God. This was followed by a spiritual warfare song: "Mía es la Victoria" (Mine is the Victory). The last song in this group was a creedal confession: "Yo confieso" (I Confess).

The congregation was seated briefly, then stood again as a woman read Matt 18:15–22. The pastor then went to the piano and played while talking about the scripture just read and its theme of forgiveness. The other musicians returned to the platform, and the congregation stood for "adoración" (worship/adoration). The pastor instructed the congregation to pray silently while he played the piano, then he prayed out loud.

This was followed by two worship songs expressing adoration and dedication: "Palabras de verdad" (Words of Truth) and "Señor yo te quiero entregar lo mejor de mi vida" (Lord, I Want to Surrender the Best of my Life to You). The pastor then prayed again, and the offering was taken. After the offering, the sermon began. The pastor's voice was very quiet, worshipful, and reverent. He never raised it or yelled.

The sermon, about revival, was based on Nehemiah 7–9. The pastor first defined revival as a group of people moved to seek God, then went on to describe this search for God. He gave some brief historic background to the section of Scripture, then compared it to the congregation's lives. Jerusalem was being restored, but there were few people in it. After this introduction, he paused to pray. He went on to relate how the people were successful in reconstructing the walls of Jerusalem, but felt something was still missing so they brought Ezra the priest, and the word of God was read to the whole assembly, as described in chapter 8. He contrasted the Israelite's attentive listening to the public reading of Scripture with people today who have short memories and pay little attention. He noted how the Israelites were moved to weep as they heard Scripture read, asking, "When will we hear? When will that day be?" He said that believers today might hear a sermon on the internet or radio and say to themselves, "Muy espiritual soy" (I am very spiritual) but still do not know or hear what God desires in their lives.

At this point the pastor asked a woman to grab the preschooler who was running down the aisle and yelling. He then continued to describe the joy the Israelites experienced as they began to understand the Law, and how the heads of families went back to study it more. He commented that men are often missing at church and proud of it. He tried to imitate a Mexican accent, saying, "No me siento bien . . . no soy digno . . . que la esposa busque pero yo no" (I don't feel good . . . I'm not worthy . . . let my wife seek but not me). He went on to say that the heads of household in Nehemiah were moved by God and this influenced their whole families.

He encouraged the congregation to seek God, to set time aside to study the Bible, and to come with a willing attitude: "Dispón tu corazón, no vengas con '¿Qué me va a decir? ya lo sé.' Somos a veces bien cara dura . . ." (Make your heart willing, don't come with "What's he going to tell me? I already know it." We're sometimes very cheeky . . .) He then went on to say, "Mi congregacion no quiere avivamiento, no quiere . . . leer la Biblia" (My congregation doesn't want revival, it doesn't want . . . to read the Bible). He went on into chapter 9, encouraging the people to have a change of heart and not let the message be just another sermon, but to provoke true change in their lives, so that people would see that this congregation understood what God wanted for their lives.

The service ended with announcements, which included women's prayer meeting and a special service on Friday. The pastor made a soccer allusion, saying, "¡Los que no están le vamos a dar tarjeta amarilla!" (If you're not there, we're going to give you a yellow card!), and the service was dismissed, having lasted about one hour and forty-five minutes.

The author and her husband visited a regular Sunday afternoon service of the Spanish-speaking congregation at Monmouth Christian Church. Though they arrived early for the service time on the website, the service had already started and the worship songs were just finishing. This church used background tapes for music and an LCD projector for word lyrics. There were three women on the worship team as vocalists: two Anglos and one Latina. When the author arrived, there were two women kneeling in prayer at the altar, and the congregation was singing "Mi universo" (My Universe), a song of dedication to God. After this, a woman led in prayer from the microphone, and many others prayed out loud at same time in their seats. Then a man in the congregation said, "Otra alabanza, Dios quiere otra alabanza" (Another praise, God wants another praise), so the worship team returned to the platform and led in singing "Ven, Espíritu, ven" (Come, Spirit, Come). The children left the sanctuary for their activities.

The pastor went forward and prayed in Spanish, and a young male interpreter translated into English. The interpreter then explained the communication card found in the pew backs. The pastor asked the author and her husband to stand and introduce themselves.

The pastor then read the text for his message, Luke 17:1–10. As he preached in Spanish, the interpreter consecutively translated into English. The pastor used many *mexicanismos* throughout his message. Basing himself on the biblical passage, he said that these were warnings about falling, and that falling was inevitable. He spoke of causing the little ones to sin, and said that the word "pequeño" was not talking about size or age but spiritual maturity, and that it would be better for those harming them to "Amarres al pescuezo . . . lo que dicimos" (Tie it to your neck . . . what we say), referring to the millstone and using a colloquial expression for 'neck.' He went on to look at the other warnings in the passage, to be careful, to repent, to forgive 490 times. He gave some historical background, saying that the Pharisees required themselves to forgive someone three times and that they thought there were very righteous for doing so. He commented on modern attitudes towards revenge: "No me lo va a hacer dos veces" (He's not going to do that to me twice). He admonished the congregation to forgive their brothers, their spouses, children, and friends seventy times seven, and said that forgiveness requires a decision and an attitude of love. He stated that no one can forgive without God's love, and that God is love, and believers, as God's children and followers, therefore, also love.

Moving on to the disciples' request that Jesus increase their faith in verse five, the pastor asked the congregation if they had made that same request. He said that Jesus's response about the mustard seed was a parable and asked the audience to decipher its message. A woman in the audience responded, remembering the previous Sunday's sermon, that faith comes by hearing, and believing in what is unseen. The pastor told the congregation that the previous day he had told his brother-in-law's grandson that he would be a pastor, and that his daughter would be a worship leader, and described these declarations as speaking with faith. He said the tree in the scripture passage would move, not by the believer's power, but by speaking in faith. He paused to ask, "¿Me están siguiendo?" (Are you following me?) and went on to say that Jesus really was not talking about a tree, but using a parable to make a point about faith. He then called on the men present, asking them what they thought, if they were speaking in faith, declaring what was unseen in their lives. He said, "La fe lo va a hacer. No es 'a lo mejor' ¿Eres profeta? Pedro va a estar sano. Así dice la palabra. Las dudas ya no tienen campo aquí." (Faith's going to do it. It's not "well, maybe" Are you a prophet? Peter is going to be healed. That's what the word says. Doubts no longer have any room here.) He was apparently making reference to a member of the congregation who was ill.

The pastor moved on to verses seven through ten, regarding duties and rights. He said that everyone likes to claim their rights, but that God owes nothing to anyone. He orders people to obey, and obedience is not in exchange for something else. He said that he was a useless servant just obeying, that in his own power, he couldn't have been there as a pastor of the church where he grew up, but that God chose his uselessness. He continued, "No nos gusta escuchar esto, verdad?" (We don't like to hear this, right?) He spoke of God's power and sovereignty, saying God chose, formed, called, and sent his people, and that no one is doing God a favor by going to church. People are either obeying or they're not. He referred to the previous week's sermon on "Here I am, send me" and asked the congregation if that was the attitude of their hearts.

The pastor turned to 1 Cor 13:4–8, saying believers do their duty out of love for Him. God is love. "God is" is a substitute for "Love is." He then named all the people in the congregation, saying that God hadn't lost hope in anyone, but that He isn't rude, isn't selfish; He respects people's choices, though He may be saddened by them. The pastor then summed up the three points of the message as sin, faith, and duty. He asked a woman in the congregation to explain the message to an Anglo man in the audience, and closed with prayer. Before the congregation left, a long informal discussion took place in which they decided where to have a potluck barbecue for an upcoming holiday.

The author and her family attended a Friday evening service of the Spanish-speaking congregation of Rogue Valley Fellowship in Medford. It was held in a large sanctuary with multipurpose chairs. The congregation was dressed casually, and many knelt in the pew as they came in, before being seated. At the beginning of the service there were about twenty-five adults present, and about thirty-five half an hour later. Before the service, several people welcomed the author and her family in both Spanish and English, and the pastor introduced himself and took their names. The worship team was made up of a young female playing the keyboard, a man on guitar and another man playing bass guitar, a young woman playing a drum set, a man playing another drum, and one man and one young woman as vocalists. An LCD projector projected song lyrics to two screens, one on the platform and another at the back of the room for the worship team's use. The worship leader was kneeling at the altar until after the third song.

The service started five minutes after the announced start time, with the pastor's admonition to applaud the Lord. He prayed and then read Psalm 62:5–8. The worship team led the song "Eres santo" (You Are Holy), that spoke of reconciliation and forgiveness through Christ's death on the cross. This was followed by "Coronado de Gloria" (Crowned with Glory), about Christ's second coming. The third song in this group was "Los cielos declaran" (The Heavens Declare) with a theme of God's majesty.

The pastor then led in prayer again, and another group of songs followed: "Revísteme" (Clothe/Cover Me), which focused on one's need of God's grace, and "Vengo a adorarte," the Spanish translation of "I Just Came to Worship," a song of worship.

The pastor read portions of Psalm 27, and the congregation sang "Otro color" (A Different Color), which spoke of gratitude and love for God. The pastor then told everyone to greet one another, which they did by shaking hands, hugging, and saying, "Dios le bendiga" (God bless you), while singing the old *corito* "Bienvenida a esta iglesia" (Welcome to This Church), which is a version of "Mi hermano serás" (My Brother You'll Be).

The leader announced that it was time for dancing to the Lord, and invited anyone who wished to do so to go forward. Four people went to the space in front of the altar (but not on the platform) where they jumped, spun, and danced during the next set of songs. One woman in the congregation let out several whoops during this time. The praise songs in this group were a *cadena de coritos*: "Quién, quién, quién como Jehová" (Who, Who, Who Like Jehovah); "Grande es el Señor" (Great is the Lord), a *corito* with a Jewish-style melody and rhythm that mentions dancing; and "Ho- ho- hosana al altísimo" (Ho- ho- hosanna to the Most High).

Announcements followed this music. They included that the childrens' ministry was looking for teachers and that there would be a baptismal service the next day in the Applegate River. The pastor gave the exact address of the park at the river, so that no one would get lost and "decir como los chinitos 'Hon Choy, ¿dónde estoy?'" (say like the Chinese, "Hon Choy, where am I?") (a phrase that rhymes in Spanish, something like "See you later, alligator"). He reminded the congregation of the worship service the following Sunday evening, meetings of the "Hogares de paz" (Homes of Peace) fellowship and Bible study groups, and that communion would be celebrated during the Sunday morning service next week. The pastor introduced the author's family, and the congregation welcomed them with applause. The children were excused from the service.

Prayer was offered for the tithes and offerings, and the congregation sang "Jehová es mi guerrero" (Jehovah is My Warrior), a song of spiritual warfare, while they were being collected. Various people in the congregation shouted out praises to God. The congregation then sang "Gracias, Jesus, por no haber bajado de la cruz" (Thank You Jesus, for not Coming Down from the Cross), which focused on Christ's work on the cross.

The pastor read 1 Cor 1:1–9, which was the first part of the text for his sermon. He said that Paul was urging people to live a consecrated, sanctified life, dedicated to reading Scripture, to prayer, and to testifying. He said the upcoming baptisms were a pact to live a consecrated life. He told a story of a Mexican in a village who was waiting for a bus. To kill time, he decided to go into the Catholic church. The sacristan saw him and showed him around the church. He indicated statues of various saints and told the man of the miracles imputed to each one. They came to a locked door, and the sacristan said that it remained lock because it held a statue of a saint that was good for nothing because it had never done any miracle. The pastor concluded the story by saying that there is no such thing as a good-for-nothing saint, that true saints always have to be in prayer.

The pastor then continued reading in 1 Corinthians chapter one, this time verses 10–17. He said that believers should be united. There may be disagreements, but these should last for moments, not for a lifetime. He urged the congregation to seek sanctification to be able to live in a spirit of unity, that there should not be divisions among them. He went on to focus on verses 17–25, observing that Paul was a man with an excellent Jewish education, but that the cross of Christ is more powerful than any degree, than any course of study. He went on to verses 18–30, asking the congregation to think about where and how they where when Christ called them. "A pesar de lo que éramos, Dios nos escogió" (In spite of what we were, God chose us). He went on to say that while most of them were not rich, they were rich in the power of the Holy Spirit, and quoted the Sermon on the Mount, "Blessed are the poor in spirit."[22] He added, "A veces a los intelectuales les cuesta entender el evangelio. ¡Hasta los niños pueden entenderlo!" (Sometimes it is hard for intellectuals to understand the gospel. Even children can understand it!) He mentioned the controversy over the age of the Earth, and the belief that people evolved from monkeys, saying that some non-biblical theories are foolishness. He stated that the gospel cannot be understood by "[e]l hombre natural . . . porque le es locura. Un doctor con licenciado no lo puede entender" (natural man . . . because it is craziness/foolishness to him. A doctor with a bachelor's degree can't understand it).

The pastor continued with verse 31, saying that no one should be proud of himself, but glory in Christ. He stated that God uses the uneducated, "lo necio" (the foolish). He said that people embarrass the doctor when he can't explain the change in x-rays when God has healed a person, that the doctor can't understand it because the power of God is different. If believers are healed, they can't take any credit for it—all the Glory goes to God. He doesn't share his Glory, and it is a shame that some seem to praise Tylenol more than God.

The pastor observed that Christ has been made wisdom for the believer, and it is Christ who justifies, sanctifies, and redeems. He stated that "Los que no saben leer, saben más de Dios algunos. Se aferran a Dios. No se glorían en su carne." (Those who don't know how to read,

22. Matt 5:3, NIV.

some know more of God. They cling to God. They don't boast in their flesh.)

He then transitioned to the topic of service, quoting Latin contemporary Christian musician Marcos Witt as saying, "El que no sirve, no sirve" (He who doesn't serve, serves for nothing). The pastor added that people who serve need to remember their service is to God, not to the pastor. He admonished the congregation to serve to please God, not their bosses, whereever they were. He imitated a woman, saying, " Mi esposo es un diablo andando—¿cómo le puedo servir?" (My husband is a walking devil—how can I serve him?) He responded, "Serve him as if serving God," adding that wisdom leads to service. He quoted Paul, "Ay de mí, si no predico el evangelio. Me es impuesta gran necesidad" (Woe to me if I do not preach the gospel. I am compelled to preach).[23] He declared that believers need to serve God and realize that the need to serve him leads to joy, adding that people should know what Christians' teeth look like because of their constant smiles. He stated that if people would understand what they are guilty of, they would be different, quoting Romans 5:8, "While we were yet sinners, Christ died for us." He said that believers don't understand that they are saved, that Christ saves from the sin that leads to sins. He said that people must give glory to God, not puffing themselves up for acts of devotion or service. He gave the example of feeling good for being invited at work to eat with "los grandes, los managers" (the big ones, the managers), and the other workers say, "Mira na' más aquél" (Wouldja get a load of that guy), when one greater than any human boss calls people to be with him. He reminded the congregation that they serve one greater than a human being, then asked the congregation whom they served: the brethren? the American pastor? or the Lord? He added that when people understand who God is, they will serve him as a privilege.

The pastor re-read verse 31, saying, "No digas 'gracias a Dios porque soy un burro'. [Diga] 'Antes era un burro pero Dios me está dando sabiduría.'" (Don't say "thank God because I'm a burro." [Say] "Before I was a burro, but God is giving me wisdom.") He then stated that Christ was left without power when he went to heaven, and that the believer must activate the power for him to act, adding that if the church does not act, people will go to hell. He said that the church has to act to release Christ's

---

23. 1 Cor 9:16, pastor's paraphrase.

power on the earth, asserting that God is all-powerful, but without the church he doesn't have power, the church has to liberate it.

He went back to verse 30 again, and told the congregation to lift their heads high because they were children of God, privileged ones. He spoke of the parade in El Salvador on September 15, for independence day, saying the marchers carry the flag with their heads lifted high. He said, "Somos extraterrestres, no somos de este mundo . . . no más estamos esperando el camión, a ver qué hora llegue" (We are extraterrestrials, we are not of this world . . . we're just waiting for the bus, wondering what time it will come). The pastor concluded with prayer, and the worship team went forward to lead in a last song, but it was not projected, and the author was unable to decipher the words.

The author and her family attended a Sunday morning worship service at New Hope Bible Church, a Mennonite Brethren congregation in Grants Pass. They were warmly welcomed in the parking lot, at the door, and as they made their way to the sanctuary. The service started at the announced time. The worship team was made up of an Anglo woman at the piano, three male Hispanic adults playing guitars, one female Anglo vocalist, one male Hispanic as vocalist and leader, and a male Hispanic teen on the drums. The lyrics for choruses and a responsive reading were projected with an LCD projector, and when hymns were sung, the page numbers for both the Spanish and English hymnals were announced. A bulletin with a sermon outline and spaces to complete was provided. Most of those present and seated in the middle of the sanctuary were middle-aged and older Anglos. There were about ten Hispanics in the pews, in addition to those on the worship team. There were also people present who appeared to be of Asian and African descent. (The pastor later confirmed that there were several immigrants from Africa in the congregation.) The attendees were dressed casually, with most women wearing dresses or skirts, but several wearing slacks. None of the women wore a head covering.

The service began with the Latino worship leader using an interpreter to call on a man in the congregation to open in prayer. He did so, in English. After the prayer, several songs, all focusing on worship, were sung. The first was the hymn "Holy, Holy, Holy," sung bilingually out of the Spanish and English hymnals simultaneously. Each person sang in the language he or she preferred, and the author observed some of the younger Anglos using the Spanish hymnal. This was followed by two worship choruses sung in English only: "Heart of Worship" and "How Great is our God." The congregation then opened both hymnals again and sang "How Great Thou Art" in both languages at the same time. This group of songs concluded with "I Love you Lord," for which lyrics were projected in English, though the congregation also sang it in Spanish without lyrics provided. This service was different from all the other Latino services attended in that none of the worshippers raised their hands during the singing.

These worship songs were followed by a prayer offered in Spanish by the worship leader. The pastor then gave a word of welcome and led the congregation in a responsive reading that was projected on the screen. The pastor spoke only English throughout the service. After this, there were announcements, which included a Spanish-language service on Friday evening, questions about a yard sale, and a reminder to check the bulletin and bulletin board for information on birthdays. The pastor asked if any had prayer requests. All those who shared requests spoke in Spanish, and they were interpreted into English for the monolingual English speakers in the congregation. The ushers received the tithes and offerings, and the pastor prayed for them and the prayer requests mentioned.

This prayer was followed by two more hymns sung in English and Spanish at the same time: "Wonderful Grace of Jesus," which focused on God's grace and "'Tis so sweet to Trust in Jesus," a hymn about trust. After this, the pastor invited the children to sit in the front rows for the children's story, which was Daniel and the lion's den. The congregation then said a formal goodbye to several students who were heading to Fresno Pacific College. This was followed by a missions report focused on Ethiopia, and a pastoral prayer.

In preparation for the sermon, the pastor asked a woman to read Daniel 6. She read off her cell phone from *The Message*[24] version of the Bible. The author observed another woman in the pews reading along on her cell phone. The pastor led in prayer yet again, directing the congregation to silently ask God to teach them. The pastor reminded the congregation they could follow the sermon outline in the bulletin, then gave some historical background about Daniel and the other Jews in exile. He said they had trust issues, as their governors and leaders were not Jewish, and they always asked themselves if the leaders could

24. Eugene Peterson, *Message Bible*, application for iPhone, Tecarta, Inc., 2010.

be trusted. He added, by way of example, "If you are a Mexican you'd like the president or vice president to be a Latino, thinking he might understand you." He told a story of jumping into his father's arms from varying heights during his childhood on a farm, and how he eventually was willing to jump a great distance because he trusted his father to catch him. The pastor then told the congregation, "Only you know the height from which God is asking you to jump into his arms. Will you jump?" The pastor likened Daniel's choices as a young man regarding following a strict diet to Daniel learning to trust God for a short jump, and his persistence in prayer as learning to hear God's voice and making longer "faith jumps." When Daniel faced the lions' den he had already trusted God to "catch" him on multiple leaps of faith. The pastor stated, "God is more concerned that we learn about him than about our happiness." He then mentioned some of the persons of great faith in Heb 12 and reminded the congregation, "If you're facing a bigger jump, God has had you make smaller ones already. The question behind every jump is 'can you trust me?'"

The service ended with a final prayer, and everyone sang "Trust and Obey" in both languages from a hymnal.

The author and her husband visited a regular Sunday evening service at Templo Betania in Ontario. There were only three people (in addition to the author and her husband) present at the announced start time, but about twenty had arrived by the time the sermon started. All the women had long hair, and most were wearing long skirts, except one younger woman who wore jeans. They knelt at their pews in prayer for a few minutes before being seated. The pastor was on vacation. The worship leader, a young man, was wearing a dress shirt and tie, though the temperature that day was over one hundred degrees, and the building was not air-conditioned. The worship leader offered cold water bottles to the researcher and her husband, as he greeted them in English by saying, "God bless you." There was Mexican-style *cumbia* with Christian lyrics as background music before the service started. There were many tambourines and English Bibles in pews, as well as a few hymnals. This church did not use a bulletin or any type of projector.

About fifteen minutes after the announced start time, the musicians had not arrived. The worship leader announced that the service would begin anyhow. He led the congregation in singing a cappella. The first chorus described heaven: "Mira que bonita es la nueva Jerusalén" (see

How Pretty the New Jerusalem Is). The second *corito* spoke of renewed strength: "Los que esperan en Jehová" (They That Wait Upon the Lord). The third song was "En la viña del Señor," the Spanish translation of "I Want to Be a Worker for the Lord," sung from a hymnal that had lyrics only. The lack of accompaniment severely impacted the musical quality of the worship songs.

At this point, the musicians arrived. They were two adult Latino men. One played a guitar and the other a bass guitar. After they had set up their instruments, they accompanied the young worship leader in several more songs, though they were obviously unrehearsed. As the congregation sang, the worship leader and a woman in the congregation occasionally yelled out praise to God. The first set of songs was a *cadena de coritos*: "Vamos a alabar a Jehová con pandero y danza," (We're Going to Worship Jehovah with Tambourine and Dance) and "Así, así, así se alaba a Dios," (This is How, This is How, This is How One Praises God) that had a theme of joyous worship. People in the congregation used the tambourines in the pews to join in with the musicians. The next song was "Yo no sé a lo que tú has venido, pero yo vine a alabar a Dios" (I Don't Know Why You Came, But I Came to Praise the Lord). This continued straight into "¡Pero qué felicidad!" (But What Happiness!)—both these songs spoke of coming to church purposefully to worship. The next song invited the Holy Spirit to come: "Bienvenido, Santo Espíritu a este lugar," the Spanish translation of "Holy Spirit, Thou Art Welcome in This Place." This was followed by a slower song "Te alabaré para siempre" (I Will Worship You Always), which focused on praise for the freedom given by God. The next song was the *corito* "El maestro de Galilea está pasando por aquí" (The Master/Teacher of Galilee is Passing Through Here); "Así se siente la presencia de Dios" (This is What the Presence of God Feels Like); "El Espíritu de Dios está en este lugar" (The Spirit of God is in This Place); and "En el principio el Espíritu de Dios" (In the beginning, the Spirit of God). All these songs proclaimed the presence of God in the worship service. The last song in the group spoke about heaven, echoing the very first song of the service: "Jerusalén, que bonita eres" (Jerusalem, How Pretty You Are).

During the last few songs, the worship leader held his hands out to the side and he began to tremble uncontrollably and emit a loud uncontrolled chattering yell in which no words were discernable, yet it did not seem like speaking in tongues. Several others sitting in the front also yelled out. When the music stopped, these manifestations also ceased. Congregational prayer followed, and then they sang two more songs: "Levanto mis manos" (I Raise my Hands), "Tú eres digno o Dios" (You Are Worthy oh God). The first spoke of finding strength despite circumstances when raising one's hands in worship, and the second of God's worthiness of worship.

Testimony time, open to anyone present, was next. A woman praised God because her hospitalized son had stabilized. The worship leader testified to getting a job at a school. Another woman read a Psalm aloud, and a third wanted to sing a song during testimony time. She launched out a cappella, expecting the guitarist to find the key she was singing in and follow her. He was unsuccessful. The song was the chorus of "Soy bautizado" (I am Baptized), focusing on setting one's self apart from the world. Another woman stated that, "desde el viernes el Espíritu Santo no me ha dejado" (since Friday night the Holy Spirit hasn't left me alone) and wanted the congregation to sing the coritos "Esta obra no va a parar" (This Work Isn't Going to Stop), "El cielo cae, cae" (Heaven Falls, Falls), and "Yo le alabo de corazón . . . con la voz . . . con las manos . . . con los pies" (I Worship Him with my Heart . . . with my Voice . . . with my Hands . . . with my Feet).

The leader then asked the congregation to share their prayer requests, which included their homes, the church, people who were on vacation, the family of a young man who had drowned, the unsaved, and everyone present. The leader asked a man in the congregation to pray, which he did. The musicians began another set of songs, after one of them asked, "¿Todos aquí hablan mexicano?" (Does everyone here speak Mexican?) This final group of songs included songs "Espíritu santo, caiga" (Fall, Holy Spirit), "Hay momentos que las palabras no alcanzan" (There are Moments When Words aren't Enough), and "Mi pensamiento eres tu Señor" (You are my Thinking, Lord). The first song encouraged the arrival of the Holy Spirit, the second focused on love for God, and the third expressed a worshipful focus on God.

The leader prayed that the Holy Spirit would fall on the service, and introduced the author and her husband as guests. The special speaker, substituting for the pastor on vacation, began preaching one hour after the service's announced start time. The sermon was roughly based on the book of Habakkuk. The preacher gave some historical background, saying that Habakkuk lived in time of Jeremiah. Habakkuk called out to God, in light of the violence of the times, as the Israelites were being overcome by the Babylonians. The speaker likened this violence to current events in Ciudad Juárez, Mexico, and Los Angeles, CA. He said that gangs, drugs, and drug cartels were the source of this violence. He stated that in Habakkuk's day, the wealthy took advantage of the poor, and that it was just the same as the present time. He mentioned the recession, the ethical failures of the banks, and government bailouts. He said that believers have always suffered and told the story of loaning one thousand dollars to a fellow believer, supposedly for two weeks, who had never re paid the loan, adding that believers get discouraged and wonder whom they can trust. The preacher said that the only trustworthy one is God. He commented on Habakkuk's prayer, which might seem irreverent, but the preacher claimed it indicated utter confidence in God. The speaker asserted that God answers prayers when and as he chooses, and told the story of God's provision of a job for him that he didn't want initially, but which turned out to be a blessing. He reminded the congregation that prayer also involves listening, and that believers shouldn't be like the child Samuel who didn't recognize God's voice.

The preacher indicated that God's answer to Habakkuk about the Babylonians was bad news for Habakkuk, and that sometimes believers get bad news—sometimes in the form of a dreaded phone call. He briefly spoke in tongues and then mentioned a grandchild. He urged the congregation to stick with God throughout suffering, stating that God uses suffering to prune out bad characteristics, and that peace is found only in God. He told a story in which God had revealed the coming death of an in-law to him, which was related to a group of witches in Veracruz, Mexico. After this, the speaker gave an altar call, and the service concluded.

DISCUSSION AND ANALYSIS

The following section is divided into three parts that could roughly be described as *who, what,* and *how.* The first subsection focuses on the participants of the worship services; the second on the elements of the services and themes emerging in them; and the last subsection describes the style of the worship services. In each subsection, observations made by other researchers about Protestant Hispanic worship services are presented, along with the information collected in the present study.

Participants

Regarding Pentecostal Hispanic churches, Soliván observes, "An appreciation of the priesthood of all believers (laymen and laywomen, as well as clergy, children, young adults, and the elderly) provides the entire congregation with an opportunity to play a role in the worship of the community."[25] Costas described Pentecostal services in Latin America as "*intensamente participatorio*" (*intensely participatory* [emphasis in the original]).[26] Darino makes a similar assertion regarding Hispanic Baptists: "A Baptist believes that the evolution of spiritual life finds its strongest foundation in the doctrinal conception of the priesthood of every believer, which shapes itself into sense and practice within the parameters of the local congregation."[27] He expands, saying, "the church is not a building, but people. So worship is an encounter with God, all together in the sanctuary, all of us responding together to the Divine Presence, with a profound sense of power and grace within. This is where the Baptist doctrinal conception of congregationalism and universal priesthood of believers is manifested. This is important because it marks the Baptist idea of worship. The Baptist worship service is a congregational service where 'everyone' participates. [These concepts] should not be considered exclusive of the Baptists, the fact remains that these have always been part of Baptist identity."[28]

The participatory nature of Latino churches was clearly observed in the churches in Oregon. Eight congregations had people playing tambourines from their seats during worship songs. Worship leaders or pastors in fifteen congregations admonished the congregation to participate by clapping, repeating a phrase, sharing a prayer request or testimony, or otherwise joining in the worship service. Teens participated actively in the worship service in eight of the services, through music or drama; one gave a missions report and another served as interpreter for the pastor's sermon. Women participated in multiple capacities: some were ushers or greeters; others led in Scripture reading or prayer; several shared testimonies or special songs; some gave announcements; served as interpreter; many participated in worship teams; some held leadership

---

25. "Hispanic Pentecostal Worship," 59.
26. "La realidad de la iglesia," 50.
27. "Hispanic Baptist Worship," 75.
28. Ibid., 78–79.

roles such as Sunday School teachers or directors; and at the Cornelius Assembly of God congregation, a woman was the invited guest preacher.

Children were active participants in the services as well. In two services, children's choirs sang specials. In four congregations, children were part of the worship team. In one church, children helped collect tithes and offerings. The importance of the children was also demonstrated in the activities provided for them, both outside of the worship service, as seen in the announcements, and during the service time. Fifteen of the congregations had special programs just for children during all or part of their services. In three cases, children were dismissed after they were called to the front and prayed over, and in one of these three, there was a special children's story time immediately prior to their dismissal.

The author regularly requires her mostly-Anglo Spanish language students to attend worship services in Spanish. They always comment about the presence of children in the services and the disruption they cause due to their movements and the noise they make. Interestingly, the author observed three services in which the pastor or the ushers directly intervened to control the disruptive behavior of children.

Soliván describes the development of lay leaders in Pentecostal churches, including children and youth, through mid-week or smaller services in which they are given opportunities to sing, lead, and speak.[29] The author observed this at Iglesia de Jesucristo in Forest Grove, the congregation that is now Vida Church, and even at a main Sunday morning service at the Iglesia Evangélica Cristo Viene in Hillsboro. Soliván also observes, "At times, local lay leaders who have demonstrated a gift for preaching are asked to sharpen their preaching gifts during weeknight services."[30] This was the case at the midweek service of Iglesia de Jesucristo, and at the regular Sunday evening worship service at the Foursquare congregation and Ontario's AOG Templo Betania.

Elements and Themes of Worship Services

Though none of the churches studied followed a "liturgy" in the traditional sense, they nevertheless had many common elements. The following section summarizes information from other researchers on Latino Protestant churches, along with observations from this study of Oregon

29. "Hispanic Pentecostal Worship," 49.

30. Ibid., 54.

churches, about the types of activities that compose worship services, and themes that emerged. Elements include:

- Baptism;
- Communion;
- Prayer;
- Collection of tithes and offerings;
- Testimonies;
- Greeting one another;
- An invitation or altar call;
- The sermon; and
- Music.

In addition, common themes expressed in various ways were otherworldliness, spiritual warfare, the desire for the Holy Spirit to be present and move in the service, and the expectation of the imminent return of Christ and his judgment.

Santillán Baert observes that water baptism is one of two sacraments consistently observed among Hispanic United Methodist congregations in the U.S. She comments extensively on it, noting the relational ties created by choosing godparents at baptism, the practice of baptizing babies, and the extended family commitments created in the entire congregation by baptism.[31] In the author's experience, few Latino Protestant churches outside of the mainline churches practice infant baptism, preferring baptism to serve as a symbol of a decision to follow Christ made consciously by an older child, youth, or adult. In two of the churches in this study, the pastors made reference in their sermons to baptism. One said that it was a step toward Christian maturity, and the other described it as a promise to live a consecrated life. Of the churches in this study, only Rogue Valley Fellowship mentioned plans for a baptismal service. Given the emphasis on baptism in Baptist churches and their proportion in this study, it is surprising that more water baptisms were not announced.

---

31. "Hispanic United Methodist Church," 62–63.

The other sacrament mentioned by Santillán Baert as a regular practice in Latino United Methodist churches is communion.[32] Gómez strongly criticizes the infrequency and method in which the Last Supper is observed in Protestant Latino churches: "In Protestant mestizo worship services, Holy Communion is an awkward attachment to a regular preaching service. Holy Communion occurs infrequently. Often the Sacrament takes place hurriedly, without mystery and power. Because of the de-emphasis on Holy Communion, the Protestant mestizo gives little attention to remembering our Lord Jesus's suffering, sacrifice, and death."[33]

Indeed, only two of the churches in this study served communion, though a third announced that it would be celebrated at a service the following week. In both services where the Last Supper was served, the pastor spent a considerable amount of time on it. At Luz del Pueblo Southern Baptist, the pastor summarized Roman Catholic beliefs regarding the bread and wine, and stressed that Protestants believe they are symbolic of Christ's sacrifice. In this congregation, oyster crackers were used for communion bread. Interestingly, Santillán Baert commented on what type of bread was used, and its cultural implications: "Tortillas have been used in some of the majority churches and by organizers of events beyond the local church, as communion bread, but I have not yet seen tortillas used in Hispanic churches. Have we as Hispanics been carefully taught that only bread can be used for communion?"[34] It would be interesting to discuss with those responsible for preparing communion at Luz del Pueblo if their use of oyster crackers had a symbolic purpose.[35]

The other church that served communion was the Christian and Missionary Alliance congregation in Hood River. The pastor was preaching through the gospel of John and had come to the narration of the Last Supper. He had put forth a lot of effort to recreate this evening meal in the upper room in the sanctuary—dim lighting, candles, a cup and bread on the front tables. The observation of communion was an

32. Ibid., 60–62.

33. "Mestizo Spirituality," 90.

34. "Hispanic United Methodist Church," 62.

35. The author associates them with seafood, especially clam chowder, and the coast. This association is undoubtedly culturally bound.

integral part of the sermon, although the pastor also read the warnings from 1 Cor 11 about proper participation in it.

All of the worship services included prayer. Most began with a prayer; however, five services did not have any kind of prayer until later in the service, just before the sermon. City Bible had no public prayer until after the message had been preached. None of the prayers were scripted; they were all spontaneous.

Costas described giving in Pentecostal services in Latin America as sacrificial: "La colecta refleja el carácter sacrificial del culto pentecostal: en ella, los fieles (la mayoría de los cuales son extremadamente pobres) se desprenden de lo poco que tienen para ofrecerlo como 'ofrenda de olor suave' al Señor." (The collection reflects the sacrificial character of the Pentecostal worship service: in it, the faithful [the majority of whom are extremely poor] give away the little that they have, offering it as a "fragrant offering" to the Lord.)[36] The author did not observe that tithes or offerings were collected in four of the churches. At Reedwood Friends, she believes this was because the congregation was a very small group that was just beginning. In two other services, she arrived after the service had already started, and it is possible that they were collected at the very beginning of the service (although this is not a common practice). At Templo Betania AOG in Ontario, the pastor was on vacation, and it is possible that the young lay leader forgot this part of the service. Prior to the collection in five of the services, a scripture referring to giving was read.

Many of the churches were involved in some type of fund-raising efforts, ranging from car washes, sale of tostadas or burritos, to raffles and yard sales. At Iglesia de Jescristo in Forest Grove, the specific need for cleaning supplies was mentioned, along with a suggested donation of $10, and people immediately went forward to make a contribution and announced publicly how much they were giving. Several mentioned special needs, including a congregation member who had lost his job, support of a radio ministry, money for the building rental, and support of a satellite campus. Some gave reports on previous giving such as missions or faith promises. In addition, one church encouraged participation in an upcoming financial management class, and at Village Baptist the congregation was told that they should not let finances keep them from attending a camp.

36. "La realidad de la iglesia evangélica latinoamericana," 51.

Beyond the Bible verses, several churches made additional comments about tithes and offerings, and money. The sermon at City Bible was entitled "Opening the Windows of Heaven" and was part of a series on finances. It included scripture passages from both the Old and New Testaments. At Salvados para Servir, the belief that "God will duplicate your tithe" was expressed. At Casa del Padre, the speaker "rebuked the devourer" as people gave their tithes and offerings. Both the pastor in Hermiston and in Forest Grove stated that it was easy to earn money in the United States compared to the countries of origin of the congregation. The speaker at Iglesia del Pueblo in Cornelius emphasized that people need Christ no matter how wealthy they are; the worship leader at Elim Restauración and the pastor of Rogue Valley Fellowship said that most of the congregation was poor, and the speaker at Templo Betania said that the wealthy oppress the poor. There was an undercurrent of resentment toward wealth, coupled with an admonition to be grateful for the opportunities to earn in this country, and a strong message of dependence on God as provider.

According to several authors, testimonies are a regular and important part of Latino church services. González describes them as a significant element in Hispanic Pentecostal worship,[37] as does Costas for Latin American Pentecostal services.[38] Soliván says that children in Pentecostal churches practice giving testimonies in smaller group settings,[39] and further explains:

> Another important part of the community's worship service is the *testimonios*. During most services the congregation is asked if anyone has a word of testimony to the love and mercy of the Lord. Testimonies of healing, economic provision, and expressions of thanksgiving for answered prayers and mercies are shared with the congregation. This is the place in the community's life in worship where both the burdens of the congregation and the joy of answered prayer are shared with others as all seek congregational support in the form of prayers. This time of testimony is also the place where one gains insight into the common and daily struggles of the community and the concrete ways God has answered their prayers.[40]

37. "Hispanic Worship: An Introduction," 12.
38. "La realidad de la iglesia evangélica latinoamericana," 50.
39. "Hispanic Pentecostal Worship," 49.
40. Ibid., 53.

Santillán Baert mentions testimony services as one special type of service held by Latino United Methodists.[41]

Eight of the congregations in this study had testimonies as part of their services. Not all of these eight were Pentecostal churches; Reedwood Friends, Iglesia de Jesucristo, Mennonite Ministerios Restauración, the Christian and Missionary Alliance church in Hood River, and Madras Conservative Baptist all had people give testimonies during their services. None of the largest cell-group churches included testimonies during the worship service, and the author postulates that this type of sharing has been shifted to the more intimate setting of the cell group.

Eight of the congregations included a time to greet one another in their services. This was most often done with handshakes, hugs, and the words "God bless you." In two congregations, an old *corito* that speaks of shaking hands and recognizing the other as one's brother in Christ, was sung during this time. In most congregations the author visited, people also greeted one another as they came in, in the same manner. Santillán Baert writes the following about greetings in Hispanic United Methodist churches:

> Does the passing of the peace during the worship service . . . have a new or deeper meaning for Hispanics? The question arises because from the time Hispanics enter the church building the passing of the peace begins with the embracing, the handshakes, and the holy kiss. And the people will do it again after the service with the same people. They do not wait until the appropriate time in the worship service, even though they will participate again in the ritual of friendship if the order of service or the liturgy so prescribes it. It is a vital part of the faith experience of Hispanics.[42]

While the author observed these friendly greetings before, during, and after the services in Oregon, she does not believe that the pastors or congregations conceive of them as a "passing of the peace"—this is more commonly practiced in mainline congregations. This practice in the churches in this study is more along the lines of González's description of the church as family: "It is rather a vast assemblage of people who are related in a multiplicity of ways, so that they have a sense of belonging, but not necessarily of excluding others."[43] The church service was an op-

41. "Hispanic United Methodist Church," 60.

42. Ibid., 64–65.

43. "Hispanic Worship: An Introduction," 22.

portunity to greet members of one's biological and spiritual families, as well as to extend a hand of fellowship and welcome to newcomers.

Soliván characterizes the altar call as the climatic point of evangelistic services in Hispanic Pentecostal churches, which are often held on Sunday evenings.[44] Costas also describes three types of sermons in Pentecostal churches in Latin America, one of which ends in an invitation: "Los sermones son mayormente de tipo 'evangelístico' (tienen como objetivo presentar los rudimentos del evangelio y llamar a una aceptación pública del mismo)" [The sermons are mostly of the "evangelistic" type (they have as their objective presenting the rudiments of the gospel and calling for a public acceptance of the same)].[45] Santillán Baert claims that in United Methodist Latino churches, "There need not be a revival or an evangelistic service for the preacher to have an altar call."[46] Darino also notes an emphasis on altar calls among Hispanic Baptists, attributing it to the denomination's origin "in the 'fire of revival.'"[47]

Only three of the churches in this study had an actual call to the altar. They were all Assemblies of God—Templo Betania in Ontario, Iglesia del Pueblo in Cornelius, and the now-defunct combined AOG-Apostolic congregation Ministerio de Vida Eterna. However, the pastors of City Bible, Nueva Esperanza CBNW in Hermiston, Luz del Pueblo Southern Baptist, Casa del Padre, and the Christian and Missionary Alliance church in Hood River all gave invitations to people to make a decision for Christ toward the end of the sermon.

Nearly all researchers describe the sermon as the focal point of Latino Protestant worship services. According to Soliván, "Probably the most important part of the service is the preaching of the Word,"[48] adding that, "The preacher in the Hispanic Pentecostal church sees himself/herself as a messenger from God with a word for the people."[49] In United Methodist services, "For many Hispanics, the sermon is the heart of the worship service. Congregations expect powerful and inspiring messages. The preacher is free to be genuinely expressive."[50] Gómez concurs:

44. "Hispanic Pentecostal Worship," 54.
45. "La realidad de la iglesia evangélica latinoamericana," 47.
46. "Hispanic United Methodist Church," 71.
47. "Hispanic Baptist Worship," 80.
48. "Hispanic Pentecostal Worship," 53.
49. Ibid., 54.
50. "Hispanic United Methodist Church," 71.

"The preached Word of God . . . become[s] important in the religious life of the Protestant mestizo."[51] Costas describes a similar importance of the sermon in Protestant churches in Latin America in what he calls "repetitive worship services" (meaning they are mostly copies of services in the home countries of missionaries):

> El culto, que responde mayormente a una situación caracterizada por la poca reflexión teológica y el énfasis en el avivamiento, gira en torno al sermón; que se espera produzca una serie determinada de respuestas determinadas. La estructura refleja una escala ascendente, que culmina con el sermon. Hay una especie de sistema controlado en el que se manipulan las variables más importantes—en este caso los himnos, las oraciones, la lectura bíblica—para asegurar el resultado que se ha predicho. Los elementos culturales simplemente "preparan" el terreno para el sermon.

> [The service, that mostly responds to a situation characterized by little theological reflection and emphasis on revival, revolves around the sermon; which it is hoped produces a set series of set responses. There is a type of controlled system in which the most important variables are manipulated—in this case the hymns, the prayers, the Bible reading—in order to assure the predicted result. Cultural elements simply "prepare" the soil for the sermon.][52]

The sermon did seem to be the high point of all the services the author attended, with the exception of Reedwood Friends, which did not have a sermon. Though Friends' Meetings sometimes practice "unprogrammed worship," this meeting was not indicated as such. Based on the pastor's comments, the author believes that he ran the service more like a Bible study due to the small group size and the fact that the majority of the group was new believers.

Thirteen of the sermons were based on passages from the New Testament (seven in the Gospels, five in the epistles, and one from Acts), nine from the Old Testament (six in the prophets, one from Psalms, and two from books of history), and two messages used portions from both Testaments. The messages ranged across many topics, but some trends emerged. Eight could roughly be categorized as describing God's faithfulness and urging the believer to trust; three dealt with humility and

---

51. "Mestizo Spirituality," 89.

52. "La realidad de la iglesia evangélica latinoamericana," 45–46.

submission to God; two focused on Christ's second coming; and two urged Christian maturity.

One of the consistent criticisms of researchers on Latin American and U.S. Latino Protestant churches is the imposition of European or U.S. worship styles, particularly in the area of music. Regarding Spanish-speaking America, Costas writes, "La música es . . . de extracción foránea." (The music is . . . of foreign extraction.)[53] He goes on to protest, "En nuestro día [1974] resulta intolerable el imperialismo cultural que impone formas que han tenido un origen extranjero y responden a necesidades de otra cultura y época." (In our day [1974] the cultural imperialism that imposes forms that have had a foreign origin and respond to the needs of another culture and era is intolerable.)[54] Darino describes U.S. Hispanic Baptist churches in the first half of the twentieth century along similar lines:

> From the cultural point of view in the majority of Hispanic contexts, worship was European-North American until the middle of this century. Hispanics worshiped according to established patterns. . . . as they opened their hearts to the gospel, they also received the forms of worship. Christian organizations that emerged from last century's revival began sending missionaries to different countries. Those missionaries . . . took not only the gospel with them, but also patterns of worship from different sources, both European and North American. In reality these patterns were transplanted . . . evidenced in hymnology, in the liturgy used at the time, and in the style of music and worship.[55]

He adds, "From a cultural point of view there are certain elements in worship such as music, for example, that the worshiper needs to own in order for the act of praise to be truly significant,"[56] and "So here we find the Hispanic Baptist, singing a hymn in church and listening to his or her 'real music' at home. It is the latter that finds an echo in the soul."[57] These criticisms imply that it is not just the translation of lyrics from English that is objectionable, but the musical style and instrumentation as well.

53. "La realidad de la iglesia evangélica latinoamericana," 46.

54. Ibid., 48.

55. "Hispanic Baptist Worship," 80.

56. Ibid., 81.

57. Ibid., 83.

On the other hand, the pre-eminent leader of Latino worship music, Marcos Witt, states specifically about Latin American churches, "Debemos honrar a ciertos grupos y denominaciones, como nuestros hermanos los bautistas, los presbiterianos y los metodistas, que por años han hecho esta labor de preparar, impulsar y apoyar a los músicos de sus congregaciones." (We should honor certain groups and denominations, like our brothers the Baptists, the Presbyterians and the Methodists, that for years have done this labor of preparing, propelling and supporting the musicians of their congregations.)[58] Indeed, the United Methodist church made serious efforts to include Latino composers in their hymnals and chorus books.[59] In more general terms of worship practices among Hispanic Presbyterians, Chávez Sauceda states, "The assumption that Hispanic Presbyterian congregations have lost all ties with their cultural heritage may move too quickly to label them cultural victims and overlook some of the strengths of the Hispanic congregation."[60]

The congregations in this study do not hold true to the accusations that their worship music is made up mostly of hymns translated into Spanish. Only six churches sang hymns translated from English. Interestingly, two hymns were heard in two different churches: "How Great Thou Art" and "Power in the Blood."

The Mennonite Brethren congregation in Grants Pass sang five hymns, more than any other congregation in this study. The use of hymns is dramatically declining in most English-speaking congregations as well, so this church is an anomaly. This is the only congregation that could be accused of "imposing" a form of worship of the dominant culture on the Spanish-speaking worshipers, but it should be remembered that Hispanics and Anglos worship together, and that over half of this blended congregation is Anglo. They accomplish this simultaneous worship by singing the same hymn in Spanish and English, out of two different hymnals. The author believes that the motivation to use these hymns, in addition to style preference, might be a practical matter. This church had an Anglo pianist, who may have needed the music provided in the hymnal to accompany the songs,[61] and using two hymnals with many of the same hymns also facilitated simultaneous worship.

58. *¿Qué hacemos con estos músicos?*, 40.

59. Santillán Baert, "Hispanic United Methodist Church," 65–68.

60. "Becoming a Mestizo Church," 91.

61. The author suggests this because of her own experience as worship leader in a Hispanic congregation several years ago, prior to the widespread use of the internet.

Seven of the churches in this study described themselves as purposefully bilingual. It would seem that these congregations would seek out songs available in both English and Spanish for use during worship services. This was the practice at New Hope Bible in Grants Pass. All but one of the songs at Iglesia del Pueblo AOG in Cornelius were Spanish translations of contemporary worship choruses in English, as were many at what is now Vida Church. However, the other bilingual congregations didn't sing in English during the services observed by the author (although at Esperanza y Vida en Jesucristo in Hood River, one of the Spanish worship songs had an English translation at the bottom of the slide).

The presence of bilingual people who lead worship has led to an interesting phenomenon. The author has observed a worship leader translating the words of a contemporary English-language worship song to Spanish, because she had heard it in English, liked it, and wanted to teach it to her congregation. This not only leads to multiple translations of English-language worship songs, some better than others, but also is strong evidence that these songs are not imposed by outsiders on the Latino congregations. Many bilingual Hispanics listen to Christian music in English and Spanish, and draw from both for their worship repertoire.

Several researchers mentioned *coritos* as an authentically Latin style of worship music. Soliván defines *coritos* as "short and repetitive spiritual songs that often tell a story, but always include praise—usually a psalm or other portion of scripture. The *corito* is an indigenous Hispanic Pentecostal singing style. . . ."[62] Aponte, in his article about this musical genre states, "The definition of *corito* is a simple one; it is a short, popular chorus sung most often in communal worship settings. While in many Hispanic Protestant congregations *coritos* have been collected into song books for ready reference, this is not how they started. Such collections are distinguished from hymnals by the Hispanic Protestant faith communities themselves."[63] He adds that, "Often the exact origin

---

She cannot play piano by ear, and with difficulty using only chord sets. She preferred to use written music, and developed a collection of worship songs with sheet music that were originally written in English and had been translated into Spanish.

62. "Hispanic Pentecostal Worship," 52–53.

63. "*Coritos* as Active Symbol," 60.

of specific songs is unknown, but they are seen to have risen from the *pueblo*."[64]

Coritos were sung in eleven of the services in this study, including AOG, Friends, Mennonite, and independent Pentecostal congregations, as well as one with ties to CBNW and one of Apostolic extraction. However, this is less than half of the congregations. What the small number of hymns and relative small percentage of *coritos* reveal is missing in the literature: a tidal wave of worship music written by Latinos in the U.S. and in the Latin America, in Spanish, has washed over the congregations since about 1995.[65] Marcos Witt wrote, in 1995, "[Dios] está haciendo énfasis hoy, que el tiempo de la canción ha venido al pueblo hispano a través de todo el mundo" ([God] is emphasizing today, that the time of the song has come to the Hispanic people throughout all the world).[66] Witt is the likely the best-known of these *salmistas* (psalmists), and was instrumental in promoting this growth through schools and conferences for church musicians throughout Latin America,[67] but there are many others. These songs were the overwhelming choice of worship leaders throughout the Protestant Hispanic churches of Oregon.

Several researchers have mentioned different types of music and instruments in Latino churches—mariachi bands, the use of maracas and drums as in the Caribbean,[68] and guitars.[69] Darino asserts,

> From a cultural point of view there are certain elements in worship such as music, for example, that the worshiper needs to own in order for the act of praise to be truly significant. For the Hispanic, a return to roots comes, perhaps, with the use of a guitar in the place of an organ or a piano. At the same time drums are introduced, reflecting a combination of influences that have shaped our culture: African, Central and South American, and

---

64. Ibid., 61.

65. This date is based on album release dates for the music mentioned in this chapter, and the interesting anecdotal information that the author noticed while researching published sheet music and hymnbooks at a Spanish language seminary—she was the first one to check out most of these worship music books since 1995! The topic of contemporary Latin Christian music begs further research.

66. *¿Qué hacemos con estos músicos?*, 45.

67. Ibid., 27.

68. González, "An introduction," 12–13.

69. Santillán Baert, "Hispanic United Methodist Church," 64.

even North American, for many of the drums used were set up in drum batteries as is common in North American popular music.[70]

There was no mariachi music in the Hispanic Protestant churches of Oregon. If guitars and drums, rather than an organ or piano, are the mark of truly Latin music, then it abounds in these churches—only two congregations did not use guitars and only three did not use drums. Monmouth Christian used music soundtracks for its worship songs and had only vocalists as musicians. Woodburn's Iglesia Menonita Pentecostés had only a keyboardist, though the author observed the pastor's wife enthusiastically and skillfully accompanying a rollicking hymn on the piano in the late 1980s. Reedwood Friends used a lone acoustic guitar. Only three churches (all Baptist, sharing a building with an Anglo congregation) used a piano in their worship music.

The presence of guitar and drums really does not mark worship music as uniquely Latin. Most of the non-mainline English-speaking churches that the author has attended have quit using the organ and the piano, too. However, there was other evidence that is more distinctively Hispanic—bongo and conga drums, maracas, and other percussion instruments, and an accordion at Iglesia de Jesucristo in Forest Grove. Tambourines were played by either the congregation or the worship team in about half the churches. The preferred style for music specials with accompaniment tracks was *tejano*, and one song used a tropical rhythm, while another was *cumbia*. Thus, with instruments typical to Latin American music, many contemporary Christian worship songs written by Latinos, a good number of traditional *coritos*, and very few hymns translated from English, the worship music in the Hispanic Protestant churches in Oregon is mostly autochthonous.

Various researchers have remarked that separation from this world is a common theme in Protestant Hispanic churches. Regarding churches started by missionary organizations in Latin America, Costas observes, "Es un culto escapista que reúne a los fieles para trasladarlos a la presencia de Dios . . . El culto es, pues, un 'apartarse del mundo.'" (It is an escapist worship service that gathers the faithful to transport them to the presence of God . . . The service is, therefore, a "setting oneself apart from the world.")[71] He goes on to define the "world":

---

70. "Hispanic Baptist Worship," 82.

71. "La realidad de la iglesia evangélica latinoamericana," 48.

"El mundo constituye el reino de las tinieblas, que se opone al Reino de Dios y del cual han salido sus súbditos. A mi juicio, esto impide que el mundo encuentre un lugar en el culto. La única relación que mantiene la Iglesia . . . con el mundo es la de un equipo de rescate."

[The world constitutes the kingdom of darkness, that opposes the Kingdom of God, and out of which its subjects have come. In my judgment, this prevents the world from finding a place in the worship service. The only relationship that the Church maintains . . . with the world is that of a rescue team.][72]

Soliván describes a similar mentality among U.S. Pentecostal Latinos: "Often Hispanic Pentecostals understand themselves as a bulwark against death and the forces of evil that are overwhelming the world. They are a fortress against the cultural forces that seek to destroy them and their value system—a system that they understand as reflecting the values of the Kingdom of God and their Lord Jesus Christ."[73] Darino agrees: "The Hispanic Christian knows well that there is a dividing line between Christian and unbeliever, which means that once crossed, one is in the world—in an alien land,"[74] adding "The vitality of the Hispanic church does not center on a style of worship, but on an understanding of the gospel. . . . never blending or mixing church with society, culture, or the world in general."[75]

This clear separation from the world was seen in several churches in Oregon in various ways. The songs "This World is not my Home" and "Down a Narrow Path" at Manantiales de Vida Eterna indicate a sense of division from the ways of the unsaved. A woman at Templo Betania AOG in Ontario sang the song "I am Baptized" during testimony time, which also focused on setting one's self apart from the world. The speaker at Iglesia del Pueblo AOG in Cornelius described various evils such as parties with beer and fights, and the "Devil internet" and urged parents to intervene and be involved in their children's lives to keep them away from "the world." The pastor at Rogue Valley Fellowship put difference from the world in dramatic terms: "We are extra-terrestrials, we are not

72. Ibid., 59.

73. "Hispanic Pentecostal Worship," 47.

74. "Hispanic Baptist Worship," 84.

75. Ibid., 86.

of this world." This focus on separation from the world did not surface in the worship services of non-Pentecostal churches.

The author relates the very conservative dress of women and the separate seating by gender in some congregations with this emphasis on otherworldliness. Women wore headscarves at Iglesia de Jesucristo in Forest Grove, Elim Restauración, Manantiales de Vida Eterna, and the combined AOG/Apostolic congregation called Ministerios de Vida Eterna. In these same congregations, and at Salvados para Servir, the women wore long dresses or skirts. Elim and Salvados para Servir have ties to Latin American denominations, which could influence this custom. Separate seating for women and men was observed only at Manantiales de Vida Eterna and Elim Restauración. While the use of headcoverings has a scriptural background (1 Cor 11:5–16), wearing long skirts could be seen as a mark of distinction from the world.

Closely related to the idea of separation from the world and the kingdom of darkness, though not mentioned in the literature on Hispanic Protestant churches, is the idea of spiritual warfare. This theme emerged repeatedly in worship music. Two songs at at Esperanza y Vida en Jesucristo in Hood River had themes of spiritual warfare: "Ganaremos la batalla de las tinieblas" (We Will Win the Battle of Darkness), and "Debajo de mis pies Satanás está," (Satan is Under my Feet). At the Conservative Baptist congregation in Newport, Nueva Esperanza, the congregation sang "Mía es la Victoria" (Mine is the Victory), which spoke of doing spiritual battle using "weapons not of this world." At Casa del Padre, they sang "Los muros caen" (The Walls Fall Down) (a reference to Jericho, though the song specifically mentions chains be-ing broken and strongholds being torn down), "Le llaman guerrero" (They Call Him Warrior)[76] and "Jehová es mi guerrero" (Jehovah is My Warrior). This latter song was also used during the service at Rogue Valley Fellowship, one of very few songs the author heard in more than one service. At Salvados para Servir, the congregation sang about their praises destroying strongholds and how God was a strong tower. The first song at Iglesia Restauración Elim Internacional was "Los enemigos de Jehová están derrotados" (The Enemies of Jehovah Are Defeated). Also, the worship leader at Rogue Valley Fellowship read all of Psalm 27, in which the first three verses speak of David's confidence in God even though he might be under military attack. The pastor of Iglesia

76. Ibid.

Pentecostés Mennonite in Woodburn referred to spiritual battles in his sermon. The Roca de Salvación pastor mentioned doing battle with the sword of the Word of God in his sermon, and indeed, used the tales of David's mighty men as an extended spiritual battle metaphor applicable to his congregation.

On the other hand, requesting and recognizing the presence of the Holy Spirit was a significant part of the service for two AOG and two Latin American-origin neo-Pentecostal churches in this study, but this theme figured less prominently for other churches of a variety of backgrounds, and was not noted in many services at all. Soliván comments that this is part of the basic expectations for U.S. Hispanic Pentecostal services: "Four general principles can be said to inform this 'open liturgy': an openness to the leading of the Holy Spirit; an environment of expectation that the Holy Spirit will meet us as we worship; an openness to be free to praise God and God's Word as it addresses us in worship; and passionate and participatory worship."[77] He adds, "Central to Pentecostal worship is the expectation that the Holy Spirit will make herself known among the people at worship."[78] Costas describes a similar theme for Pentecostal churches in Latin America: "Su foco es el poder de Cristo que viene a través del Espíritu; poder que libera de los vicios, sana las enfermedades del cuerpo, salva al hombre de la muerte y lo capacita para la evangelización." (Their focus is the power of Christ that comes through the Spirit; power that frees from vices, heals those sick in body, saves man from death, and enables him to evangelize.)[79] Various metaphors are commonly used to indicate the Holy Spirit, such as fire, wind, and a flowing river.

Templo Betania AOG in Ontario sang many songs that invoked the Holy Spirit's presence and then encouraged the congregation to recognize it: "Bienvenido, Santo Espíritu a este lugar," the Spanish translation of "Holy Spirit, Thou Art Welcome in This Place"; "El maestro de Galilea está pasando por aquí" (The Master/Teacher of Galilee is Passing Through Here); "Así se siente la presencia de Dios" (This is What the Presence of God Feels Like); "El Espíritu de Dios está en este lugar" (The Spirit of God is in This Place); and "En el principio el Espíritu de Dios" (In the beginning, the Spirit of God); "Espíritu santo, caiga" (Fall, Holy

77. "Hispanic Pentecostal Worship," 51–52.

78. Ibid., 55.

79. "La realidad de la iglesia evangélica latinoamericana," 50.

Spirit); and "Levanto mis manos" (I Raise My Hands). This latter song described feeling "the fire" during worship. A woman requested the congregation sing "El cielo cae, cae" (Heaven Falls, Falls), and the second verse of this song speaks of the "fire falling." Prior to the message, the leader prayed that the Holy Spirit would fall on the service.

The now-defunct Iglesia de Vida Eterna, a combination Assembly of God and Apostolic congregations, also sang many songs recognizing or inviting the Holy Spirit: "Dios está aquí" (God Is Here); "Déjale que se sienta" (Let it [the Holy Spirit] Be Felt), a variation of "Déjalo que se mueva" (Let it [the Holy Spirit] Move); "Prepárate para que sientas el Espíritu de Dios" (Get Ready to Feel the Spirit of God); followed by the *cadena de coritos* that included "El río de Dios" (The River of God); "Va bajando ya" (It's Already Coming Down); "Que no se acabe" (Don't Let It Stop); and "En el principio, el Espíritu de Dios" (In the Beginning, the Spirit of God). "The River of God" centers on deeply experiencing God's presence.

At Iglesia Restauración Elim Internacional, the congregation sang three songs recognizing or inviting the Spirit's presence: "En la presencia del Señor hay libertad" (In the Presence of the Lord there is Freedom); En el principio el Espíritu de Dios," (In the beginning, the Spirit of God); and "Ven, Espíritu, ven," (Come, Spirit, Come). The worship leader told the congregation to pray and sing while seated, in recognition that the Holy Spirit was present and moving among the worshipers.

At Casa del Padre in Portland, they sang "Dame de beber" (Give Me to Drink), which focuses on one's need to sense God's presence; "El río de Dios" (The River of God); and "Donde está el Espíritu de Dios hay libertad" (Where the Spirit of God is There is Freedom).

Two churches sang only one song about the Holy Spirit's presence. The Madras Conservative Baptist church sang "Siento tu Gloria" (I Sense Your Glory). "El rubio de Galilea pasando va" (The Blond from Galilee is Passing By), sung at Manantiales de Vida Eterna, speaks of "letting Him touch you."

Soliván described a focus on Christ´s return and the subsequent world judgment as part of Hispanic Pentecostal thinking: "This worldview [of the church in constant battle against the evil world] plays an important part in the ethos of their worship, which is fueled by an eschatological—at times even apocalyptic—vision of the future."[80] Several

80. "Hispanic Pentecostal Worship," 47.

churches in this study did mention Christ's return, the final judgment, or heaven in their services. The sermon at Luz del Pueblo made reference to the great white throne judgment in Revelations, and urged people to make sure they were truly God's children while they still had the chance. The first congregational song in Madras was "When the Trumpet Sounds the Church Will Rise," referring to Christ's second coming. The sermon at Hermiston's Nueva Esperanza CBNW church was titled "Signs Before the Coming of Christ." At Rogue Valley Fellowship, the congregation sang "Crowned with Glory," alluding to Christ's triumphant return. The pastor later said in his sermon that Christians are "just waiting for the bus, wondering what time it will come," referring to believers' departure for heaven. The congregation at Ontario's Templo Betania sang two songs that described the beauty of heaven. The pastor of Salvados para Servir directed the congregation to read John 14:1–3 which speaks of Jesus's preparation of "many rooms" in heaven.

To summarize, the author saw few references to the traditional sacraments of baptism and communion in the Hispanic Protestant churches of Oregon. Prayer, collection of tithes and offerings, testimonies, a time of greeting one another, scripture reading and a sermon were common elements in nearly all the services. A few gave an invitation or altar call, though the sermon was not particularly evangelistic. Most of the music was composed by Latinos, sung in Spanish, and sometimes included Latin rhythms and instruments commonly used in Latin America. The themes of otherworldliness, eschatology, and the Holy Spirit's presence, noted by other researchers, were also prevalent in some of the Oregon churches. A related theme of spiritual warfare was observed, though not described by previous authors.

Style of Worship

This section describes *how* the congregations in this study worshiped. It includes observations from previous researchers about worship style when pertinent. The aspects of worship covered in this section are:

- Time;

- Freedom, which is related to the following three;

- Enthusiasm;

- Dance;

- Charismata;
- Use of technology, symbols, and text;
- Pastors' speaking style; and finally,
- Pastors' references to Hispanic cultures.

Santillán Baert observes, regarding Hispanic United Methodist services, "Worship services are not restricted to one hour. It is not that time is not important to Hispanics, but rather that when the Spirit of God is given control of the worship experience, God cannot be bound by time and space. Hispanics stay around until they have greeted all their friends after the service, even though many greeted one another before the service. There is no rush to beat the Baptists to the cafeteria line."[81] Soliván describes a similar attitude among Latino Pentecostals in the U.S.: "The typical message lasts at least forty-five minutes—on special occasions at least an hour to an hour and a half. . . . The people come to worship expecting to spend at least two to three hours, especially on Sundays."[82]

The author noticed that over half of the services started at the announced service time. Three had worshipers who had arrived earlier and were singing or praying in the meeting place before the service started. Monmouth Christian had changed its start time without updating its website, starting thirty minutes before announced. The rest of the services started later than their announced times—ranging from five minutes to thirty minutes later. The latter occurred at Manantiales de Vida Eterna, where everyone was present, but sharing a meal down the hall in the kitchen. The author also observed that in many congregations, more people continued to arrive over the first thirty minutes of the service.

The average service length was two and one half hours, with the Pentecostal churches tending to closer to three hours, and Reedwood Friends' small group having the shortest service at just over one hour. Most churches dedicated just under one hour to worship music, prayer, and announcements, with the sermons starting about fifty minutes into the service. Exceptions to this were Hillsboro's Iglesia Evangélica Cristo Viene, which had only five minutes of congregational singing (probably due to the many special activities for Mother´s Day), and Iglesia de Jesucristo in Forest Grove, which spent twenty minutes on announce-

81. "Hispanic United Methodist Church," 70.
82. "Hispanic Pentecostal Worship," 55.

ments alone. The Christian and Missionary Alliance Esperanza y Vida en Jesucristo in Hood River, Casa del Padre in Portland, and Iglesia Restauración Elim Internacional in Hillsboro had about ninety minutes of music before the sermon began. The average sermon length was fifty minutes, although the special speaker at Iglesia del Pueblo in Forest Grove spent fifty minutes speaking and singing before she started her sermon.

Freedom in worship is an important component for Hispanic churches. Costas calls Pentecostal worship in Latin America "spontaneous": "el culto pentecostal es un culto *espontáneo, creativo e intensamente participatorio.*" (The Pentecostal worship service is a *spontaneous, creative and intensely participatory* service [emphasis in the original]).[83] He goes on to describe this spontaneous freedom in greater detail:

> el culto de tipo pentecostal hace aparecer a la iglesia como *una comunidad que quiere ser ella misma.* Como he indicado, es un culto intensamente participatorio donde los fieles se sienten en casa y pueden echar a un lado sus defensas e inhibiciones y entregarse de lleno a la alabanza. Crea una experiencia liberadora porque permite una expresión espontánea y total. El creyente adora con todo lo que tiene, y cuando no halla palabras suficientes para expresar sus sentimientos y preocupaciones más íntimas, tiene acceso a la glosolalia y a las otras manifestaciones carismáticas.
>
> [the Pentecostal type of worship service makes the church appear as *a community that wants to be itself.* As I have indicated, it is an intensely participatory service where the faithful feel at home and can cast aside their defenses and inhibitions and give themselves fully to worship. It creates a liberating experience because it allows complete and spontaneous expression. The believer worships with all he or she has, and when he or she cannot find sufficient words to express his or her feelings and most intimate worries, he or she has access to glosolalia and the other charismatic manifestations.][84]

Regarding Hispanic Pentecostal churches in the U.S., Soliván comments, "Usually laypersons are the ones who lead the community in worship and are free to lead as they feel led to by the Spirit and on the basis of the tradition of worship they have observed in their congrega-

83. "La realidad de la iglesia evangélica latinoamericana," 50.
84. Ibid., 54.

tions and in other Pentecostal Hispanic congregations."[85] He adds that the non-creedal stance of Pentecostals "is an affirmation of the singular authority of Scripture, and the freedom of the Spirit to lead the church today in its worship in a similar manner to that of the apostolic church,"[86] and the third of his four principles of Pentecostal worship is "an openness to be free to praise God and God's Word as it addresses us in worship."[87]

Darino recognizes the influence Pentecostal congregations have had on Latino Baptist churches, stating, "In a very special way the charismatic and neopentecostal movements have made a significant impact on the life and development of Hispanic churches,"[88] and adding that this has caused Hispanic Baptist churches to discuss what is appropriate in their churches.[89] However, he asserts that freedom in worship is an historic mark of Baptist congregations: "Nevertheless, before the historic birth of Pentecostalism, worship among Baptists was distinguished by its spontaneity . . . ," including the ability to follow the leadership of the Holy Spirit for worship services.[90] He goes on to lament that, while the freedom of the Spirit is part of the Baptist heritage, its substance is rarely seen in present-day Anglo Baptist services,[91] though "In the majority of Hispanic Baptist churches there is a growing fervor in the expression of worship."[92]

At Restauración Elim Internacional, the congregation sang a song that spoke of God's presence as the source of freedom to worship: "En la presencia del Señor hay libertad" (In the Presence of the Lord there is Freedom). During other songs at this church, the audience was urged to clap and to use their freedom to worship. At Casa del Padre, they sang "Libre, Tú me hiciste libre" (Free, You Made Me Free) and "Donde está el Espíritu de Dios hay libertad" (Where the Spirit of God is There is Freedom). At Roca de Salvación, which was an AOG mission at the time of the site visit, the congregation sang "Libre, yo soy libre" (Free, I Am

85. "Hispanic Pentecostal Worship," 51.

86. Ibid., 50.

87. Ibid., 52.

88. "Hispanic Baptist Worship," 74.

89. The author observed this at Luz del Pueblo Southern Baptist, where the pastor emphasized studying Scripture and not being swayed by emotionalism.

90. "Hispanic Baptist Worship," 74.

91. Ibid., 80.

92. Ibid., 88.

Free). At Ontario's Templo Betania, they sang "Te alabaré para siempre" (I Will Worship You Always), which focused on praise for the freedom given by God.

Freedom in worship is related to the idea of worship as *fiesta* or celebration. González remarks, "First of all, because worship is a *fiesta* rather than a performance, it may be planned but not rehearsed. Oftentimes, Hispanic worship seems chaotic."[93] Costas also uses the idea of celebration when describing services in what he terms "renewal" churches in Latin America (charismatic churches of many denominations, excluding traditional Pentecostals): "Es un gran festival donde se alaba y se rinde tributo a Cristo el Señor. Reaccionando fuertemente contra el individualismo que caracteriza el culto Pentecostal clásico, los renovados hacen hincapié en el carácter comunitario del culto. Este es concebido en términos de una gran celebración familiar." (It is a great festival where Christ the Lord is worshiped and rendered tribute. Reacting strongly against the individualism that characterizes the classical Pentecostal worship service, the renewed churches emphasize the community nature of the service. This is conceived of in terms of a great family celebration.)[94]

González describes elements of the church service as *fiesta*: "A fiesta is characterized by movement and sensuality. . . . The people move around. They dance. They embrace. They shout. They cry. They laugh. . . . When we enter, there is always sound—not always soft music—reminding us that this is the fiesta of God."[95] He also notes, "Sometimes people in the dominant culture complain that our worship is too emotional, too festive."[96]

Soliván characterizes Hispanic Pentecostal worship services as "passionate and participatory."[97] He goes on to note that the issue of passion is not just a difference between Anglo mainline and Pentecostal churches, "but even more so between Anglo and Hispanic Pentecostals. The expression of passion is not only a matter of degree among Hispanic Pentecostals; passion is a constituent makeup of Hispanic culture. Most

93. "Hispanic Worship: An Introduction," 20–21.

94. "La realidad de la iglesia evangélica latinoamericana," 50.

95. "Hispanic Worship: An Introduction," 23.

96. Ibid., 22.

97. "Hispanic Pentecostal Worship," 52.

that we do is done with enthusiasm, whether it be socializing, working, or praising God."[98]

Santillán Baert claims that even some staid mainline churches demonstrate this passion in worship: "One of the characteristics of Hispanic Methodist worship is the religious fervor that is manifested by believers. They sing with overflowing joy and seem never to tire even after a long period of singing or even if hymns have five or more stanzas. Enthusiasm seems to be the natural climate in worship, especially in the more charismatic congregations where more *estribillos* (choruses) rather than hymns are sung. People are often moved to clap as they sing, raise their arms in praise, and play tambourines. Such lively participation is spontaneous, unavoidable, and contagious. It indeed becomes a celebration."[99]

As previously mentioned, Darino claims that "In the majority of Hispanic Baptist churches there is a growing fervor in the expression of worship."[100] He adds his view that "the church has caused people to be 'spectators' of what is called worship, performed by a few people behind a pulpit. . . . When Anglos watch Hispanics worship they feel there is something in these people that brings great joy to their church life. And so there is."[101] He further asserts that "In a way, this is just being felt by the Anglo-Saxons as they watch our worship. Their religious life is being permeated by the manifested need of many to become not only spectators, but protagonists in the worship experience. Although there will always be Hispanics who will wish to cover up this reality, it is something latent . . ."[102]

Fervor, enthusiasm, uninhibited passionate participation, *fiesta*, festival, family celebration—all of these could describe several of the worship services observed by the author. Probably the incredibly loud volume used at Restauración Elim and Salvados para Servir was one outcome of this fervor, as was the "clamor unto God" pre-service prayer behind closed sanctuary doors at Casa del Padre. Passionate participation could be seen in the dancing, both spontaneous and directed by the worship leader. For example, when the author arrived at Rosa de

---

98. Ibid., 55.

99. "Hispanic United Methodist Church," 60.

100. "Hispanic Baptist Worship," 88.

101. Ibid., 85.

102. Ibid., 86–87.

Sarón Foursquare before the service started, the pastor was dancing to the worship music. At Rogue Valley Fellowship in Medford, there was a specific time in the service to dance unto the Lord, accompanied by a song that spoke of dancing. Four congregants went forward to the front near the altar and danced, spun, and jumped, and one of them joyously whooped while dancing. At Casa del Padre, many people danced in their places in the congregation, until the pastor himself went forward, dancing to the song "El río de Dios" (The River of God). At this point many of the congregation made their way up toward the front and danced, sang, applauded, jumped, and whistled during four more songs, two of which specifically mentioned dancing. At Ministerio de Vida Eterna, the pastor danced to a series of old *coritos*, and the children danced during worship music at the back of the fellowship hall. However, these churches were in the minority, and the enthusiasm in most churches was demonstrated by clapping, raising one's hands, playing the tambourine, or shouting out "Amen."

Charismata, such as speaking in tongues, being slain in the Spirit, or other such manifestations of the Holy Spirit, are related both to the idea of fervent and free worship and the expectation that the Holy Spirit move during the worship service. These events are most common in Pentecostal churches. Soliván comments that "[A]ll Pentecostals emphasize the Baptism of the Holy Spirit as evidenced by speaking in tongues, along with healing, and the return (*parousia*) of the Lord."[103] He goes on to indicate that *charismata* are the distinctive mark in Pentecostal services: "Among most Pentecostal communities there is an accepted order for these expressions of charismata. Central to Pentecostal worship is the expectation that the Holy Spirit will make herself known among the people at worship. It is the presence of the charismata in the life of the congregation in worship and in mission that characterizes Pentecostal Christianity."[104]

Only five services in this study had these charismatic elements. At Casa del Padre, the pastor and a few others very briefly spoke in tongues. It appeared that someone dancing up front was slain in the spirit, but the author did not have a clear view. The pastor also made reference to a prophetic dream he had had about the church's ministry during the sermon,

103. "Hispanic Pentecostal Worship," 44.
104. Ibid., 55–56.

and during the pastoral interview his wife cited a prophetic word spoken about the church's multicultural mission.

At Iglesia del Pueblo AOG in Cornelius, the special speaker asked groups of people to come forward for prophetic prayer at the end of the service. This included praying out loud individually for each person at the front, saying "I'm going to give you a blessing in Jesus's name," admonishing the men that they were chosen as priest of their homes, lightly passing her hands over the arms, stomachs, heads, and chests of the women who went forward, and giving them a little push backwards after praying for them. Some of those who went forward prayed out loud, and some spoke in tongues as they prayed. Several were slain in the spirit and someone caught them as they fell backward.

While the congregation sang a worship chorus repeatedly at Restauración Elim Ministerio Internacional, a man began to speak in tongues, then interpret what he called a prophetic word—"dice el Señor" (the Lord says). He was given a microphone, but because he spoke in singsong sobs the author was not able to understand him.

In Ontario, at Templo Betania AOG, after many worship songs had been sung invoking the presence of the Holy Spirit, the worship leader was "caught by the Holy Ghost"[105]—holding his hands out to the side, he began to tremble uncontrollably and emit a loud uncontrollable chattering yell in which no words were discernable, yet it did not seem like speaking in tongues. Several others sitting in the front also yelled out unintelligibly. When the music stopped, these manifestations also ceased. The guest speaker at this church very briefly spoke in tongues during the sermon.

The pastor at Monmouth Christian Church also referred prophetically to the healing of someone in the congregation, and a call for another to become a pastor, reflecting a "name it and claim it" theology in his sermon.

Though González claims that worship is planned but not rehearsed because worship is a *fiesta*,[106] well-known worship leader Marcos Witt disagrees with him, at least in reference to the musicians:

> Se nota que hay una actitud muy descansada con respecto a
> ensayar, preparar y organizar su música. Reina más una actitud

105. Use of this term clarified by Hjamil Martínez, e-mail message to the author, November 9, 2011.

106. "Hispanic Worship: An Introduction," 20–21.

de espontaneidad y desorden, en algunos casos, que el orden, preparación y buena ejecución. Muchos han creído que si alguna música se ensaya y se prepara mucho, no va a dar lugar a que se mueva el Espíritu Santo. Pero, podemos ver en la Biblia que no fue así. Hubo mucho orden y muchísima preparación en el área musical . . . y en medio de ese orden, el Señor se movía de una manera extraordinaria. El ensayo y la preparación sólo nos ayudan a estar listos y prestos para fluir con lo que el Espíritu quiere hacer. Muchas veces hemos visto cómo el Espíritu Santo es "apagado" (1 Tesalonicenses 5.19), precisamente por la falta de preparación del grupo de alabanza, o por una alabanza mal tocada, mal ejecutada, fomentado de esta manera la confusión y el caos en el momento de ser interpretada.

[One notices that there is a very relaxed attitude toward practicing, preparing, and organizing their music. More of an attitude of spontaneity and disorder reigns, in some cases, than one of order, preparation, and good execution. Many have believed that if some music is practiced and prepared a lot, it will not leave room for the Holy Spirit to move. But, we can seen in the Bible that this was not so. There was much order and very much preparation in the area of music . . . and in the midst of that order, the Lord moved in an extraordinary way. Practice and preparation just help us to be ready and prepared to flow with what the Spirit wants to do. Many times we have seen how the Holy Spirit is "put out" (1 Thessalonians 5:19), precisely due to the lack preparation by the worship team, or by worship music poorly played, poorly executed, promoting in this way confusion and chaos at the moment of its presentation.][107]

The only service where the author observed this lack of preparation by musicians was Ontario's Templo Betania. Not only were they late, but their instruments weren't tuned, and they obviously did not have a plan as to what songs they would use for the service.

The author was intrigued by the use (or lack of use) of technology, visual aids, and text in the churches. This was not commented on in the literature. Three churches had videos of worship music or worship services playing before their services. Four of the churches also videotaped part of their services. Seventeen of the churches used an LCD projector for song lyrics, and one church used an overhead projector. One church projected a responsive reading with an LCD system, and three also used

---

107. *¿Qué hacemos con estos músicos?*, 54–55.

it for announcements. Two pastors projected images such as photos or paintings to illustrate their sermons. Of the churches that did not project song lyrics, one used a hymnal for a few songs. Otherwise, the congregation sang from memory; no songbooks were provided. Other than reading Scripture, four congregations used additional written materials: three provided a sermon outline with blanks for note-taking in the bulletin, and one handed out photocopies of a Sunday School lesson, which the pastor read out loud as his sermon.

About one third of the congregations in this study, then, did not provide words for the congregation to follow in singing, and few used text for any purpose beyond reading the Bible in the service. There are several plausible explanations for this. One could be lack of technological resources—the author attended a Spanish-speaking church (not included this study) that did not have the resources to buy an LCD projector, nor did the pastor know how to use a computer to create the files to be projected. Another explanation could be lower literacy levels among the congregants—the author has heard several Latino Christians living in the U.S. say that they learned to read at church or by reading the Bible at home, and has personally observed Hispanic believers struggle to read out loud during Sunday School classes. The author also observed that the preachers used non-standard Spanish, such as "nojostros," "haiga," "ansina," "nadien," "hágamos," and "dígamos"[108] in three of the congregations that used very little text (although there was another pastor who used similar expressions in a congregation that projected song lyrics). A third reason could be that many Latinos come from a background of oral tradition—knowledge is handed down verbally. A fourth explanation could be that the cultural shift away from text toward image noted by observers of U.S. culture[109] is impacting the Latino population as well. The two pastors who projected visuals for their sermons were availing themselves of non-text methods to communicate with their congregations.

The Latino pastor's role and style have been commented on by other researchers. In Latin American Pentecostal churches, "Normalmente

108. In standard modern Spanish, these words are "nosotros," "haya," "así," "nadie," "hagamos," and "digamos" respectively.

109. Presentation made by Leonard Sweet at PALCON conference, Nampa, ID, July 2010. Sweet proclaimed that the Gutenberg era (of texts in books) is over, and learners now receive their information through visuals such as icons and videoclips, having entered the "Google era."

el pastor constituye la principal autoridad profética de la congregación. Su entrada al púlpito resulta siempre algo impresionante." (Normally the pastor constitutes the main prophetic authority of the congregation. His entrance to the pulpit is always something impressive.)[110] Regarding congregations in the U.S., Soliván writes, "In most Hispanic Pentecostal churches, the preaching of the gospel is open to men and women, lay and ordained. What is required is the community's affirmation that one should possess a preaching gift and preach with 'anointing'—that is, with clear signs that one is led by the Holy Spirit. The preacher in the Hispanic Pentecostal tradition sees himself/herself as a messenger from God with a word for the people of God."[111] For U.S. United Methodist Latino congregations, Santillán Baert claims, "For many Hispanics, the sermon is the heart of the worship service. Congregations expect powerful and inspiring messages. The preacher is free to be genuinely expressive."[112] Darino traces Baptist preaching style back to denominational beginnings during a period of revival, describing services as "characterized by powerful preaching with the purpose of giving conviction of sin."[113]

These descriptions of the pastoral style do fit many of the messages observed for this study. For example, when the service began at Casa del Padre, the pastor was not on the platform or sitting on the front row. Part way through the congregational singing, he entered through a side door, and a murmur went through the crowd. Later, he danced to the front during a song about desiring to fully experience God and led others in dancing in worship. Costas's description of an impressive entrance to the pulpit is entirely apt in this instance.

Several pastors were very expressive in their preaching. The AOG pastor of Iglesia de Jesucristo Ministerios de Vida Eterna had a very loud, dynamic preaching style. The pastor at Ministerios Restauración Mennonite was very active as he preached—walking about, gesticulating, but not yelling. The female guest speaker at Iglesia del Pueblo AOG in Cornelius was also a very dynamic, active preacher who used many gestures as she spoke. She alternately spoke very fast, shouted, whispered, and paused. She also stated, "I bring a word from God" as she

110. Costas, "La realidad de la iglesia evangélica latinoamericana," 63.

111. "Hispanic Pentecostal Worship," 54.

112. "Hispanic United Methodist Church," 71.

113. "Hispanic Baptist Worship," 80.

took the pulpit, clearly following in the prophetic tradition referenced by Solivián. The pastor preaching at Salvados para Servir spoke very loudly and animatedly, nearly yelling. Interestingly, though the congregation sang many energetic praise songs with great enthusiasm, just before the message at Salvados para Servir, the worship leader admonished them to listen respectfully and reverently to the sermon.

Other pastors tended to the opposite end of the spectrum. Pastor Kuroda of Newport's Nueva Esperanza preached in a voice that was very quiet, worshipful, and reverent. He never yelled or even raised his voice. Pastor Macias at Reedwood Friends likewise had a very calm manner as he led the service for his small flock. Due to his disability, Pastor Reyes struggled to read his sermon and relied on the congregation to help him. Most of the pastors tended to a more moderate style, using jokes or colloquial expressions to keep the attention of the congregation.

In fact, it is through these jokes, sayings, and references to life experiences of the audience that one can measure how firmly the pastors located themselves within the cultural reference of the congregants. Solivián claims that Pentecostal tradition can do this especially well: "This 'open liturgy' or 'free liturgy' lends itself for incorporating into the service the particularity of the community and its cultural expressions."[114] Costas strongly criticized many Protestant worship services in Latin American in the 1970s for not recognizing the context of the community: "El culto dramatiza, además, la interacción de la iglesia con la cultura. . . . Esto implica que todo culto debe ser "indígena," debe ser el reflejo de una Iglesia que surge, vive y actúa en medio de un ambiente cultural determinado." (The worship service dramatizes, moreover, the interaction of the church with the culture. . . . This implies that every worship service should be 'indigenous', it should be the reflection of a Church that arises, lives, and acts in the midst of a particular cultural environment.)[115]

There were cultural references of one type or another in twenty of the twenty-five sermons in this study. One of the ways pastors acknowledged the cultures of their congregations was through reference to typical foods. The former pastor of Madras Iglesia Bautista Conservadora Bilingüe, who is Dominican, demonstrated his understanding of Mexican culture by referring to *jitomates*, a word used by Mexicans for toma-

114. "Hispanic Pentecostal Worship," 51.
115. "La realidad de la iglesia evangélica latinoamericana," 39–40.

toes. The Mexican pastor at Hermiston Nueva Esperanza Conservative Baptist spoke of *tortillas* and a *comal*, the traditional griddle used to heat tortillas. The Mexican-American pastor of Monmouth Christian helped his congregation decide where they were going to have a picnic that would include *carne asada* and a *gallinazo*.[116] The Salvadoran pastor at Salvados para Servir mentioned the belief that babies are born liking chile pepper because they grew accustomed to it from their mother's diet during pregnancy. The guest preacher at Iglesia del Pueblo AOG in Cornelius told the families to "go without *tortillas*" in order to invest in their childrens' lives, and also decried the parties with *carnitas*[117] and *cerveza*. The pastor of the Southern Baptist congregation Luz del Pueblo told of being invited to "have a cold one" while out calling.

Another way preachers recognized the cultural context of their congregations was by making reference to their status as immigrants, including crossing the border via the desert, with the time of immigration serving as a divider of life "back home" and "in this country." When the scripture passage referred to a desert, both the preacher at Manantiales de Vida Eterna and in Madras alluded to the desert as a border crossing. The latter went on to describe snakes and "bad men" (meaning the border patrol, or perhaps *coyotes* who guide people across the border for exhorbitant fees). The pastor of City Bible mentioned trusting God to help with immigrant status, and described Joseph's exile as a type of forced immigration. The pastor of Village Baptist spoke several times of his own status of immigrant, making multiple references to his past, prior to immigration. The pastor of Iglesia Evangélica Cristo Viene in Hillsboro remembered how children used to work on coffee plantations, while others lived off what they found in the garbage dump, in his native Guatemala. The pastor in Hermiston referred to feeding a large family on one hundred dollars and working in the fields as a child with his father in Mexico. The pastor in Woodburn recalled frequent break-ins to his former house in Costa Rica. Medford's pastor of Rogue Valley Fellowship described independence day parades in his native El Salvador. The speaker in Cornelius relayed growing up in a remote area of Mexico where there was no school, and playing with paper boats in

116. Mexicans often use *gallina* instead of *pollo* to refer to chicken meat, whereas other groups use it to refer to live chickens. Here *gallinazo* meant something like "a chicken feast."

117. Mexican-style spicy braised pork.

puddles. The pastor at Ministerios Restauración Mennonite mentioned that his church "back home" had had many teachers in attendance. The pastor of Luz del Pueblo said that his brothers, who remain in Mexico, accused him of being "brainwashed" into conversion in the United States. Several preachers also claimed that life in the U.S. was financially much easier than it had been prior to immigration; one compared the value of Mexican *pesos* to the U.S. dollar. Others referred to the humble social status of the Latino immigrant.

The reality of immigration from Latin America to the U.S. has linguistic consequences. English has strongly influenced the Spanish language, so much so that a new lexicon has emerged—Spanglish. The preacher in Madras and Woodburn both spoke of working in the *fil* instead of the *campo*, the proper Spanish word for "field." The latter also mentioned employment in *norserías*, (plant nurseries), instead of using the standard term *invernaderos*. The speaker at Iglesia de Jesucristo used false cognates in Spanish or literal translations from English: *sentencia* instead of *oración* or *frase* for "sentence," *caer en su lugar* for "fall into place" instead of *acomodarse* or *ponerse en su lugar*. The pastors of Casa del Padre, Ministerios Restauración in Portland, and Hermiston Nueva Esperanza inserted phrases or sentences in English in their sermons. This has the effect of both emphasizing a point and identifying with the host culture. The pastor at Salvados para Servir used the congregation's common experience of learning English to illustrate the point that skills must be practiced to be maintained.

At other times, pastors used words unique to one region or country, or colloquial expressions to establish cultural connections. The preacher in Madras explained the word used in the Dominican Republic for "fire hydrant," but he also clearly was familiar with Mexican usages, like *zopilote* for buzzard. He also said "Patita, ¿pa' qué te tengo?" a colloquial expression that is literally "Little paw, what are you good for?" that means "Let's get out of here fast!" The Costa Rican pastor in Woodburn used the Mexican term for short stature, *chaparrito*. Both the pastor in Newport and Medford imitated Mexican accents for a few sentences in their sermons, and the latter spoke of *ser burro*, which literally means "to be a burro" but is understood as "to be stupid." The speaker in Cornelius used several phrases which she called *dichos de la abuelita* (Grandma's sayings). The sermons preached by the pastors at Roca de Salvación and

Luz del Pueblo, who are both Mexican, were peppered throughout with Mexican colloquialisms.

Beyond word choice, many preachers alluded to Latin television, such as the channel Univision (described as *carnevision* "fleshvision"), the horoscope reader Walter Mercado (as Walter *Pecado* "Sin"), and animator Raul Velasco of the popular program "Siempre en domingo" (Always on Sunday). Another mentioned the moustache of Mario Moreno Cantiflas, a prolific Mexican comedian and film star.

Many sermons mentioned events in Latin America, including wars and guerrilla attacks, natural disasters, and leaders such as Simón Bolívar, Hugo Chávez, and Evo Morales, and a group of witches in Mexico. There were multiple references to Roman Catholic traditions, such as seeing images of Christ in various public places, images of saints, the veneration of the Virgin Mary, and Catholic beliefs regarding the elements of communion.

The speakers also mentioned *machismo* or male dominance; soccer; large families; ready acceptance of children born out of wedlock; the expectation that grown children provide for their parents; gangs and drug use; and the role of a mother as providing emotional support. These elements are often associated with Hispanic cultures, but by no means are exclusively related to them. However, these themes were all used by Latino preachers as sermon illustrations.

The Anglo pastor in Grants Pass made an overture to the Mexicans in the congregation at the beginning of his sermon on Daniel as an exile, saying that Mexicans would probably like a Latino president or vice president to be elected, because they would feel that this leader would understand them better.

The speakers in Madras and Woodburn clearly understood the kind of employment their congregations had and made reference to them. The former pastor in Madras, the pastor of Reedwood Friends, and the pastor at Roca de Salvación in Portland made references to the people in their congregation by name and other characteristics, such as having a well-tended garden.

While the majority of sermons were placed firmly in the cultural experience of the congregations, the message at Hood River's Christian and Missionary Alliance, and that at what is now Vida Church, did not. These two sermons were very closely tied to the biblical text, including historic information, but made no reference whatsoever to the cultural experiences of the listeners.

CONCLUSION

The Protestant Hispanic churches in Oregon have highly participatory and enthusiastic worship services. There were few instances of the traditional sacraments of baptism and communion in the Hispanic Protestant churches. Prayer, collection of tithes and offerings, testimonies, a time of greeting one another, scripture reading and a sermon were common elements in nearly all the services. Several gave an invitation or altar call. The themes of otherworldliness, the Holy Spirit's presence, and an emphasis on eschatology, noted by other researchers, were also prevalent in some of the Oregon churches. A related theme of spiritual warfare was observed, though not described by previous authors. Many churches included teachings on money and its use.

Though the congregations in this study welcomed visitors before the service, from the pulpit, and included a special time to greet one another during the service, two elements made the author feel excluded. The first was variation from published service times, and the second was the lack of written lyrics to follow during congregational singing. While she sensed that the congregation and pastor both more or less knew when services were going to begin, an outsider seeking to participate could not reasonably know when to arrive based on information posted on the building or the Internet in a small percentage of the churches visited. Perhaps this does not indicate a desire to exclude newcomers, but rather that the method of outreach is mostly through personal invitation from members of the congregation who know what time services really begin. Likewise, not providing lyrics for congregational singing had the effect of excluding newcomers from participating in worship. Everyone else was "in the know," having memorized the songs. However, a Latino visitor might have a different perspective on both these points.

Most of the music was composed by Latinos, sung in Spanish, and sometimes included Latin rhythms and instruments commonly used in Latin America. The vast increase of available worship music written by Latinos is a fecund area for further research. The majority of pastors used many references to their congregations' status as immigrants, and included colloquial sayings and comments uniquely understood by Latinos. Thus, by and large, the churches of Oregon are not mere copies of Anglo worship services translated into Spanish—they reflect and respond to their own cultural environment.

6

Conclusion

THE HISPANIC POPULATION IN the U.S. is growing rapidly, and Oregon is no exception. Persons describing themselves as Hispanic or Latino now make up nearly 12 percent of the state's population, a 300 percent increase over the past twenty years. In Oregon, most Latinos are Mexican or of Mexican descent, followed by people from Guatemala. Despite this growth, there are very few published studies about the Latino population of Oregon.

Not all U.S. Latinos are Roman Catholic. A growing number, perhaps one-third, are *evangélicos*. Previous publications on U.S. immigrant churches, and particularly Hispanic churches, describe much conflict between Anglos and the immigrant or minority group. They also note the interior diversity of Latino churches in terms of age, country of origin, and generation of immigration; cite a need for Hispanic churches to forge their own identity; and report a tendency of the churches toward independence from denominations.

The majority of early church-planting efforts among Oregon Hispanics were denominationally based. The Conservative Baptists and Assemblies of God were most active in starting Hispanic churches prior to 1990, while mainline churches have not sustained efforts to create Latino congregations in Oregon. There was a dramatic increase in Protestant Latino churches in the state in the late 1990s. Most of them were independent groups, but there are several Latin American-origin churches operating in Oregon. Though there are now over 200 Protestant Hispanic churches in the state, many groups are not yet consolidated—moving often or having several false starts. The churches in this study suggest that denominational ties contribute to longevity and stability.

Oregon's Protestant Latino churches are mostly representative of the Latino population, and thus are relatively homogenous because the great majority of the Latino population is mostly first-generation immigrants from Mexico. The rural churches are much less diverse than those in the Portland metropolitan area, reflecting the settlement patterns of immigrants to the state. The Hispanic churches in the state are young, both in terms of existence as organizations and the ages of those attending. As the congregations establish themselves, and the number of Protestant Latino churches increases, doctrinal differences are becoming more important, and churches are entering into competition for members.

Most congregants in the Oregon churches converted to Protestantism after immigration, though many Guatemalans are the exception to this finding. Churches provide emotional and occasionally material support to their congregations, and opportunity for personal growth and leadership development. Like English-speaking congregations, Latinos in Oregon tend to worship with persons of similar educational and employment backgrounds. Within the limited diversity of the Hispanic population in Oregon, national origin and ethnicity do not seem to be determining factors in where people choose to worship. Pastors indicate that they are dealing with these potential divisors directly through teaching and preaching. The pastors overwhelmingly indicated a pressing need for legal information and immigration reform for the members of their congregations.

Most pastors in this study have availed themselves of training at a seminary or Bible school, though some Pentecostal pastors have no formal training and do not see it as necessary. For Oregon Hispanics who have a call to ministry, several options for face-to-face pastoral education are available in Spanish in the state.

Meeting space has been an obstacle for many Oregon Protestant Latino churches. Few have their own building for worship. Most congregations have moved several times, seeking adequate facilities and a positive relationship with those with whom they share a building. Several congregations have shared space with other minority congregations. Significantly, more than one-third of the congregations in this study reported sharing not only a building, but a unified vision for ministry with a larger church body. This unity has not been described in any previous studies of Protestant Hispanic churches in the U.S.

These nine churches notwithstanding, the tendency to independence described in the literature was also seen in many churches in this study, and a few pastors indicated that the opinions of Latinos were not heard at the denominational level.

The Latino congregations in this study were not very politically involved. This is likely due to a focus on individual salvation and purity, instead of collective social responsibility, typical of Pentecostal churches and other denominations represented in this study. It is probably also related to the legal status of some of the churchgoers who are hesitant to draw attention to themselves by participating in public forums.

All the Latino churches in this study are dealing with the issue of what language to use for worship services, educational programs, and other activities. A minority of the churches has chosen to do everything entirely in Spanish, thus fostering cultural and linguistic preservation. One-third of the churches have made the decision to be bilingual, operating in both English and Spanish. Most of the churches have a blend of programming—mostly in Spanish, but some activities (particularly those for children and youth) in English. Those with bilingual programs have more second- and third-generation immigrants in attendance. As the Latino population in Oregon grows older and the subsequent generations speak less Spanish and more English, the language issue will become more pressing. Several pastors observed reduced participation by younger generations, with high school graduation being a significant juncture.

Like their counterparts across the country, the worship services in the Protestant Latino churches of Oregon are highly participatory. The leaders encourage audience participation from the platform in a variety of ways. Children, youth, and women regularly contribute in the services. One common form of participation is giving a testimony of God's work in one's life. This was seen in many of the services, but not in the large cell-group congregations. A minority of the churches mentioned or observed baptism (of adults) and communion. All the services in this study included prayer, and all but three collected tithes and offerings. One-third had a specific time in the service for greeting one another. The Assemblies of God included an altar call in their services, and five additional pastors presented the congregation with an opportunity to make a decision for Christ. The sermon was the focal point in all the services. Many of the messages had a theme of God's faithfulness, urging

people to trust him. Other themes included teaching on money, separation from the world, asking the Holy Spirit to be present in the service
(especially in the Pentecostal and neo-Pentecostal churches), Christ's
second coming, and spiritual warfare.

Time (both in terms of beginning and ending the service) was less
important in the Hispanic churches than it generally is in Anglo congregations. There was an emphasis on freedom, both for the Spirit to lead
the service, and for people to worship spontaneously and enthusiastically. The congregations in this study tended to use less text during the
worship service than the author has observed in Anglo services—the
only written source used by one-third of the congregations was the Bible.

Previous studies of Latino churches in the U.S. have issued a call in
to make worship services in these churches reflect their unique identities. Whether purposefully or unconsciously, the congregations in this
study have done so. The worship services in all but one of the congregations in this study were culturally U.S. Latino. Many congregations
were bilingual and deliberately chose worship songs available in both
languages. Nearly all used worship songs written by Latinos living either in the U.S. or in Latin America, and very few churches used only
hymns. A significant number, but not a majority, also sang *coritos*. Both
the traditional *coritos* and the new wave of worship music composed in
Spanish are fertile ground for further study. Most pastors made overt
cultural connections through language use, jokes, and references to
public figures from Latin America or common experiences prior to or
during immigration. For the most part, they were not copies of English-
speaking Anglo churches. Neither were they copies of congregations in
Latin America. They reflected the unique realities of Latinos living in the
U.S., with varying degrees of bilingualism and participation in majority
society.

In many areas, the Protestant Hispanic churches of Oregon dif-
fer from those described in other parts of the country. Some of these
differences are certainly due to the short length of existence of these
organizations and to the relatively brief period in which a significant
number of Hispanics have lived in the state. Other differences, such as
the extensive use of worship music written by Latinos, simply reflect
recent changes that are occurring across the country but have not yet
been documented in published studies. This may be the case as well for
the Spanish-speaking congregations that participate as equals in a larger

church body with a unified vision for ministry. On the other hand, it is possible that these churches are leading the way for Hispanic and Anglo congregations across the country, working through issues of communication and power towards unity in the body of Christ.

Appendix

Questions Used in Pastoral Interviews

PLEASE remember that you are free to decline to answer any of these questions.

ORIGIN OF CHURCH AND DENOMINATIONAL TIES

What denomination are you associated with, if any?

When did this church or ministry begin?

Describe its beginnings.

For those that have denominations:

Please describe your denomination's administrative structure for Hispanic churches.

Please describe your interaction as pastor with your church's administrative structure whether it is a formal denomination or not? How frequent? In what language? Who initiates?

Do you see a struggle for Latino churches/pastors to be included in your denomination?

DEMOGRAPHICS OF MEMBERS

About how many people attend your weekly Sunday worship services?

Would you say that your congregation is growing, staying the same size, or losing people?

Briefly describe the age breakdown of those who attend.

Tell me about the church attendance or participation of the adolescents in your church?—do they stay actively involved here, attend a different church, or drop out altogether?

Do any Anglos or other non-Hispanics attend your church? If yes,

Do the Anglos speak Spanish?

Why do you believe that they have chosen to attend this church?

Are they women or men?

Are they married to a Hispanic?

What percent of the active church-goers are first generation immigrants?

What countries are they from?

Of your immigrant population, what percentage of your congregation would you say attended an evangelical church before immigrating?

Could you give a few examples of the (spiritual or travel) journeys of some in your congregation regarding church attendance?

Would you say that most people in your congregation started attending here immediately after conversion, did they attend awhile before conversion, or were they attending another evangelical church before coming here?

If your church has people from different Latin American countries of origin, how does this affect the church body?

Do people from different countries mingle socially or stay separate?

Do you observe a sense that one group of origin looks down on another?

Do you think the pastor's country of origin impacts whether people from other countries also come here or don't come?

What percentage of your regular attendees are from a rural background in their home country?

What percentage is from an urban background?

If your church has both recent immigrants and second or third generation immigrants, how does this affect the church body?

What type of employment do church-goers have?

What percentage of the adult members has completed elementary school only?

What percentage of the adult members has only completed high school?

What percentage of the adult members has completed a bachelor's degree?

What countries did they complete this education in the U.S. or elsewhere?

Please describe the country of origin and educational achievement of your board members.

Could you estimate the percentage of your congregation that is here legally? (Please remember that you don't have to answer this question if you're uncomfortable doing so)

LOCATION

Where and when do you meet for worship services?

Do you pay rent for this facility?

If you share a church building, where specifically in the building do you hold your services?

Do most people in the congregation live in the community where the church building is?

What percentage of the congregation live in a rural community?

What percentage live in an urban area,

What percentage live in a suburban area?

FINANCES

Is this church financially dependent on an Anglo denomination or church and if so, in what way?

If your church depends financially on an Anglo church or shares an Anglo church building, tell me how this has affected your ministry?

PASTORAL LEADERSHIP

Are you bivocational?

If you are bivocational, what is your other job?

What percentage of your time is given to the ministry?

What percentage of your personal income comes from the church?

Describe the relationship between the Hispanic church and the Anglo church?

Do you think this sharing has impacted the Anglo church, and if so, how Pastor's beginning/training/call

How did you come to pastor at this church?

Were you already living in this area when you were called to be pastor here?

Were you a pastor in your country of origin?

Describe your pastoral training.

Have you completed this pastoral training?

Where was it?

Was any of the coursework online?

Was the instruction in English?

Was it in your denomination's institutions?

Did it prepare you to work in ministry to a culturally diverse immigrant population?

Were you ordained? If yes, by whom?

What percentage of your ministry is primarily spiritual?

What percentage is devoted to meeting other needs, such as helping find employment, housing, etc.

Describe your church or denomination's program to identify and train new pastors to work in Hispanic churches in the US.

LANGUAGE

Which language does the church use for these events:

Sunday School?

For worship services?

At informal activities?

How did you arrive at the decision to have your services in English or Spanish?

INTERACTIONS/COMMUNITY

Does your church interact with other congregations?

Which ones?

Why these particular churches?

How often and for what reasons?

If your church belongs to a denomination, does your church participate in denominational activities such as statewide youth activities or women's conferences? Describe.

Describe your church's activities regarding missions.

What kinds of ministries does your congregation have? Do these ministries serve only Hispanics? If not, tell me about those who participate. (Include both "spiritual" and "social" ministries)

Do you or other church members participate actively in the community in non-church related activities (such as school meetings, etc.)?

What needs would you say your congregation has that are not being met by existing organizations or programs?

What needs would you say the greater Hispanic population in this area has that are not being met by existing organizations or programs?

What do you feel is a strength of this church?

Do you participate in a ministerial association? If so which one, if not, why not?

Do you see a struggle for Latino churches/pastors to be included in the Christian community of Oregon? (for example, a mayor's prayer breakfast).

Do you ever feel excluded?

Do you ever feel that decisions are made for you and your church that you had no input on?

Could you refer me to one or 2 laypersons with whom I could do a similar interview?

Can you give me the names and address of any other Hispanic churches in this county that you are aware of?

Bibliography

Aguilera, Michael, et al., "Work and Employment for Immigrants in Oregon." In *Understanding the Immigrant Experience in Oregon: Research, Analysis, and Recommendations from University of Oregon Scholars*, edited by Robert Bussel, 69–73. Eugene, OR: University of Oregon Labor and Research Education Center, 2008.

Alabanzas infantiles. Puebla, Mexico: Ediciones las Américas, 1973.

Argüello, Ramón. *Historia de Primera Iglesia Hispana Ebenezer y las iglesias pioneras del área metropolitana de Portland*. unpublished mss., nd.

Armendariz, Rubén. "The Protestant Hispanic Congregation: Identity." In *Protestantes/ Protestants: Hispanic Christianity within the Mainline Traditions*, edited by David Maldonado Jr., 239–54. Nashville: Abingdon, 1999.

Aponte, Edwin. "*Coritos* as Active Symbol in Latino Protestant Popular Religion." *Journal of Hispanic/Latino Theology* 2, no. 3 (1995): 57–66.

Aponte, Edwin. "Hispanic/Latino Protestantism in Philadelphia." In *Re-forming the Center: American Protestantism, 1900 to the Present*, edited by Douglas Jacobsen and William Vance Trollinger Jr., 381–403. Grand Rapids: Eerdman's, 1998.

Atencio, Tomás. "The Empty Cross: The First Hispano Presbyterians in Northern New Mexico and Southern Colorado." In *Protestants/Protestants: Hispanic Christianity within Mainline Traditions*, edited by David Maldonado, Jr., 38–59. Nashville: Abingdon, 1999.

Barton, Paul. "Inter-ethnic Relations Between Mexican American and Anglo American Methodists in the U.S. Southwest, 1836–1938." In *Protestants/Protestants: Hispanic Christianity within Mainline Traditions*, edited by David Maldonado, Jr., 60–84. Nashville: Abingdon, 1999.

Berho, Gonzalo B., comp. *Cantad a Jehová cántico nuevo*. Quito: Imprenta del Nazareno, n.d.

Bussel, Robert, ed. *Understanding the Immigrant Experience in Oregon: Research, Analysis, and Recommendations from University of Oregon Scholars*. Eugene, OR: University of Oregon Labor and Research Education Center, 2008.

Chávez Sauceda, Teresa. "Becoming a Mestizo Church." In *Alabadle: Hispanic Christian Worship*, edited by Justo González, 89–99. Nashville: Abingdon, 1996.

———. "Race, Religion and La Raza." In *Protestantes/ Protestants: Hispanic Christianity within the Mainline Traditions*, edited by David Maldonado Jr., 177–93. Nashville: Abingdon, 1999.

Cleary, Edward and Hannah Stewart-Gambino, *Power, Politics, and Pentecostals in Latin America*. Boulder, CO: Westview, 1997.

Cohen, Robin. *Global Diasporas*. Seattle: University of Washington Press, 1997.

Comiskey, Joel. *Passion & Persistence: How the ELIM Church's Cell Groups Penetrated an Entire City for Jesus*. Houston: Cell Group Resources, 2004.

Conde-Frazier, Elizabeth and Loida Martell Otero. "U.S. Latina Evangélicas." In *Encyclopedia of Women and Religion in North America*, edited by Rosemary Skinner Keller and Rosemary Radford Ruether, 477–84. Bloomington: Indiana University Press, 2006.

Cortés, Carlos, ed. *Protestantism and Latinos in the United States*. New York: Arno, 1980.

Costas, Orlando. "La realidad de la iglesia evangélica latinoamericana." In *Fé cristiana y Latinoamérica hoy*, edited by René Padilla, 35–66. Buenos Aires: Ediciones Certeza, 1974.

Darino, Miguel Angel. "What is Different about Hispanic Baptist Worship?" In *Alabadle: Hispanic Christian Worship*, edited by Justo González, 73–88. Nashville: Abingdon, 1996.

Department of Church Planning and Research, Protestant Council of the City of New York. *A Report on the Protestant Spanish Community in New York City*. New York: 1960. A facsimile of the first edition in Cortés, Carlos, ed. *Protestantism and Latinos in the United States*. New York: Arno, 1980.

Ebaugh, Helen Rose and Janet Saltzman Chafetz, eds. *Religion Across Borders*. Walnut Creek, CA: Altamira, 2002.

———. *Religion and the New Immigrants* Walnut Creek, CA: Altamira, 2000.

———. "Dilemmas of Language in Immigrant Congregations: The Tie that Binds or the Tower of Babel?" *Review of Religious Research* 41, no. 4 (2000): 432–52.

Elizondo, Virgilio. *The Future is Mestizo: Life Where Cultures Meet*. Bloomington, IN: Meyer-Stone Books, 1988.

Epps, Garrett. *To an Unknown God: Religious Freedom on Trial*. New York: St. Martin's, 2001.

Escobar, Samuel. *Changing Tides: Latin America & World Mission Today*. Maryknoll, NY: Orbis, 2002.

Espinosa, Gastón. "The Pentecostalization of Latin American and U.S. Latino Christianity." *Pneuma: The Journal of the Society for Pentecostal Studies.* 26, no. 2 (Fall 2004): 262–92.

Espinosa, Gastón, et al. "Hispanic Churches in American Public Life: Summary of Findings." *Interim Reports, 2003* (2). Notre Dame, IN: Institute for Latino Studies.

Freston, Paul. "Contours of Latin American Pentecostalism." In *Christianity Reborn: The Global Expansion of Evangelicalism in the Twentieth Century*, edited by Donald M. Lewis, 232. Grand Rapids: Eerdmans, 2004.

Freston, Paul and Virginia Garrard-Burnett. "Christianity and Conflict in Latin America." Panel at symposium on Religion, Conflict and the Global War on Terrorism in Latin America. Sponsored by the Pew Forum and National Defense University's School for National Security Executive Education, National Defense University, Washington, D.C., April 6, 2006.

Gamboa, Erasmo. "Chicanos in the Pacific Northwest: Expanding the Discourse." America's Review 23, no. 3 (1995): 15–25.

———. *Mexican Labor and World War II: Braceros in the Pacific Northwest, 1942–1947*. Seattle: University of Washington Press, (1990), 1999.

———. "Mexican Mule Packers and Oregon's Second Regiment Mounted Volunteers, 1855-1856." *Oregon Historical Quarterly* 92 (Spring 1991), 41–59.

Gamboa, Erasmo and Carolyn Buan, eds. *Nosotros: The Hispanic People of Oregon: Essays and Recollections*. Portland, OR: Oregon Council for the Humanities, 1995.

García-Treto, Francisco. "Reading the Hyphens: An Emerging Biblical Hermeneutics for Latino/Hispanic US Protestants." In *Protestantes/ Protestants: Hispanic Christianity within the Mainline Traditions*, edited by David Maldonado Jr., 160–73. Nashville: Abindgon, 1999.

Garrard-Burnett, Virginia and Paul Freston. "Christianity and Conflict in Latin America." Panel at symposium on Religion, Conflict and the Global War on Terrorism in Latin America. Sponsored by the Pew Forum and National Defense University's School for National Security Executive Education, National Defense University, Washington, DC, April 6, 2006.

Gjerde, Jon. "Conflict and Community: A case study of the immigrant church in the United States." In *American Immigration and Ethnicity: A 20 Volume Series of Distinguished Essays*, edited by George Pozzetta, vol 19, 181–97. Hamden, CT: Garland Publishing, 1991.

Gómez, Roberto. "Mestizo Spirituality: Motifs of Sacrifice, Transformation, Thanksgiving, and Family in Four Mexican-American Rituals." *Apuntes*, 11, no. 4 (Winter 1991): 81–92.

Gonzales-Berry, Erlinda and Marcela Mendoza. *Mexicanos in Oregon: Their Stories, Their Lives*. Corvallis, OR: Oregon State University Press, 2010.

Gonzales-Berry, Erlinda, et al. "One-and-a-half Generation Mexican Youth in Oregon: Pursuing the Mobility Dream." Report, Forum on Immigration Studies, Oregon State University Department of Ethnic Studies. Corvallis, OR, April 2006.

Gonzales-Berry, Erlinda with Dwaine Plaza. "'We are Tired of Cookies and Old Clothes': From Poverty Programs to Community Empowerment among Oregon's Mexicano Population, 1957–1975." In *Seeing Color: Indigenous Peoples and Racialized Ethnic Minorities in Oregon,* edited by Jun Xing et al., 93–113. Lanham, MD: University Press of America, 2007.

González, Justo, ed. *Alabadle: Hispanic Christian Worship*. Nashville: Abingdon, 1996.

González, Justo. "Hispanic Worship: An Introduction." In *Alabadle: Hispanic Christian Worship,* edited by Justo González, 9–27. Nashville: Abingdon, 1996.

Gonzalez Pino, Barbara and Frank Pino. "Serving the Heritage Speaker across a Five-Year Program." *ADFL Bulletin,* 32, no. 1 (2000): 27–35.

Greeley, Andrew. *The Denominational Society: A Sociological Approach to Religion in America*. Glenview, IL: Scott, Foresman and Co., 1972.

Hernández, Edwin I. "Moving from the Cathedral to Storefront Churches: Understanding Religious Growth and Decline Among Latino Protestants." In *Protestantes/ Protestants: Hispanic Christianity within the Mainline Traditions*, edited by David Maldonado Jr., 216–38. Nashville: Abingdon, 1999.

Himnos de gloria y triunfo. Miami: Editorial Vida, 1985.

Holland, Clifton. "Chronology of Protestant Origins in Guatemala, 1824–1980." PROLADES -RITA database, http://www.prolades.com/historiografia/2-Guatemala/guate_ chron.pdf (updated March 18, 2011; accessed June 3, 2011).

Hurh, Won Moo and Kwang Chung Kim. "Religious Participation of Korean Immigrants in the United States." *Journal for the Scientific Study of Religion* 29, no. 1 (March 1990): 19–34.

Isasi-Díaz, Ada María and Yolanda Tarango. *Hispanic Women: Prophetic Voice in the Church*. New York: Harper & Row, 1988.

Jenkins, Philip. *The Next Christendom: The Coming of Global Christianity*. New York: Oxford, 2002.

Karny, Yo'av. *Highlanders: A Journey to the Caucasus in Quest of Memory*. New York: Farrar, Straus, Giroux, 2002.

Lara-Braud, Jorge. "A Profile of Hispanic Protestant Pastors." In *Protestantes/ Protestants: Hispanic Christianity within the Mainline Traditions,* edited by David Maldonado Jr., 255–67. Nashville: Abindgon, 1999.

Lawson, Ronald. "From American Church to Immigrant Church: The Changing Face of Seventh-Day Adventism in Metropolitan New York." *Sociology of Religion* 59, no. 4 (1998): 329–51.

Lewis, Donald, ed. *Christianity Reborn: The Global Expansion of Evangelicalism in the Twentieth Century.* Grand Rapids: Eerdman's, 2004.

Liprinzi, Colleen. "Hispanic Migrant Labor in Oregon: 1940–1990." Master's thesis, Portland State University, 1991.

Lobdell, William. "Latino Exodus From Catholic Church Rising, Study Says," Los Angeles Times, May 5, 2001.

Lobdell, William. "Building Respect for Latino Protestantism," Los Angeles Times, June 16, 2001.

Luebke, Frederick. "German Immigrants and Churches in Nebraska, 1889-1915." In *American Immigration and Ethnicity: A 20 Volume Series of Distinguished Essays,* edited by George Pozzetta, Vol 19, 210–24. Hamden, CT: Garland Publishing, 1991.

Machado, Daisy. "Latinos and Protestant Establishment: Is There a Place for Us at the Feast Table?" In *Protestantes/Protestants: Hispanic Christianity within the Mainline Traditions,* edited by David Maldonado Jr., 85–106. Nashville: Abindgon, 1999.

———. *Of Borders and Margins: Hispanic Disciples in Texas, 1888-1945.* New York: AAR/Oxford University Press, 2003.

Maduro, Otto. "Religion and Exclusion/Marginalization: Globalized Pentecostalism among Hispanics in Newark, NJ." *Revista Cultura y Religión* III, no. 1 (2009): 35–50.

Maldonado, Jorge E., ed. *Cántico nuevo de alabanza, adoración y compromiso.* Quito: Iglesias del Pacto Evangélico/EIRENE, 1989.

Maldonado Jr., David, ed. *Protestantes/Protestants: Hispanic Christianity within the Mainline Traditions.* Nashville:Abingdon, 1999.

Martin, David. "Evangelical Expansion in Global Society." In *Christianity Reborn: The Global Expansion of Evangelicalism in the Twentieth Century,* edited by Donald M. Lewis, 273–94. Grand Rapids, MI: Eerdmans, 2004.

Martin del Campo, Ismael. "Asamblea Apostólica de la Fe en Cristo Jesús." In *Iglesias Peregrinas en Busca de Identidad: Cuadros del Protestantismo Latino en los Estados Unidos,* edited by Juan F. Martínez and Luis Scott, 51–75. Buenos Aires, Argentina: Ediciones Kairos and CEHILA, 2004.

Martinez Jr., Charles R., et al., "Latino Immigrant Children and Families: Demographics, Challenges, and Promise." In *Understanding the Immigrant Experience in Oregon: Research, Analysis, and Recommendations from University of Oregon Scholars,* edited by Robert Bussel, 56–67. Eugene: University of Oregon Labor and Education Research Center, 2008.

Martinez, Jr., Charles R., and J. Mark Eddy. "Effects of Culturally Adapted Parent Management Training on Latino Youth Behavioral Health Outcomes." *Journal of Consulting & Clinical Psychology,* 73, no. 5 (October 2005): 841–51

Martínez Guerra, Juan, and Luis [Lindy] Scott, eds. *Iglesias peregrinas en busca de identidad: Cuadros del protestantismo latino en los Estados Unidos.* Buenos Aires: Kairos, 2004.

McLagan, Elizabeth. "A Very Prejudiced State: Discrimination in Oregon from 1900–1940." In *Seeing Color: Indigenous Peoples and Racialized Minorities in Oregon*, edited by Jun Xing et al., 78–92. Lanham, MD: University Press of America, 2007.

McLeary, Rachel and José de Jesús Pesina. "Religious Competition, Protestant Syncretization, and Conversion in Guatemala since the 1880s." Conference paper presented at the annual meeting of ASREC, April 2011, Arlington, VA.

Miller, Eugene D. *Latinos and the Development of Community: Philanthropy, Associations, and Advocacy.* Multicultural Philanthropy Curriculum Guide 7. New York: CUNY Center for the Study of Philanthropy, 1999.

Mohl, Raymond A. and Neil Betten. "The Immigrant Church in Gary, Indiana: Religious Adjustment and Cultural Defense." In *American Immigration and Ethnicity: A 20 Volume Series of Distinguished Essays*, edited by George Pozzetta, Vol 19, 269–85. Hamden, CT: Garland Publishing, 1991.

Nusz, Nancy and Gabriella Ricciardi. "Our ways: History and culture of Mexicans in Oregon." *Oregon Historical Quarterly* 104 (2003): 110–23.

O'Connell Killen, Patricia and Mark Silk, eds. *Religion and Public Life in the Pacific Northwest: The None Zone.* Charlotte, N.C.: Rowman and Littlefield, 2004.

Oregon Center for Public Policy, *Undocumented Workers are Taxpayers, too.* Silverton, OR: Oregon Center for Public Policy, April 2007.

Orozco Hawkins, Olga. "Hispanic/Latina Women in Agriculture." In *Hidden Stories: Unveiling the History of the Latino Church*, edited by Daniel Rodríguez-Díaz and David Cortés-Fuentes, 117–24. Decatur, GA: Asociación para la Educación Teológica Hispana, 1994.

Pascoe, Peggy. "'A Mistake to Simmer the Question Down to Black and White': The History of Oregon's Miscengenation Law." In *Seeing Color: Indigenous Peoples and Racialized Minorities in Oregon*, edited by Jun Xing et al., 27–43. Lanham, MD: University Press of America, 2007.

Pew Hispanic Center, "Demographic profile of Hispanics in Oregon, 2008." http:// pewhispanic.org/ states/?stateid=OR.

Pozzetta, George, ed. *American Immigration and Ethnicity: A 20 Volume Series of Distinguished Essays.* Vol 19. Hamden, Conn: Garland Publishing, 1991.

Ramírez, Daniel. "'Call Me Bitter': Life and Death in the Diasporic Borderlands and the Challenges/Opportunities for Norteamericano Churches." *Perspectivas*, Hispanic Theological Initiative Occasional Papers, Princeton Seminary (Fall 2007): 39–66

Recinos, Harold. "Mainline Hispanic Protestantism and Latino Newcomers." In *Protestantes/Protestants: Hispanic Christianity within the Mainline Traditions*, edited by David Maldonado Jr., 194–215. Nashville: Abingdon, 1999.

Rodríguez-Díaz, Daniel and David Cortés-Fuentes, eds. *Hidden Stories: Unveiling the History of the Latino Church.* Decatur, GA: Asociación para la Educación Teológica Hispana, 1994.

Sanchez-Walsh, Arlene. *Latino Pentecostal Identity: Evangelical Faith, Self, and Society.* New York: Columbia University Press, 2003.

Sanneh, Lamin. *Whose Religion is Christianity? The Gospel Beyond the West.* Grand Rapids: Eerdman's, 2003.

Santillán Baert, María Luisa. "Worship in the Hispanic United Methodist Church." In *Alabadle: Hispanic Christian Worship*, edited by Justo González, 57–71. Nashville: Abingdon, 1996.

Savage, Roberto C., comp. *Cofre de cánticos: solos, duos y coritos evangélicos.* Grand Rapids: Singspiration, 1968.

———, comp. *Himnos de fe y alabanza.* Cucutá, Colombia: Asociación El Sembrador/Singspiration, 1966.

———, comp. *Preludios celestiales:solos, duos y coritos evangélicos.* Grand Rapids: Singspiration, 1954.

Sepúlveda, Juan. "The Pentecostal Movement in Latin America." In *New Face of the Church in Latin America: Between Tradition and Change,* edited by Guillermo Cook, 68–74. American Society of Missiology series; no. 18. Maryknoll, NY: Orbis, 1994.

Smith, Timothy. "Religion and Ethnicity in America." *American Historical Review* 83, no. 5 (December 1978), 1155–85.

Soliván, Samuel. "Hispanic Pentecostal Worship." In *Alabadle: Hispanic Christian Worship,* edited by Justo González, 43–56. Nashville: Abingdon, 1996.

Stephen, Lynn. *Transborder Lives: Indigenous Oaxacans in Mexico, California, and Oregon.* Durham, NC: Duke University Press, 2007.

Stephen, Lynn and Marcela Mendoza. "Oregon." In *Latino America, A State-by-State Encyclopedia,* edited by Mark Overmyer-Velazquez, 667–68. Westport, CT: Greenwood, 2008.

Stevens-Arroyo, Anthony. *Recognizing the Latino Resurgence in U.S. Religion.* Boulder, CO: Westview, 1998.

Stevens-Arroyo, Anthony, and Ana María Díaz-Stevens, eds. "Density, Diaspora, and Diversity: Interpreting the 2000 U.S. Census for Its Pastoral Implications." *The National Survey of Leadership in Latino Parishes and Congregations: A Summary Report parts I & II.* 2003. New York: RISC. http://depthome.brooklyn.cuny.edu/risc/Essay%2010-15-02.pdf.

Stevens-Arroyo, Anthony, and Gilbert Cadena, eds. *Old Masks, New Faces: Religion and Latino Identities.* New York: Bildner Center for Western Hemisphere Studies, 1995.

Stout, Harry. "Ethnicity: The Vital Center of Religion in America." In *American Immigration and Ethnicity: A 20 Volume Series of Distinguished Essays,* edited by George Pozzetta, vol 19, 374–94. Hamden, CT: Garland Publishing, 1991.

"Tejano." *Encyclopædia Britannica. Encyclopædia Britannica Online Academic Edition.* Encyclopædia Britannica, 2011. http://0-www.britannica.com.catalog.georgefox.edu/EBchecked/topic/1163291/Tejano. Accessed Oct. 17, 2011.

Thompson, Robert D., Jr., "Racialized Minority Demographics of Oregon." In *Seeing Color: Indigenous Peoples and Racialized Minorities in Oregon,* edited by Jun Xing et al., 22. Lanham, MD: University Press of America, 2007.

Troyer, L. E. *The Sovereignty of the Spirit. Revealed in the Opening of our Mexican Missions of the South-West.* Los Angeles: Students Benefit Publishing Co., 1934. A facsimilie of the first edition in Cortés, Carlos, ed. *Protestantism and Latinos in the United States.* New York: Arno, 1980.

Tucker, Kathy. Caption of photo "Women & Children outside Farm Labor Camp." Oregon Historical Society, 2004. No pages. Online: http://www.ohs.org/ education/oregonhistory/historical_records/dspDocument.cfm?doc_ID=000AE35B-711E-1ED6-A42A80B05272006C.

Vasquez, Manuel A. "Pentecostalism, Collective Identity, and Transnationalism Among Salvadorans and Peruvians in the U.S." *Journal of the American Academy of Religion* 67, no. 3 (Sep., 1999), 617–36.

Wadkins, T. "Pentecostal Power: Conversions in El Salvador." *Christian Century* 123, no. 23 (November 14, 2006): 26–29.

Warner, R. Stephen and Judith Wittner, eds. *Gatherings in Diaspora: Religious Communities and the New Immigration*. Philadelphia: Temple University Press, 1998.

Warren, Rick. *Una Iglesia con propósito: Cómo crecer sin comprometer el mensaje y la misión*. Translated by Cecilia de De Francesco. Miami: Editorial Vida, 1998. Originally published as *The Purpose-Driven Church*. (Grand Rapids: Zondervan, 1995).

Warren, Bruce L. "Socioeconomic Achievement and Religion: The American Case." *Sociological Inquiry*. 40 (Spring 1970): 130–55.

Williams, Philip J. "The Sound of Tambourines: The Politics of Pentecostal Growth in El Salvador." In *Power, Politics, and Pentecostals in Latin America*, edited by Edward Cleary and Hannah Stewart-Gambino, 179–200. Boulder, CO: Westview, 1997.

Wilson, Everett A. "Sanguine Saints: Pentecostalism in El Salvador." *Church History* 52, no. 2 (June 1983): 186–98.

———. "Guatemalan Pentecostals: Something of their Own." In *Power, Politics, and Pentecostals in Latin America,* edited by Edward Cleary and Hannah Stewart-Gambino, 139–62. Boulder, CO: Westview, 1997.

Witt, Marcos. *¿Qué hacemos con estos músicos?* Nashville: Editorial Caribe, 1995.

Xing, Jun. "Introduction: From the Legacy of Ing 'Doc' Hay to Reading Ethnicity in Oregon History." In *Seeing Color: Indigenous Peoples and Racialized Minorities in Oregon,* edited by Jun Xing et al., 6–7. Lanham, MD: University Press of America, 2007.

Index of Protestant Hispanic Churches of Oregon